Special Relationships

Special Relationships

People and Places

∾

Asa Briggs

Frontline Books
London

First published in 2012 by Frontline Books,

an imprint of
Pen & Sword Books Ltd.,
47 Church Street, Barnsley, S. Yorkshire, S70 2AS.

Visit us at www.frontline-books.com, email info@frontline-books.com
or write to us at the above address.

ISBN 978-1-84832-667-5

CIP data records for this title are available from the British Library.

Typeset i   6XN

'A man will turn over half a library
to make one book.'

Samuel Johnson

'"What is the use of a book," thought Alice,
"without pictures or conversations?"'

Lewis Carroll

This book is dedicated to my children.

Katharine

Daniel

Judith

Matthew

Contents

Illustrations

Acknowledgements

I acknowledge the great help given to me in far from easy times by many people in many different places. I owe a special debt within Frontline Books to my publisher, Michael Leventhal, to Stephen Chumbley and to Donald Sommerville. There would have been no book at all without Judy Grant. I would never have been able to write it without the support of Pat Spencer. Without the skills of Andra Nelki there would have been no illustrations. My wife Susan has given me invaluable assistance in arranging them and in writing captions. In my early writing of the book I recognise the great help given me by the present Vice-Chancellor of the University of Sussex, Michael Farthing, and by the University as a whole. Likewise, the Vice-Chancellor of the Open University, Martin Bean, and his colleagues in Milton Keynes. They have been helpful all the way through.

Asa Briggs
Lewes, 2012

Chapter 1

Why This Book?

I started writing this book on an exceptionally cold day in January 2010. It is the first book about myself that I have ever written. Judy Grant, widow of Sir Alistair Grant, urged me to write it. She is a treasured friend and neighbour, as was Alistair until his untimely death in 2001. My book, however, is not an autobiography in any conventional sense of the word. I was exceptionally fortunate to have Paul Thompson, pioneer of oral history, to record my memoirs at length, some years ago. I feel no urge in 2011 to bring them up-to-date myself in print. Nevertheless, my book has an autobiographical dimension to it as I recall my relationships with the extraordinarily wide range of people and places that I have come to know in different phases of my life.

I trust that it will be published in 2012, within the year following my ninetieth birthday, which, as I write, I have already celebrated on 7 May 2011. When I started writing it I was not sure that I would still be alive to celebrate this landmark date. I included in the provisional title of my book, therefore, the sub title 'Asa with or without me'. Now, after clambering over a few hurdles, I have given it a completely new main title, 'Special Relationships', a title that has nothing directly to do with birthdays. I seek in it to trace those personal relationships which have most shaped my work as an historian and, indeed, my whole life, although my last chapter concentrates on the curious convergences of the year 2012.

My perspectives are not those of an autobiographer. They have more in common with those of a diarist. Throughout I try to focus the spotlight on the people with whom I developed these relationships rather than on myself. I agree with the nineteenth-century German historian Wilhelm Dilthey that 'progressive identification with the mental and emotional life of others creates higher levels of self-awareness than unaided self-examination'. I approach history in this spirit. I also focus in my book as much on particular places which have influenced my sensibilities as on people who have influenced my ideas and my behaviour. I have a very strong visual sense, and whenever I think either of individuals or of institutions I recall particular scenes. For me there are vantage places, therefore, as well as vantage points in time.

The words 'special relationships' in my main title have been employed by historians to identify relations between politicians, like that between Winston Churchill and Franklin D. Roosevelt, and between countries over a longer period of time, like Britain's so-called 'special relationship' with the United States. This topic hit the headlines while I was half way through the writing of this book. Is the relationship between David Cameron's Britain and Barack Obama's United States really special? Or is it better described as 'essential', like the very different and now strained relationship between the United States and Pakistan?

In my own life some of the personal relationships which I select have been essential to me or to the other person. Some, nevertheless, have been special in either a narrower or broader way. It is probably easier for an individual to point to special relationships in his or her own life than it is for journalists (or even historians) to identify special relationships in the history of nations. In the latter case there will seldom be consensus between them. Nor should there be. One of the taken-for-granted phrases in regular use which most irritates me is 'history will show'. A distinction should be drawn between 'the past' and the critical study of history.

What is called the verdict of history is really the verdict of historians, and they, like journalists, may disagree about the past in their books as journalists do about the present in newspapers and on radio and television. Increasingly some journalists argue with each other in more than one medium, a phenomenon which is seldom discussed. What the lessons of Libya or, more generally, of the so-called 'Arab Spring' really are is a question that many journalists are asking as I finish this book, some of them relating the current question directly to the question of what are (or were) the lessons of Iraq. Before that it was what are (or were) the lessons of Vietnam. Books figure more prominently than newspapers or magazine articles in this book, as the first motto which I have chosen to precede it indicates. I have turned over more than a quarter of the books in my own substantial library while writing it. When I reflect on the past, the subject of most of my books, I emphasize the role of oral and visual history in dealing with it – I co-operated closely with Paul Thompson to develop the idea of a National Life Story Collection in 1986, the first brochure of which read:

> Every man and woman in the country has a story to tell of his or her own life. Those stories are the raw material of our history and our understanding of change today: the millions of threads which together make the fabric of our collective experience.

Oral and visual converge. History for me is a tapestry, which continues to be woven as both individuals and institutions come and go. There are many threads both in personal and in institutional lives. Some are 'threads that bind' but there are also some that break. I am glad that my wife collects tapestries and embroideries. I am equally glad, however, that she loves illustrations and is a good photographer. Photography, particularly through film and television, has transformed history more profoundly than earlier modes of visual communication such as effigies and medals. Yet, in a year when we are rightly celebrating the quarto-centenary of the King James Bible, I note the beauties not only of language but of stained glass windows and their power to communicate. So do churches and their graveyards. I believe that it is necessary for an historian to be able to 'read' both

3

ancient and new objects and buildings as wholes as knowledgeably and as critically as he reads books. They are adapted through time and sometimes (controversially) restored. Significantly Paul Thompson concerned himself not only with oral history but with architecture. I have been inspired by the extensive writings of John Ruskin and William Morris on interiors and exteriors, and I am very proud of the selected writings and designs in my Morris anthology which appeared in 1962.

The relationship between buildings and their surrounding is always a special one for me. I began to think about this very early in my life in my home town, Keighley, an industrial town, surrounded by moors, on the small River Worth which joins the River Aire there. Built largely out of Pennine stone, it grew rapidly during the Victorian years, and when it was incorporated as a borough in 1888 it chose for its coat of arms the words 'By Worth'. Was it, I have often asked myself since the 1960s, the coexistence of smoking chimneys and heather among the bracken in the hills that somehow turned me into an historian of the nineteenth century?

Such an inference seems plausible, yet Herbert Butterfield, an historian from my school in Keighley, whose father was a mill accountant and who lived in Oxenhope, a remote moorland village beyond Haworth, wrote history which was largely unconcerned with the nineteenth century. This seems more surprising to me than the fact that R. H. Tawney, whom I followed in 1958 as President of the Workers' Educational Association (WEA), founded in 1903, wrote not about the society and culture of the working-class students who attended his tutorial classes in the Potteries but about Tudor and Stuart history.

I would have been very surprised, however, if Arnold Bennett had not written novels about the five towns of the Potteries, which he knew so well, or, indeed, if the Brontës had not written about the moors which they knew perhaps equally well. I never once heard Butterfield refer to the Brontës or Tawney to Bennett, although as an under-graduate at Sidney Sussex College, Cambridge between 1938 and 1941, I frequently heard both Butterfield and Tawney lecture, and I was enthralled by Butterfield's lectures on early modern European history and Tawney's lectures on religion and pre-industrial capitalism. They were both to play an important part in my life, although after completing my Cambridge degree, I did not take up an invitation to go to Peterhouse, Butterfield's college, as a Research Fellow, nor did I go to the London School of Economics (LSE) where I had been awarded a Gerstenberg Studentship in 1941 and where Tawney was one of the most prominent professors.

Before I went up to Cambridge I never even dreamed of becoming an historian, I loved history as a schoolboy though I was not exclusively interested in it. I never have been. In 1941, when I completed my degree, I wanted above all to be a writer. In my ninetieth year I retain my passion for writing, and I am unhappy if I write fewer than a thousand words a day.

The most thorough and conscientious of my teachers in Keighley Boys' Grammar School was Kenneth Preston, born in 1902, known by his nickname 'Prut', who taught us English Literature. Under his influence I read more English poetry and fiction, and scholarly books about both, when I was in the sixth form than I would now read if I were studying English Literature in a university. I read lots of Matthew Arnold, for example, and wrote poems which were too strongly influenced by him. Preston patiently and helpfully read and commented on them outside school hours. He would then bicycle back to his home. He had himself been a pupil at Keighley Trade and Grammar School, as it was then called, when the headmaster was T. P. Watson. He had been Butterfield's headmaster too, and Butterfield, who never wrote a line about trade, always stated with unusual consistency that he had been a boy at the 'Trade School', a unique name, abandoned in the 1920s. Preston owed as much to Watson as I owed to my headmaster Neville Hind, whom I have described at some length in my parallel volume to this on Bletchley Park, *Secret Days*. A Cambridge historian, Hind would not allow his brightest boys either to go to Oxford or to read English Literature. He also preferred them to go, as I did, to his own college, Oliver Cromwell's college, Sidney Sussex. He was a Benthamite, so that we learned not about Anglicans or Nonconformists but about Utilitarians in scripture lessons which he himself, twirling his gown, gave for the sixth form.

Isaac Holden, a mill owner, who was chairman at the opening of the Trade School in the old Mechanics' Institute building, was to become Keighley's first Member of Parliament in 1885. It was a Gothic landmark and when its clock tower was burnt down in a disastrous fire in 1962 it was as big an event in my own personal life, although I was then living miles away in Lewes, as the devastating fire in the Crystal Palace in 1936 had been for Londoners. It made me recall other great fires in history including the 'Great Fire of London' in 1666 and the cruel fires of the Blitz which destroyed the area round St Paul's but kept the dome intact.

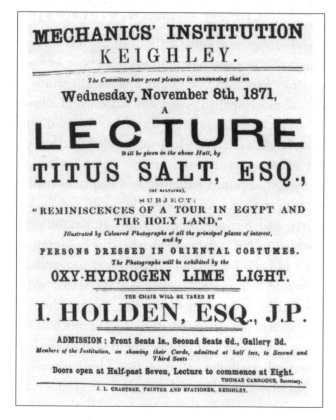

Advertisement for a lecture at the
Mechanics' Institute in 1871.

When I turned to social history in the late 1940s, it was a social history which took full account both of men as different as Isaac Holden and Christopher Wren and of other natural disasters besides fires, like earthquakes and floods. I came to love the great bookshop in New York where the whole of human knowledge was divided between topics, one of which was 'disasters'. I appreciated that there was creative fire too that inspired men and women to do great things. My approach to social history was different from that of G. M. Trevelyan, whose *Social History* had been a wartime best-seller. I barely knew him when I was an undergraduate and never heard him lecture. Nevertheless, like him, I believed as an undergraduate and indeed as a schoolboy that we must always relate literature to history. It did not just provide 'background', a word I have never liked.

I made something of a reputation for myself as a young reviewer when after the war I confronted Trevelyan's proposition that social history was history with the politics left out with my alternative judgement that it was economic history with the politics put in. I later produced two editions of Trevelyan, who was a major author for the publishing house of Longman. I had other differences of approach to social history, however, from his. Thus, I did not want to write social history and leave the economics out. I studied economic history in some depth at Cambridge and was taken up by M. M. Postan who succeeded Sir John Clapham as Professor of it. Clapham made me investigate facts, which he collected meticulously. Postan, born in Bessarabia not in Yorkshire, primarily but by no means exclusively interested in medieval history which was the staple of my undergraduate studies, encouraged me to bring together economic theory and economic history. For him 'the facts of history, even those which in historical parlance figure as "hard and fast" are no more than relevances: facets of past phenomena which happen to relate to the preoccupations of historical inquirers at the time of their inquiries'. I did not see relevance in quite such a deterministic way. I knew too that Postan's own economic theory was quirky. He would have been no more drawn to the theories of Alfred Marshall than to Clapham

One of my favourite historians, whose writing I admired, Jacob Burckhardt, rejected what Hugh Trevor-Roper (whom I also admired when I got to know him, though until his last days never well) called the 'cramping systems' which have imprisoned universal history. I was convinced that Burckhardt was right to acknowledge in the preface to his *Civilization of the Renaissance in Italy* (1860) that

> In the wide ocean upon which we venture, the possible ways and directions are many, and the same studies which have served for this work might easily, in other hands, not only receive a wholly different treatment and application, but lead also to essentially different conclusions.

In this statement I liked the humility, a quality Trevor-Roper never practised or extolled, but I also liked the word 'venture'.

Trevor-Roper himself deliberately chose the University of Sussex to deliver defiant lectures on medieval history, not his own specialist subject, soon after it opened. He expected a fashionable audience, but I had to mobilize schoolchildren from local schools to ensure that he had a sizeable number of television viewers on the spot. I was inspired by Hugh's clarity of mind more than by his television performance. He was no A. J. P. Taylor. Their careers converged and crossed at many points and I am delighted that a Sussex graduate, Adam Sisman, has written well-received biographies of both of them.

While I was at school in Keighley I enjoyed browsing through biographies in Keighley's Public Library. Indeed it was there that I first learned what browsing meant. This was a building in an early Renaissance style 'freely treated', which was endowed by the American multi-millionaire Andrew Carnegie and opened in 1904 by the Duke of Devonshire. All its original stock of books came from the Gothic Mechanics' Institute on the other side of the Skipton Road, as did its first librarian. He was appointed 'for the time being' but stayed in the post for forty-two years.

I used to read newspapers in the great news room of the Library on the ground floor, which could seat 150 people, but I best enjoyed working after school in its reference library which had incorporated the library of Philip Snowden, the Labour politician, who was born in the moorland village of Cowling on the way to Colne. It was there that I first studied the politics that I was to introduce into my own version of social history. Karl Marx did not have a prominent place in it. Indeed, later in my life, like most historians of my age group, I read most of the works of Marx. Unlike some of them, however, I never became what was called a Marxist. Nor, of course, did Trevor-Roper or A. J. P. Taylor. Nevertheless, I worked with Marxists more easily than they did, and I came to the conclusion that there were as many varieties of Marxism as there were of non-Marxist history.

As far as I know, I was never taught by a Marxist teacher at school, though I was taught by Roman Catholics as well as Protestants, and mathematics (very well) by a member of the Plymouth Brethren. It was one of the advantages of Keighley Boys' Grammar School when I was a pupil there that boys came to the school not only from the industrial town of Keighley and its suburbs but from villages, some of them also industrial, in the moorland countryside. I had friends both in Cowling and in Haworth, and when I went up to Cambridge one of my friends in Caius College came from Nelson, beyond Colne. We worked out highly original theories of choice together. They were influenced neither by Marx nor Burckhardt. They reflected nonetheless my first acquaintance with economics.

It was a boy at the Grammar School with me, Leo White, born near the middle of Keighley, with whom I used to go for long walks in the moors around the town, who persuaded me in 1938, the year I went up to Cambridge, to take an external London University Inter-BSc(Econ) at the same time as he did so that we could talk over the answers to likely examination questions. I had general reasons for taking up economics at that stage in my life which had nothing to do with examinations. Since Keighley was a depressed town during the 1930s, my own family, involved in small-scale retailing, suffered from the effects of the great depression in my own immediate locality. I believed that economics might help me to understand the causes of depressions everywhere and at all times.

I was lucky that in 1937, the year that I won a scholarship to

Cambridge, which was renowned for its economists, the most famous of them, J. M. Keynes, had just published his *General Theory of Employment, Interest and Money* which was concerned with the kind of economic issues that were directly relevant to me. Sadly, while an undergraduate, I only once heard Keynes lecture. He was too busy to do so, particularly after 1939 when he was advising wartime governments. It was only later that I read his fascinating essay on Marshall, a flight of thought which made it clear what he thought of the study of economics as a subject:

> The study of economics does not seem to require any special gifts of an unusually high order. Is it not, intellectually regarded, a very easy subject compared with the higher branches of philosophy and pure science? Yet good, even competent, economists are the rarest of birds. An easy subject at which very few excel. The paradox finds its explanation, perhaps, in that the master economist must possess a rare combination of gifts . . . He must combine talents not often found together. He must be mathematician, historian, statesman, philosopher – in some degree. He must understand symbols and speak in words. He must contemplate the particular in terms of the general, and touch abstract and concrete in the same flight of thought. He must study the present in the light of the past for the purposes of the future.

I have never ceased to be inspired by this 'flight of thought'. I note how important Keynes thought biography was, and I am delighted that my friend Robert Skidelsky, who lived and worked for a time in Keynes's house and library just out of Lewes, has written a brilliant biography of him.

Keynes did not talk of destiny – or luck – in this 'flight of thought' or of the importance to a writer of being in the right place at the right time. I was really lucky that during the war the LSE was evacuated to Cambridge and that I was given as open an access to LSE lectures as to those on the Cambridge lecture lists. I never understood F. A. Hayek's lectures on the rate of interest, however, and I had no idea that in 1942, the year of the Beveridge Report, with a brilliant career as a philosopher before him, he would write a devastating book, *The Road to Serfdom*, which I fully understood but totally disliked. I read it in Bletchley Park when I had little time to read economics. It was to be a book that itself made history at the general election of 1945, the first such election for ten years.

The LSE lectures which I found most interesting were those of Harold Laski, who every Saturday morning lectured brilliantly on politics to an attentive audience which included housewives with shopping baskets. He never used a single note. He was to be the chairman of the Labour Party's executive in 1945. I also listened to Eileen Power, the best lecturer on economic history whom I have ever heard, to Lance Beales, whose name I knew then mainly through his editorial connection with Penguin Books, and to Tawney. I will never forget Eileen's lecture on the golden road to Samarkand. At the end of it I dared to ask her if she would get us tickets to travel there together the next day.

I never told my tutor in Sidney Sussex College or the Director of the London School of Economics, Alexander Carr-Saunders, that I was taking a London University external BSc(Econ) degree in parallel to the History Tripos. I had learned to keep my own secrets, therefore, before I went to work at Bletchley Park as a code-breaker. There I had to sign the Official Secrets Act and took secrecy for granted. In Cambridge there had to be subterfuge. If I had told my tutor at Sidney Sussex what I was doing, the College would have undoubtedly stopped me from doing so. It had the power. Happily for me when I got Firsts in parallel both in Cambridge and in London University my Cambridge supervisors were delighted. So was Carr-Saunders, who invited me to dinner in Peterhouse, Butterfield's college, where the LSE was evacuated. All things connect.

I took my External BSc(Econ) examination neither in Cambridge nor in London but in Bradford, by a coincidence near the site of what was to become post-war Bradford University, which was to confer upon me an honorary doctorate in 1978. I had the first of my big surprises in my academic life one week before the results of the

BSc(Econ) were announced. I received a telegram from Laski asking why I had not applied for the Gerstenberg Studentship, which was awarded to the best student in the examination. When he asked me whether I would like to apply now quite unsurprisingly I said yes and was duly awarded the Studentship.

Although I never took up the Studentship because I was offered a Fellowship at Worcester College, Oxford, in 1944 while still in uniform at Bletchley Park, nevertheless, I retained links with the LSE which survived all my other institutional allegiances. Thus, I was on the LSE committee which watched over (not always with his approval) the writing of LSE history by Ralph Dahrendorf, its Director from 1974 to 1984. I had tried to attract Dahrendorf to Sussex University when I was Vice-Chancellor there from 1967 to 1976. I had heard him trounce the great American sociologist Talcott Parsons, who became a friend of mine, at an International Sociological Conference in Washington.

I had turned to sociology myself as well as to social history even before I arrived at Sussex, and in the University of Chicago, which I regarded as my second university, I was thought of as much as a sociologist as an historian. Everett Hughes was a friend, and I succeeded in attracting to Sussex for a substantial spell David Riesmann, author of *The Lonely Crowd*, who had turned down invitations from Oxford. Meanwhile, in the LSE David Glass drew me into studies of social mobility, while his wife Ruth worked with me on urban sociology. With her I got to know well the architect William Holford, who was devising reconstruction plans for the war-shattered area round St Pauls. I was increasingly interested at this time in the past, present and future of cities, and became very critical of a much admired book by Lewis Mumford, *The Culture of Cities*, which had appeared before the war. In particular I disliked his use of the word *alias* in describing industrial cities. He thought wrongly that they were all the same.

Some of the implications of these criticisms and of my special relationships with places and people I will examine more fully in later chapters. In 1987, eleven years after I had moved from Sussex back to Oxford after a long break, Dahrendorf was himself to become Warden of an Oxford College, St Antony's, with which I had had much to do when it was founded in 1947. From the start I had two very special relationships there. Its founding benefactor, Antoine Besse, was a benefactor to Worcester College also, and its first Warden, William (Bill) Deakin, whom I introduced into my *Secret Days* when he was working with Tito in Yugoslavia, presided over a team of historians reading the proofs of Winston Churchill's *History of the English-Speaking Peoples*, which he had started before the war.

I admired Churchill's great literary gifts and his willingness to turn aside from politics, if temporarily, to paint landscapes. I also admired his skill as an historian in dealing with those distant periods of history that I had studied in Cambridge but had now largely abandoned. It was not those pages, however, that I was required to comment upon, but his chapters on the eighteenth and nineteenth centuries. These covered American as well as British history, and I had the mischievous pleasure of telling him that in one of them he was presenting too Marxist an interpretation of the American constitution. Deakin's helpers never met as a team, but I got to know another man who figured later in my life, Alan Hodge, wartime secretary to Brendan Bracken, the Minister of Information, who was very close to Churchill. In 1951 Hodge was to become co-editor of the new magazine *History Today*. Its title was thought up by Bracken.

When the *History of the English-Speaking Peoples* appeared, I pondered on whether to keep the cheque signed by Winston for, I believe, £200, which he sent me along with signed copies of the different volumes. I needed the money, however, for life was not easy for me in the years of post-war austerity. When I joined Worcester College I was paid only £400 a year from which furniture rent was deducted, and it took a few years of pressure and changes of personality in the College to raise Fellowship stipends. The leader of the pressure group in Worcester was an Australian lawyer, Alan Brown, back from the war, whom I thought of at the time as a worthy successor to George Canning who had given his name – or had his name taken – by Oxford's famous political club. Provost J. C. Masterman, who replaced the 83-year-old Provost, C. J. Lys, in 1947, would go no further than say when a few of us interviewed him in his rooms in Christ Church that he would look into stipends after he had settled in the College Lodgings.

Lys, who liked me if only because I was young, amazed me at the first College meeting that I attended in 1945 by cataloguing his wartime privations and reading a list of his household expenditures during the war, I remember one item on it – 'small clothes'. Many stories gathered round him and his snobbish wife. He kept his study on the first floor of the Lodgings in a room which my wife and I made our main bedroom when I became Provost in 1976; and on one autumnal day in 1945 the Bursar, Bobby Milburn, an alumnus of my old Cambridge college, already a good friend, the first dedicated diarist that I had ever met and Chaplain of the College as well as Bursar with a distinguished ecclesiastical career ahead of him, passed an ashen-faced Vice-Provost, the historian Paul Roberts, aged seventy-five, coming down the stairs. The Provost's first words to the Bursar were 'I am afraid poor old Roberts is losing his powers'.

Given both their ages and a personal relationship which went back for nearly thirty years, it is evidence that Oxford under its so-called old statutes was a very different place from what it became later in the twentieth century. No one retired except of their own volition. Lys subsequently dwelt on many of his experiences in the Worcester College he knew in a privately printed and informative booklet, which he described as an account of a stewardship. The Dean of the College in 1945, Cyril Wilkinson, gave me a copy of it; he had marked 'rubbish' against some of the passages of the text. Forty years on I had a message from the Bodleian Library saying that there was a parcel there for the Provost of Worcester College marked 'strictly confidential' and only then to be sent to him. I opened it with anticipation only to find that it contained twenty copies of *Account of a Stewardship*. Lys, like Wilkinson, had given me one in 1945.

When I was a young don at Worcester – it took me time to recognize myself as such – I owed less to Lys or to his successor Masterman than to G. D. H. Cole, a socialist very different from Tawney and Laski, who had never had anything to do with Worcester.

At a crucial point in my life he put his trust in me. It is a curious Oxbridge story. An effort was made in 1949 to get me back to Cambridge as a reader in economic history, and I went over to Cambridge several times to be looked over both by economists and by historians, taking the train through Bletchley that I had so often travelled on during the war. The fact that I was teaching both economics and politics in Worcester College, then a most unusual dual commitment, greatly appealed to Cambridge dons. So did the fact that at an unusually young age I had been made a member of the editorial board of *Oxford Economic Papers*.

In 1947 I knew Austin Robinson, economics fellow of my own old College, and, rather better, his wife Joan, who was one of the most formidable economists I have ever met. She had introduced me to the whole idea of imperfect competition which had not figured in any of the textbooks that I had read for my LSE final examinations in economics. I also knew Richard Kahn and Denis Robertson, economists of quite different persuasions, both of whom, for different reasons, were anxious to get me back to Cambridge. I confess that I was flattered.

They failed in their efforts, however, as did Postan, but this was only after my closest economist friend in Oxford, David Worswick, told Cole about the Cambridge talks and insisted, another surprise to me, that in his view Oxford needed me. I was writing an essay on post-1945 social policy for a book on the British post-war economy, edited by him and Peter Ady, who was later to become a Fellow of St Anne's. Cole, whose socialism had gone through many phases, had his own political group in Oxford, to which I never belonged and which he never tried to persuade me to join. What mattered most to him about me was that, like him, I believed in PPE, the Honours School of Philosophy, Politics and Economics, 'Modern Greats', which had been founded in the year of my birth, 1921.

Cole himself straddled all three disciplines, and, when told about my talks in Cambridge, he decided that a new readership should be created in Oxford, a Readership in Recent Social and Economic History, and that I should fill it. I had been secretary of a group of academics teaching economic history in Oxford and had seen a lot of the Chichele Professor of Economic History, Keith Hancock, an Australian, whom I had first met when he was a Professor in Birmingham. Hancock had recently left Oxford, though he still had close contacts with All Souls, but I do not think that he had anything to do with Cole's initiative.

It was as important to Cole as it was to me that the word 'social' should appear before the word 'economic' in the title of the readership. The limits of the adjective 'recent' he deliberately and fortunately left undefined. I was already spanning present and future in my work as well as present and past, and I was already introducing literature as well as economics into my published work on social history, as Cole himself did. I turned back, for example, to the Brontës and, knowing their local connections, re-examined Charlotte's novel *Shirley* which introduced the Luddites. Like Cole, I was also to write a brief biography of William Cobbett, whom I had read avidly in Cambridge as an undergraduate when I chose a 'special subject', 'Utilitarianism and Tory Democracy'. The first half of its name took me back in spirit to Neville Hind. In Cambridge this was my one intellectual excursion outside the Middle Ages, and the subject was well taught by R. J. White, the second White in my life, whose approach to history (and to politics) was profoundly different from Cole's.

After marrying Susan in 1955 and moving from Oxford to Leeds I discovered that White's daughter Judith had been one of my wife's school friends and that Susan had stayed with the Whites in a holiday house at Sheringham. Almost the only thing that White and Cole had in common, I felt, was that they liked listening to records on their gramophones. I did not know that White wrote novels as well as histories, but I did know that Cole wrote detective novels, in his case co-authored with his wife Margaret. They both suffered from insomnia. I did not.

I wish in retrospect that while my relationship with Cole was fresh I had written a book comparing the intellectual and temperamental characteristics of Cole, Laski and Tawney as socialists. (I never called any of the three by their first names.) I found Cole the most difficult to assess. I realized that behind his often icy way of expressing his thoughts there was a deep passion: he was always concerned with the consequences of thought for action. There was no one the least bit like him in Worcester College or in his own Oxford college, All Souls, to which he moved when he became a professor.

The college which meant most to me in Oxford was Magdalen, Worswick's college. No one in it, least of all A. J. P. Taylor or indeed its President, Henry Tizard, seemed to want to cut themselves off from the world. They were actively engaged in it, Tizard fighting a continuing war with Churchill's main adviser on science, Frederick Lindemann, whom Churchill had made Lord Cherwell. He was ensconced in Christ Church, a college with which I had little to do.

One of the attractions of post-1945 Oxford for me was that I was in no way tied to my own college. Indeed, most of my friends were Fellows of other colleges, the closest of them Neville Ward-Perkins with whom I organized economic history seminars in Pembroke College. One of the research students attending them was an Australian, Max Hartwell, who was to succeed me in the readership. He too became a friend, and I travelled to Italy with him, his wife and their very young baby. The Italians loved the baby, and our trip, the third of many which I was to make to Italy, included Florence and Siena. My first trip had been to Venice in 1950 where I stayed for a whole long vacation in a delightful palazzo in San Trovaso at the back of the Academia. Ward-Perkins was an active Liberal as was Peter Wiles, a Fellow of New College, and they were leading figures in an Unservile State Group (USG) founded in Oxford in 1953.

Another college where I dined frequently was Exeter. One of my fellow tutors in politics, Herbert Nicholas, became a good friend with whom I examined once or twice. I also examined once with Eric Kemp, whom I was to meet years later when he was Bishop of Chichester. In 1953 I was made a Faculty Fellow of Nuffield College, where I saw a lot of Philip Williams who was working on French politics and with whom I made a short visit to Lyons, a city which I was studying in detail, comparing its politics during the 1830s with those of Birmingham. Philip, a friend of Tony Crosland, was later to write a biography of Hugh Gaitskell.

By 1955 when, entirely of my own choice, I left Oxford with its dreaming spires for Leeds with its smoky chimneys I had played almost as active a role or series of roles in Oxford as Cole himself. Undergraduates were always members of my *dramatis personae*. I taught almost as many undergraduates from Exeter College as from Worcester, and many women undergraduates from St Anne's and Somerville. I visited some of them in their homes during vacations. Their names live for me. I greatly enjoyed visits to Simon Lee in Ledbury and Robin Midgely in Wensleydale. They were both pupils of mine in Worcester College. John Pettifer and Maurice Bard were with my on my 1950 trip to Venice.

The arrangement of my chapters in this book is not chronological, nor is my treatment of my experiences in each chapter. Although I believe that chronology is a necessary foundation for all history I am a lateral thinker myself, and my mind seldom moves in straight lines. It assembles facts and ideas in curves and circles, although I have never belonged to any circle, political or literary. I became interested in cycles too, among them trade cycles and cycles in historical thinking, even before I became a Fellow of Worcester. When I dined in Magdalen I used to talk a lot to the philosopher Gilbert Ryle, author in 1949 of a much discussed book *The Concept of Mind*, and he soon came to know that I was deeply interested in Giambattisto Vico, the eighteenth-century Italian historian – and much more. I bought every book by or about Vico that I could, most of them in Italy, but a few of them off Paris bookstalls by the Seine. Nevertheless, I was alarmed when Ryle asked me to talk about him to his philosophy seminar. It was with trepidation that I crossed the portals of the third PPE mansion, philosophy. Cole approved.

In my next chapter I will move back in time to my beginnings in the West Riding of Yorkshire in 1921. I was given a highly distinctive first name by my parents, who had no awareness of what the implications of their choice might be. It certainly helped me as a writer and in a more profound way almost guaranteed that throughout the changes of my long life I would always be sure of my own identity.

Chapter 2

What's in a Name?

Why was I called Asa? Only in Oxford was I called Briggs. This is the question which I am most often asked about myself. The most obvious answer that I give – 'for family reasons' – never satisfies my questioners. The more specific answer, 'My mother's younger brother, who was called Asa, died just before I was born,' usually does. But supplementary questions then multiply. The most common of them, 'Where does the name "Asa" come from?' sometimes tempts me to reply Scandinavia. The correct answer – 'from the Bible' – inevitably demands further explanation.

I have met priests who, for all their clerical calling, do not think immediately of the connection. I have had to point out even to a Brighton clergyman that in 2 Chronicles, 14, we learn that 'Asa, the son of Abijah, did what was good and right in the sight of the Lord his God . . . He commanded Judah to seek the Lord, the God of their fathers and to keep his laws and commands.' 2 Kings confirms the account given in Chronicles. I have paid enough attention in my own reading to the special relationship between Judah and Israel for me sometimes to be treated as an authority on it.

What more virtuous start could there be to this book? Sadly, however, that was not quite the end of the Bible story. In the second part of his reign Asa transgressed. Cursed with great pain in his feet, he put his trust not in the Lord but in his physicians. I appreciated the relevance of the second part of the story when, during the 1990s, I too was smitten by great pains in my feet. Although I continued to put my trust in the Lord, as I had been taught to do in my childhood, I notwithstanding accepted an invitation to write a volume on the post-1945 history of the Royal College of Physicians, a very old institution, founded in 1518. I was following in the footsteps of the very non-Biblical historian G. N. Clark, who in 1945 was Provost of Oriel College, where there had once been intense discussions about the authority of the scriptures. The Oriel Provost I knew best was Zelman Cowen, a wonderful person and an astute Governor-General of Australia, who had children who settled in Israel.

I had not started to write Volume 4 of the physicians' history when, in 1991 on the eve of my leaving the Provostship of Worcester College, Oxford, after fifteen years, the then Chaplain of the College, Tom Wright, who was later to become Bishop of Durham and is now a Professor at the University of St Andrew's, preached the only sermon about King Asa that I have ever heard. Tom wisely concentrated on Asa's good years. I did not tell him that there is a window in Chartres Cathedral which I saw as a boy that tells Asa's story. It is too high up in that great cathedral for me ever to have seen it in detail. I do not know whether it covers his bad years as well. Chartres Cathedral has always fascinated me. It was so different from the Nonconformist chapels that flourished in my home town of Keighley when I was young.

I was to get to know the cathedrals of France as well as I knew the cathedrals of England. Although I often went to York with my grandfather, I was doubtless more interested then in the Roman walls of the city than in the Minster's great windows. I went to Lincoln several times as a boy, long before the Chaplain of Sidney Sussex in my undergraduate years, Kenneth Riches, became Bishop there, to be followed by a friend with whom I often stayed, Simon Phipps. Long before that I had come to love Rouen Cathedral, as Morris had done, and I was to be moved by Richard Cobb's 'first sketch' of Rouen written in 1975 and published in his *The End of the Line* years later in 1997. I first visited the city in 1934, when I also visited Caen and Bayeux. Richard was fortunate to be in Rouen on an Easter Sunday and to attend a pontifical High Mass celebrated by the very old archbishop. He was 'fascinated and repelled'. I know that I would have been simply fascinated.

In my earliest childhood, before I first went to France, I had not been keen on the name which my parents had given me. Nevertheless, before I left school I came to appreciate their choice. Asa is such an unusual name that I never had a nickname then or later in my life, although an American friend shortened the name to Aze. There are two ways of pronouncing the s, as an s and as a z: my mother and father always used the s. I began to be called Asa, pronounced both ways, not Briggs, during the 1930s when first names were not in general use. My teachers used it as happily as my friends. So did librarians, including, after the war, the librarians in Paris's Bibliothèque Nationale. Long before I became a writer I realized that an unusual name was an advantage. The French always pronounced it with a short, sharp A. How can three letters sound so different?

In Scandinavia, where Åsa is a woman's name, I found that my male gender could cause confusion. On an early visit there I had booked a sleeper from Oslo to Stockholm and found myself placed in a carriage with three women. They urged me to stay! Scandinavia has played a big part in my life. I used to go to Sweden often to meet Swedish WEA colleagues and I was a leader in developing the IFWEA, an international federation of WEAs. In that capacity I got to know well a young Olof Palme long before he became prime minister. He was not living then in the historic district of Stockholm but in a kind of new town.

Later in my life I travelled around Norway more than once to the new northern university of Tromsø, founded in 1968. In 1990 I was a member of a Norwegian evaluation committee examining the state of English studies in Norwegian universities, and on one occasion I was an 'adversarial' examiner for an Oslo University doctoral thesis. Sadly, I had lost touch by then with my first Norwegian friend, Hans Dahl, who, like me, was interested in communications and in broadcasting in particular. I explored Trondheim on my own, and went fishing there – lots of fish – in a group of fishermen among whom I was the only Englishman.

In Denmark I was a member of a small Organization for Economic Co-operation and Development (OECD) team, a unique experience for me, reporting on the future of higher education there: they had produced a report, which they called the U-90, broad-ranging in its recommendations, and we were called upon to discuss it with university teachers and students. We spent most time in Copenhagen and in Aarhus, and I found time to explore the streets and buildings of the capital city. I was interested not only in Danish university education but in the distinctive history of adult education in Denmark, where the great names were very different from Tawney or Albert Mansbridge, the founder of the WEA.

In Denmark, Norway and Sweden I combined learning with the delights of Scandinavian food and drink. Copenhagen's Tivoli Gardens introduced me to some of them. The Rector of the University of Copenhagen, a communist, produced an excellent old brandy from his cellars. In Aarhus I stayed with a wine merchant. There, and in Stockholm and Oslo, I got to like various brands of aquavit, confidently comparing their qualities, and on one unforgettable visit to Uppsala, drinking excellent aquavit (expensive) and eating crayfish, I took part in a ceremony where we all pledged our eternal friendship. Thereafter in Sweden I came to be called in the second person 'thou' as, indeed, I sometimes was in my native Yorkshire. In Denholme, an industrial village, where my mother was born and one of her brothers and his family lived, the word 'you' was uncommon.

Getting to know Finland through broadcasting contacts was last in my Scandinavian journeys of discovery, although when I gave my Jubilee Address to the WEA at Harrogate in 1953 the IFWEA speaker was Reino Oittinen from Finland. It was in Helsinki that I got to enjoy saunas and to listen to the music of Sibelius, which I had first begun to appreciate at a WEA summer school in Wales where there was an excellent music tutor. My often mischievous Finnish hosts were anxious for me to get out of Helsinki, travel north, and see (and eat) reindeer. On one trip with them I got to a point in the far north where the signpost pointed to Murmansk. I broadcast from a radio station using only Lapp, and felt then that I was in communication with Arctic peoples on both sides of the Atlantic. Perhaps I should have spent more time in Iceland and Greenland. I did not travel round Iceland in William Morris's footsteps, but I was taken to some magnificent sites, including glaciers and hot springs.

There is more to names than travel anecdotes, and back at home there remained many questions for me to ask about my own name. Why was my uncle Asa called Asa? I don't know. His own son was called Jack. How much did my parents know of other Yorkshire Asas, like Asa Lingard, a Bradford shopkeeper? I myself knew how common Old Testament names were in whole of the West Riding of Yorkshire, not least the mining towns, in one of which my very learned great uncle William lived, which were very different from the textile towns which I knew best. Coal was their life. In Leeds, a far older city than Bradford, there was a very similar pattern of names. On the other side of my family. my father's father, born in Leeds, was called Abraham. All his brothers had Biblical names, among them Samuel, except for the name which was given to my father, William.

This was the one non-Biblical name used on both sides of my family: my mother had a brother called William. Curiously the two names William and Briggs were linked in the late eighteenth century in a Thompson family which has claimed connections with my own. William Briggs, an excise official, who died in 1791 was the father of Philothea Perronet Briggs who married Thomas Thompson and whose second child was Thomas Perronet Thompson, radical author of a well-known *Corn Law Catechism*, who figures in the history of Chartism and, most memorably, invented the first ballot box. That was before the first Ballot Act.

My mother, born Jane Spencer, lived mainly in a family with Old Testament names. As I have noted, it was a family of thees and thous. She had an uncle called Eli and a cousin called Hannah, both of them speaking what to me as a boy was the broadest of local dialects. Her oldest brother, a John, married a Leah. We had a neighbour called Jesse. I knew several Joshuas and Nathaniels and one Zephaniah. It was not only personal names that were Biblical. Around Keighley place-names included not only Alma and Sebastopol but Palestine and more comprehensively near East Morton, the village where my father's father lived throughout my childhood, the Holy Land. He and my father were non-worshipping Anglicans. Meanwhile, Nonconformity, a term more frequently used in Keighley than Dissent, which was dominant on my mother's side of the family, seemed to me to look back more to the Old Testament than to the New.

The first time that I heard the name Asa in a far broader setting then the West Riding was when I saw Al Jolson in the first talkie, *The Jazz Singer* (1927). Jolson was called Asa, and it was strange to hear his mother calling him Asa by name on the screen. Asa was not a common Jewish name. I have subsequently got to know around ten Asas on both sides of the Atlantic, two named after me, one a singer called Asa Murphy, a Liverpudlian whom I met and listened to on a cruise, another the baby son of a resident of Paddington, London, whom I met at North Westminster Community School, where many languages were taught systematically to a high level while Michael Marland from Sidney Sussex was its very lively headmaster. I once met the Labour politician Ken Livingstone there at a highly eclectic evening concert. That part of London has changed dramatically since those days. Marland himself, who has written many books, became director of a new Heinemann School Management series of books in 1971. There had been little talk of school management before that date.

The American Asa with whom I have most been involved since his birth, Asa Firestone, the son of the Aspen Institute's Director of Communications, got his name, as I did, from his mother's side of the family. Year by year in the 1980s we would stand together below the mountains of Aspen, Colorado, to have our photographs taken and our heights measured. Asa has long towered high above me. My own father and grandfather used to compare their heights with mine too. At the age of fifteen, without being likely ever to tower above anyone, I nevertheless looked likely to be the tallest of the three. Instead, I stopped growing, and thereafter there was the minimum of difference between the three of us.

Being already an historian, if only in the making, I attributed this stoppage, as did my grandfather, a retired engineer who was deeply interested in history, to the influence of the industrial revolution. That was a subject that I was to write much about in the future. I was also to chair a broadcast series about it and to take part in a symposium on it organized by the pioneering history journal, *Past and Present*. The term 'industrial revolution', often used loosely, has a long history and a complex historiography; I do not like to see it printed with capitals. I have preferred too to use the term industrialization, which emphasizes process, and I have lectured on industrialization in many places, among them Japan and Brazil, although I was drawn to the imaginative term used by a Dutch historian, 'industrious revolution', to cover an earlier period of economic history than that which T. S. Ashton brilliantly summarized in his little book *The Industrial Revolution*. My successor as Reader in Recent Social and Economic History in Oxford, Max Hartwell, whom I introduced in the last chapter, stuck with the name and was to make the subject very much his own.

On both sides of the Atlantic in the twentieth century I usually came across Asa in acronyms, almost all of which, except for the Advertising Standards Authority, were not remotely connected to industrialization. Whenever I see the acronym ASA being employed for the American Security Agency I go back to my Bletchley Park days, while the Amateur Swimming Association and the Advertising Standards Authority are the most prominent on this side of the Atlantic. As an historian I have been more interested in advertising than in swimming, and I once addressed the A(d)SA on advertisements as a source for historians.

In reading old newspapers, another invaluable source, I have often found the advertisements in them more fascinating than the news items or the editorial leaders. I have used them lavishly, particularly in *Victorian Things* (1987), to help delineate cultures, treating artefacts as witnesses. Advertisements bring back phases in my personal life too. As a very young child I ate and drank some of the first 'branded' products and studied early posters of railways and holiday resorts. As an adolescent I purchased nationally advertised toothpaste, soaps, deodorants and after-shaves. Through being a board member of

Southern Television I learned that there were some products which our much-married chairman, Sir John Davies, objected to advertising, and I have followed the long and absorbing history of the restrictions and ultimate ban of smoking.

American research on advertising history has been far more probing and thorough than British, although in 1986 Brian Henry, the able and enterprising director of sales at Southern Television, edited an invaluable book on television advertising. It covered both verbal and visual history. (I wish that he had also been able to write a history of Southern Television as a whole.) Interested as I became in popular culture, a term to be studied in depth, one of the places in the United States which I would still love to visit is the Hartman Center for Sales, Marketing and Advertising History at Duke University. In 2011 it launched a digital collection of 27,000 outdoor advertising images spanning the 1900s to the 1980s.

Sadly I have only been able to visit once the older and pioneering Center for Popular Culture at Bowling Green, Ohio, but I maintained a friendly correspondence for many years with a professor there, Asa Berger – another AB – whose interests in 'pop' were even more comprehensive (and uninhibited) than mine. I cannot do full justice to him in this book. My relationship with him was very special. We both felt this.

I like shared initials, particularly with Asa in front of them. Like W. H. Auden, however, I have been uneasy about the ubiquitous presence of unexplained acronyms in the media. Nevertheless, during the war I accepted the name NAAFI (Navy, Army and Air Force Institutes) without bothering about what the initials stood for, and there are many acronyms in the University of Sussex that go back to my own Vice-Chancellorship, among them IDS and SPRU, the Institute of Development Studies and the Science Policy Research Unit. It was in my Sussex years, long after the war, that the Inland Revenue – and sometimes the Royal Mail – found it difficult to understand that I am called Asa. Doubtless knowing that I am not a living acronym, they put full stops between A, S and A in their correspondence with me, treating the three letters as initials.

Sometimes, if rarely, acronyms rest on personal names. A post-war ASA, Anthony Shiel Associates Ltd, described itself in 1962 as a 'new literary agency, with both a strong nucleus of established authors and promising new writers'. I have never voluntarily employed agents, and had nothing personally to do with ASA nor it with me. I have always disliked and mistrusted football agents too bargaining for particular players. The most prominent Asa, who came into public view when I was in Sussex University, was a footballer, Asa Hartford, known as the 'hole-in-the-heart soccer star', who interested Leeds United, then a team of stars, the fortunes of which I continue to follow. I have a copy of the front page of the *Sun* for 8 November 1971 which bears the large headline 'Asa's 48 Hours of Agony'. I myself was so affected by Asa's plight that I wrote to him offering my sympathies and good wishes for the future, and after a few weeks he replied in a long letter, which my two sons, Daniel and Matthew, then thought was the most important letter I had ever received. There have been recent newspaper headlines referring among sportsmen to both a Daniel Briggs and a Matthew Briggs, one a cricketer, the other a footballer. 'Danny Briggs proves star turn for Hampshire', one of them read in August 2011 while I was writing this book.

My wife and I chose Biblical names for three of our four children, to whom this book is dedicated. We resisted any impulse to follow King Asa who gave his son the name Jehosophat. If we had had a third son, however, we would have called him Joshua. Our choice of Judith as the name of our second daughter had more recent historical echoes than the Bible in my wife's family. When my wife as a baby was christened in Keevil Church in Wiltshire, far away from the West Riding, the church where she and I were to be married, the officiating clergyman refused to allow her to be christened Judith. Without any warning he whispered to my wife's mother, Edna, that Judith was a wicked woman and that Christian names had to be derived from women who were good.

Taken completely by surprise, Edna, who had herself been unblessed by a biblical name, hesitated to offer an alternative name to Judith but eventually mumbled the name Susan. This name he accepted, although it lacked the inherent goodness in Puritan names like Prudence and Patience which were not always 'lived up to' by those people given them. Within the range of names Hope was a safer choice. Mercy was – and is – doubtless the name that should have been most in demand. One problem with Susan is that there are often so many Susans in the same room that it is difficult for them to know which Susan is being addressed. There has been at least one Susan Briggs on my side of the family. I have a Bible which she presented to William Fawcett Briggs in May 1866.

I myself was christened by a neighbouring Congregationalist layman, but I could never have foreseen that the Congregationalist mission church, Marlborough Street, which my mother attended in Keighley would in the twenty-first century become a mosque. My mother used to sing in the Marlborough Street choir, and I occasionally pumped the organ there. More actively in my teens I became a Sunday School Superintendent and a local preacher. In that role I addressed Congregationalists and Methodists alike, sometimes during university vacations. The experience taught me the arts of public speaking. It also taught me about the vagaries and varieties of social life in a medium-sized town. One person I got to know slightly through this activity was Mollie Sugden who was to make her reputation on the TV comedy series *Are You Being Served?*

Before the war I bought a book, *Old Asa and Other Stories*, written by W. Riley and published by the Methodist Epworth Press in 1936, which is concerned primarily with local preaching, and I enjoyed following Asa around what Methodists called his circuit. I was very surprised, however, on re-reading the book while I was writing this one in the summer of 2010 by what seemed a very strange coincidence. Old Asa, a very poor man, preached what he knew was the sermon of his life in a small rural chapel blessed with a harmonium, not an organ. 'There's "grip" in our friend Asa's sermons', a fellow local preacher notes. 'He doesn't go flounderin' about with a lot of new-fangled notions and high sounding words.' On re-reading the book I was not surprised by this judgement on Asa, but I was really surprised to be told of another fellow local preacher's judgement of old Asa which I had completely forgotten. 'I felt my faith strengthened', he says, 'an' I said "Thank God for sending Asa Briggs here tonight".' Asa Briggs! My own first and second names were placed together in a novel. Why had I not noted this coincidence before?

It is not the only curious coincidence in naming that I have encountered. I have frequently got letters, the latest of them dated 18 February 2010, telling me about objects that the letter writers have inherited or purchased bearing the words 'Best wishes Mr and Mrs Asa Briggs, April 6 1906'. Some of my correspondents want to sell their objects to me. Others have given them to me. I have now quite a collection. Nevertheless, there is no family connection of any kind between the Mr and Mrs Asa Briggs, of Clayton Manor, their house near Bradford, whose names appear on labelled objects, the best of them a large silver cigarette case, and my wife and me. Nor was there any family connection between them and my parents. The name Asa in my case, as I have explained, came from my mother Jane Spencer's side of the family, not from my father or his father's side. The idea that my mother's father had chosen the name Asa as a possible family name because he had read of Mr Asa Briggs of Clayton Manor is unlikely. The dates do not fit. This, therefore, is another coincidence.

It was not until the 1980s that I first became aware of many other Yorkshire Briggses and of the founding of a Briggs Family Society. It was run by Noel Currer-Briggs, then living in the Dordogne, and it concentrated on the Briggs collieries in Normanton, Yorkshire, to which I had drawn attention when I had written about profit-sharing in nineteenth-century industrial relations. For a time Noel Currer-Briggs and I were both at Bletchley Park, but we never met there. After the war he was to serve for a time with the Intelligence Coordination Staff at the Foreign Office, and later for three years he was to be Secretary of the Three Choirs Festival at Gloucester. He was deeply interested in genealogy.

The surname Briggs figured less in my own childhood than Brigg, without the 's'. At the Grammar School one of the houses was called Brigg House, and naturally I was placed in it. More remarkably – or so it seemed at the time – the twin sons of Sir John Brigg, a mill owner, who was Liberal MP for Keighley from 1895 to 1911 and gave his name to the house, took a personal interest in my school and university achievements. They invited me to their impressive house, Kildwick Hall, and gave me copies of articles that they had written for the *Bradford Antiquary* on local place-names and on Keighley history. Former textile mill owners, deeply involved in local Liberal politics, they were, like my mother, zealous Congregationalists. When I won a scholarship to Cambridge they treated this as a family triumph, but they never met either my parents or grandparents or asked me any questions about them.

I have never been a committed genealogist myself. Nevertheless one of my ancestors that I know about, Williamson Briggs, left behind him a commonplace book written in the first decades of the nineteenth century, which quoted lines about those of his contemporaries who crossed the Atlantic to find a home in a new country. Four of the lines have lingered in my mind, I know them by heart:

> Brave men are we and be it understood
> We left our country for our country's good;
> And none may doubt our emigration
> Was of great value to the British nation.

It was a strange feeling to hear them in a play written by the Australian novelist Thomas Keneally.

I have a sheaf of letters sent to me from America, which suggest that I had American relatives long before Williamson wrote those lines. One of them, from Donald Briggs Johnson, dated 13 June 1973, told me that 'the Briggs line appears first in 1750 in Berkley, Massachusetts, in the form of one Asa Briggs'. There had been one famous American Asa with whom I have no family connections, the distinguished nineteenth-century American scholar, Asa Gray (1810–82), from 1842 Professor of Natural History at Harvard, who wrote a *Manual of Botany* (1848) which appeared in a much revised centenary edition. Drawn into many public debates about evolution, Gray was both an exponent of it and a critic. He was interested, as biologists and botanists were, in naming as well as in names, and so, of course, are historians like me, who look not only at names of plants but at names of all kinds, including those of dolls and matches, locomotives and steam ships. Names were easily transferred from one category to another, among them plants and flowers. Thus, there was a shrub rose called 'The Great Western' and another called 'Queen Victoria' (1872).

Place names, like house names, tell us as much about social and cultural history, as the researches of the English Place Names Society and *The Concise Dictionary of English-Place Names* (first edition 1935) show. Some of the names are so-called nature names: they were often attached to rivers. The name of the river that rises in the Yorkshire Dales, the Aire, which flows through my own town, where the Worth joins it, through to Kirkstall Abbey and Leeds, is Celtic in origin, as is the name Leeds itself. The name is linked to the verb 'to flow', although near where the rivers Aire and Worth met the Aire was so badly polluted when I was a boy that it scarcely seemed to be flowing at all. Another river name that I was curious about as a boy, the Tyne, which I already associated with Newcastle and the far north, I now associate more with a second smaller river which is part of the name Tyning-hame where I now live when I am in Scotland.

House names and street names are influenced, as are other proper names, both by political and military history, by travel and by fashion. Some take the names of flowers and trees, like Acacia Avenue and Laburnum Grove: some, like pub names, refer back to past monarchs and politicians. The name of our eighteenth-century house in Lewes, The Caprons, is derived from the name of a Sussex family. The person who first built a house there was not a Capron but the musician Nicholas Yonge. It was the Pelhams, however, a prominent family with political ambitions, who gave the house unchallenged local status. An inn, the Pelham Arms, was to bear the family name. There are many other Pelham echoes in Lewes.

As I look backwards over time, long before I came to Lewes, I am fascinated by the fact that many of the names of mountains in the Lake District, which I knew well as a boy, were not old. They were popularised through guide books. There were curiosities, however. The 'Old Man' in Coniston has nothing to do with an aged human being. It referred to a stone cairn marking a summit. I got to know the Lake District well because my father's father left Leeds, where he was born, to work first in London and then in Barrow-in-Furness at the Vickers-Armstrong plant, and my father went to grammar school in Barrow and stayed to work there too. One of the most memorable events in my ninetieth year has been a visit to Barrow. It was a journey of exploration, and it was entirely appropriate that I should explore it with an admiral. Sir John Kerr and his wife have reintroduced me to many places that I knew well as a boy, among them Kirby Lonsdale, where I love Ruskinian views, and Sedbergh, where I love the bookshops. There must have been an equal sense of exploration for both my father and grandfather when they moved back to Yorkshire after the First World War, not to my grandfather's birthplace of Leeds but to Keighley, the town where my mother lived and where I was born.

Keighley figures in Domesday Book, a matter of local pride, but its name then, Chichelae, bore little immediate resemblance to its present name, often mispronounced. The Ch was replaced by multiple names beginning with K, starting with Kichalais. It was not until the sixteenth century, however, that the present name Keighley was first used. In 1513 a number of men from the town travelled north from Skipton to 'Flodden Field' to join the English troops led by Lord Clifford of Skipton, to fight against the Scots led by King James IV. The English soldiers included a Brigg and a Butterfield.

The town's first known historian, the Reverend Miles Gale, Rector of Keighley from 1680 to 1720, wrote an unpublished history of the Free Grammar School as well as an account of his parish. A traveller through it, he explained, 'shall not meet with half a mile of level ground save a field of plain earth to the east' where horse races took place. Within that 'field of plain earth' William Sugden was to build his home, Eastwood House, in 1819 which sixty years later was put up for sale and acquired as a public park. Opened in 1893, it was called Victoria Park. The courtyard of the house was extended to house a museum which displayed not only butterflies and stuffed birds but an Egyptian mummy. Nature and history were conjoined.

On 7 May 1921 I was born not more than 200 yards away from what were called 'the Park Gates'. Victoria Park Methodist Chapel was on the way. The infant department in the elementary school which I first attended – there were no primary schools then – was even nearer to my home than Victoria Park. It was called Eastwood.

Chapter 3

What's in a Place?

I have never ceased thinking of Keighley as my 'home town' although
I have not lived in it since I went up to Cambridge University in
1938. During the war when I went home on leave, it was not to
Keighley but to East Morton where my father's mother lived, and after
my father's death in 1950 that was the village where my mother lived
too. There had once been industry there but the industrial frontier
had receded. It was a largely non-industrial village, unlike Denholme,
where my mother was born, or Haworth not far away from it across
forbidding moors.

East Morton was located in the more friendly hills that rose above
the Aire Valley, with the moors behind and beyond them. It had a
beautiful bridge across the Morton Beck and a Victorian church, St
Luke's, consecrated in 1851. Below it, through Micklethwaite, where
my father and I would love to have lived, was what William Keighley,
author of *Keighley Past and Present* (1858), then called the
'contiguous' parish of Bingley. Nevertheless, a long stretch of the
road from Keighley to Bradford lay between them. Trams from
Crossflatts through Bingley to Bradford were still in use when I was
a boy, which gave Bingley a quite different geographical orientation
from Keighley.

Clever boys from East Morton went to Bingley Grammar School,
not to Keighley Grammar School, and I knew some of them well,
among them Eric Hutchinson, who years later became a Professor of

Chemistry at Stanford. I travelled with him to Cambridge in 1938. One of the most famous Bingley alumni, whom I greatly admired, was Fred Hoyle, the astronomer, who straddled science and literature. I compared him in my own mind with Herbert Butterfield, who turned to the history of science with an almost boyish enthusiasm after 1945.

Perhaps because there was a sense of educational rivalry between Keighley and Bingley, perhaps because the topography and buildings of the two places were quite different, I became deeply interested as a boy in local, even parochial, history. It was only later that provincial history, a term that I was not then aware of, came to matter to me. I knew, of course, that parishes and towns were linked together. The Leeds and Liverpool Canal, authorized by an Act of Parliament in 1770, passed through both Keighley and Bingley. The stretch of canal linking Bingley and Keighley was opened in March 1774 when there was a general holiday, church bells were rung, a brass band played, and guns were fired by the local militia.

During the 1930s I used to walk by myself along the canal bank from just below East Morton to Bingley. The famous Five-Rise Locks, which raised boats ninety feet, were an impressive sight. They figured in national history books. Indeed, they were considered to be 'one of the grandest engineering achievements in the world'. The whole canal had not been completed until 1816. By the 1930s the volume of commercial traffic had greatly diminished, but at holiday times, 'parish feasts' as they were always called in Keighley, great barges carried local people on excursions. Sunday schools made regular use of them for 'outings', usually moving west beyond Skipton and seldom towards Leeds.

Leeds and Bradford, rival cities, were not linked by water, and though they were each served with trams you could not get from one city to the other without changing from one tramway system to another. It was a Leeds writer, Richard Hoggart, author of *The Use of Literacy*, a friend of mine, whom I have been writing about elsewhere this year, who was to describe trams as gondolas of the people. In Keighley it was not until 1889 that a tramway company laid rails between Ingrow and Utley and expanded its horse-tram services. It failed to make a profit, however, and sold all its equipment to the Town Council, saddling it with thirty horses and a stable.

The railway pattern was complicated. Rival railway companies, using different lines, did not find it easy to co-operate. There was no problem, however, in going either way by rail between Bingley and Keighley. The first Keighley railway station, an attractive building, known to the Brontës, and the first Bingley station were opened in the same year, 1846. The first scholarly articles that I read about local railways were by the Brigg twins, as were the first articles I read about Roman roads. It was in a lecture to students at Bingley Training College on the far side of East Morton, an institution where I once lectured myself, that one of the twins told his audience that when the railway was built through Bingley in 1846 the 'Bingley Bog', once a prehistoric lake, swallowed up tons of material before it was 'subdued'.

The most famous of all local railways, which the Briggs never wrote about, was the Keighley and Worth Valley, the setting for *The Railway Children* and, through the efforts of dedicated volunteers, a thriving vintage steam railway which has attracted thousands of visitors to Keighley and Haworth. In my Keighley childhood it brought lots of boys to the Grammar School, most of them less interested in enjoying the delights of the line than in finishing their homework before they got to school. The Keighley station of those days was far less attractive than the good-looking first station, but Station Bridge was a local landmark.

The Keighley and Worth Valley Railway, backed financially by mill-owning directors, had opened in 1867 to carry goods from Oxenhope to join the Midland Railway at Keighley, travelling through Ingrow and Damems, the latter a very curious name. Its opening inspired William Wright, usually known as Bill o' th' Hoylus End, to write dialect poetry:

> So strike up yor music an' give it sum month.
> An' welcum all nashuns fra north to th' south . . .
> An' all beyond th' Tiber, th' Baltic, or Rhine,
> Shall know at we've oppen'd th' Worth Valley Line.

I have never been greatly inspired by dialect poetry, but I would hate to see 'Ilkley Moor bah't 'at' pass into oblivion as it is threatening to do. In better days I have had to sing it by myself at international gatherings to try to prove that a Yorkshireman far from home can still sing when he is ordered to do so.

In my boyhood it was necessary for Keighlians, as we called ourselves, to take account not only of Leeds and Bradford but of the great tract of moorland, Rombald's Moor, which lay between Airedale and Wharfedale with Ilkley beyond it. Climbing up Street Lane above East Morton you reached West Morton and the edge of the moor. My grandfather collapsed and died there in the open air in 1940. Above that point was the Roman road to Ilkley, passing Upwood, the once great house of a prominent local squire and for a time MP, William Busfeild, a Tory radical who supported textile workers in their fight to settle by law the length of their working day. What in my boyhood looked the most splendid inn in East Morton was called the Busfeild Arms. Motor buses to and from Keighley and Bingley began and ended their routes there. In buying a ticket you asked for the Busfeild. Uninformed visitors thought the name was mis-spelt.

Near Upwood there was a meeting of four roads known as Four Lanes End. Long after I went to Oxford in 1945 I would wake up in the night after mysterious dreams in which this curious junction figured. Then later in my life the dreams suddenly stopped as did equally mysterious dreams about a cleaner and more beautiful River Worth in old Keighley behind the Parish Church. On one of the roads which started in Keighley and crossed at Four Lanes End was Ilkley Gate, a real gate. You could go no further than the gate if you were travelling by car. It was a road that you had to walk on. I used often to walk up it in solitude, but from time to time I went across the gate to Ilkley in a noisy group of young people. This we called hiking. On the road from Keighley to Upwood was Riddlesden, the place which Denis Healey, a near contemporary of mine, who was a boy at Bradford Grammar School, chose as part of his title when he became a peer.

The name Riddlesden, which appeared in the Domesday Book, is usually associated also with East Riddlesden Hall, which in its seventeenth-century prime had been one of the largest, if not the largest, and most costly residences in the Aire valley. It had a spacious fish pond and, an unusual feature in Airedale, a well-built peacock house. Eventually it had become a commonplace, ultimately dilapidated, farm. It would have been demolished and turned into a private housing estate in 1933 had not the Brigg twins come to the rescue and presented it to the Keighley Borough Council.

In Victorian times the inhabitants of Keighley and Bingley, fascinated by 'origins', liked to go back long before the seventeenth century to the Romans and the Druids, and one of the first craggy beauty spots which they used to visit was called Druids' Altar. A local poet, John Nicholson, 'the Airedale Poet', lovingly described a woodland place

> where the majestic oaks their branches spread
> And the Druids form'd a sacred shade.

The 1825 edition of his poems has as its frontispiece a picture of 'Ancient Britons sacrificing at the Altar'. I never read his poems as a boy. Nor did I learn much at school of local history after the arrival of the Saxons and Danes. I knew Druids' Altar well, however, and loved to walk there.

I had been told about the great bonfire lit there to celebrate Queen Victoria's Diamond Jubilee and about the crowds that watched it blaze. Later I learned that Disraeli had once paid a visit there. There were sinister stories too of people committing suicide by throwing themselves from the top of the Altar crag. There was a strong undercurrent of superstition in the daily life of Keighlians. It was stronger than anything that I detected later in life in Lewes, although the bonfires of Lewes, diligently organized by local bonfire societies on 5 November, blaze brighter than the 1897 bonfire at Druids' Altar.

Fireworks are now more sophisticated but can be just as dangerous in the wrong hands as they were in 1897. I love them best when they are on a big scale as they were to be on the Thames when I travelled on a boat at the time of George VI's jubilee. I had to make do with little 'sparklers', but there were public firework displays in Victoria

Park. The main regular attraction in what we always called simply 'the Museum', placed within the park, was the Egyptian mummy. I never went through the park without going to look at it.

I did not learn much about ancient Egypt even in the junior forms of the Grammar School. Nor, indeed, about ancient Greece and Rome, scarcely represented in the Museum. I knew, however, when I was fourteen that no one could enter Cambridge (or Oxford) University without Latin, and before I took my matriculation examination I idolized my Latin teacher who seemed to me to be a real scholar. He taught me about Romulus and Remus (and Augustus and Nero), but I did not acquire much knowledge of Latin grammar from him. In the sixth form it was a forceful Welsh Latin teacher, not claiming to be a scholar, who at last greatly improved my Latin and in the process gave me a taste, which he never questioned me about, for Virgil and Ovid. I now began to learn Latin poetry by heart as I learned English poetry. Horace did not figure in my reading or in my reciting, and I greatly regret now that he did not.

I note that in a book I now turn to regularly, *Local History in England* (1959, thoroughly revised in 1970) its author W. G. Hoskins prefaced his text with a quotation from Horace, '*Illa terrarum mihi praeter omnes Regulus ridet*' which he translated as 'It is that corner of the world above all others which has a smile for me'. Hoskins did more to encourage the study of local history in England than any other historian. Leicester was the university which came to specialize in it. There was indeed what may be correctly described as a Leicester school of historians. I kept in close touch with them after Hoskins left Leicester for Exeter.

Until I reached the sixth form of my Grammar School I did not read the local books about local history which I came to treasure just before the war, among them the works of Harry Speight, author of *Through Airedale, The Craven Highlands, Nidderdale* and, my favourite, *Chronicles and Stories of Old Bingley: A Full Account of the History, Antiquities, Natural Productions, Scenery, Customs and Folklore* (1898). Profusely illustrated, it tempted me to find out more both about natural as well as human history. I have been reading it again as I write this book, discovering new features in it, like its first chapter 'Primeval Bingley', which Speight preceded with a quotation not from a Latin poet but from Deuteronomy. It does not now seem to me at all pertinent to his text, and he wisely preceded his third chapter 'wanderings among wild flowers' with a quotation from a poem written by himself.

His book, which listed the people, not all of them local, who had subscribed to it, was published by Elliott Stout, unknown to me, whose address was to become very well known to me, Paternoster Row, London EC, very near to the premises of the Longman publishing company, which were to be destroyed by fire in 1940. The list included a Beanland, a local name that survives along with Beanlands, in East Morton, a Hind, a Hutchinson (from Catterick), a Jowett, a Rowntree (from Scarborough), a Scruton, two Baldwins, five Wrights, one a Professor at Oxford, six Butterfields (one from Oldham), six Longbottoms (one living in Graniteville, Massachusetts), fourteen Shackletons (one from Sydenham, home after 1851 of the Crystal Palace) and fifteen Smiths. For me two first names stand out on the list – Pharaoh and Aethelbert.

There were three Briggses – William Briggs (in Glasgow), Briggs Brothers, printers in Silsden, who in the 1930s were to print the Keighley Grammar School magazine, and thoroughly at home in the list Mrs Briggs of Bingley, given no other distinction. There was also W. A. Brigg in Kildwick Hall. He was to become Mayor of Keighley in 1912, staying in that office until 1916.

Foreign subscribers to Speight's book included Charles Banks in Washington, William Hill in Philadelphia, W. H. Holmes in Truro, Nova Scotia, John Foulds (a good local name in Keighley) in Cape Town, and a Mrs Cox in Hong Kong. Library subscribers included the Bingley, Leeds, Blackburn and Rochdale Free Libraries, the Edward Pease Public Library in Darlington, and Dewsbury, Halifax, Leeds and Manchester Public Libraries. Other institutional subscribers were Bradford Historical Society, the Thoresby Society in Leeds, Yorkshire Archaeological Society, the Salt Schools in Shipley, the Bradford and Wakefield Mechanics' Institute, the only mechanics' institute on the list, and the Wakefield Book Society. 'Big names' included the Earl of Cranbrook, Lord Hawkesbury, Lord Howard of Effingham, Lord Masham and the Lord Bishop of Oxford.

While I enjoyed books like Speight's, which are now described as 'antiquarian', my lasting concern with the future of local history, a story which brings together professional and non-professional historians, did not rest on solid local foundations. I did not know, for example, until I read *Cliffe Castle . . . An Illustrated Guide*, published by Keighley's Art Gallery and Museum in 1965, that the owner of the mock-Elizabethan Cliffe Castle in Keighley, Henry Isaac Butterfield, had been a strong supporter of the re-naming of Eastwood Park as Victoria Park after the aged Queen Victoria in 1893. Indeed, he had generously subscribed half the purchase cost, adding as a condition of his subscription the closure of Dark Lane, for him a troublesome public right of way across his huge Cliffe Castle estate which extended far along Skipton Road beyond the limits of built-up Keighley.

I never saw Cliffe Castle as a boy, but I knew that it included fountains surrounded in marble and conservatories where within memory bananas and muscat grapes had been grown. I also knew that part of Butterfield's bedroom furniture had belonged to the musician Rossini. In 1962 I became a vice-president of the newly formed Friends of Cliffe Castle. So had a quite different Butterfield, Herbert, who had never shown the slightest interest in local history. Sir Bracewell Smith, a former school teacher who, with great and largely unappreciated generosity, had given the Castle to the borough of Keighley, was the first president of the Friends, a term I liked, and I was happy to follow him. My chairman was John S. Bell, then a county alderman, a Labour councillor whom I had known while at the Grammar School. The Friends were pledged not only 'to stimulate public interest in Cliffe Castle' but 'to encourage and promote appreciation of the Fine Arts'.

By then Keighley Boys' Grammar School had ceased to exist. The premises of what became a new comprehensive school had moved out of the centre of Keighley, the appearance of which had been changing since the early 1960s.

It is difficult to see any merits in some of the physical changes that took place in the topography of Keighley, another subject delighted in by antiquarians. The Hippodrome Theatre was thoughtlessly pulled down in 1961: I used to go there often during the late 1930s when it provided exceptionally good repertory. A new shopping centre, opened in 1968, had none of the character of the old market, demolished in 1971, which had been divided into two parts, the upper part selling food, the lower part clothes. I loved the old market. I had one favourite food shop where huge barrels of cheese were on display and where you could always have a taste of what you fancied. I was impressed too by greengrocers who before the war assembled weekend parcels that usually included a rabbit. A tripe shop, where many varieties of tripe, including thick seam and dish clout, were sold, had attracted huge queues during the war.

I am sure that the new market is more hygienic than the old and that the new comprehensive, Oakbank, in what I thought of as the suburbs, has far better physical facilities than the old Mechanics building, which also incorporated what was always called the Municipal Hall. The school had moved out before it 'went comprehensive' and I felt honoured when its last headmaster told me that a building on the new site would be named after me, my first. There have been several since, the most interesting of them Asa Briggs House in South Kensington, named after me by Richmond College, an international university in London, the board of governors of which I chaired. In devoting an immense amount of time to its affairs I kept in touch with university problems long after I left Oxford in 1991. We had very impressive governors at first, among them Ernst Gombrich and Randolph Quirk, a great lexicographer. I had a very special relationship with him. The man who made it all possible, Cyril Taylor, was a fascinating person. He was a dedicated but unconventional London conservative.

Meanwhile, back in Keighley, the politics of the town as well as its demography had changed long before it was incorporated in Bradford. My friend Ivor Thomas, chosen as its wartime MP without having to fight an election, a key figure in my life whom I introduced in *Secret*

Days, left the Labour Party controversially in 1948 and turned Independent. Although he was succeeded by a Labour MP, Charles Hobson, Marcus Worsley won the seat for the Conservatives in 1959. During these years Keighley was becoming a marginal seat in national politics. John Binns recaptured it for Labour in 1964; Joan Valerie Hall, close in politics to Edward Heath, won it back for the Conservatives in 1970.

The switch in that year from a Labour government headed by Harold Wilson to a Conservative government headed by Heath was followed by Britain's entry into what the British almost always called the Common Market. Heath, when he found himself in the midst of an international oil crisis in 1973 and concurrently at war with militant coal miners, could not cling to power. In 1974, a year of two general elections, the borough of Keighley ceased to exist. This was a consequence not of economic and political conflict but of the government's implementation of a highly controversial reorganization of local government. Keighley now became a constituent part of Bradford Metropolitan District. The name Keighley was retained for a parliamentary constituency, and Bob Cryer became its MP. After a period of Conservative control from 1983, Bob's wife Ann regained the seat for Labour in 1997. Their son was educated at Oakbank and is himself now a Labour MP.

I had little to do with the daily life of my home town during the 1990s, but in 1983 I took part in a Keighley Conversazione, a term with many cultural resonances, to celebrate the twenty-first anniversary of the Friends. The Cons, so-called, had been held each year in the old Municipal Hall. I wish that I had been able to visit an exhibition arranged by the Friends a year earlier which was devoted to 'The Fall of Zion'. It dealt with northern chapel architecture. In the same year the Friends purchased two stained glass windows from the old Temple Street Methodist Church. They had been made in the William Morris factory. I had not known that when I went to services in Temple Street with Leo White.

I knew a little more then, but not much, about the great house up Spring Gardens Lane owned by Keighley's great textile engineering employer, Prince Smith, because some of the masters at the Grammar School, those who were involved in amateur dramatics, asked me to deliver messages there. I even got inside it. The first name of its owner, Prince, seemed entirely appropriate, although his textile engineering works, not far from my home, known unromantically in the town as the Sheds, covered far more space than his house and garden. Situated on the other side of the railway from Cavendish Street, the grandest street in Keighley, bearing an appropriately aristocratic name, they dominated the central area of the town, although they were no more open to public view than his house. Their owner's main residence was some distance from Keighley, in Driffield, in Yorkshire's East Riding, a place I never visited then or later. It kept Prince Smith apart from the town. I never heard him speak and only rarely saw him. I had no intimation that in 1960 he would dispose of his property and never be heard of again.

On 'our side' of his Sheds during the 1920s and 1930s Bingley Street was utterly plebeian. On the main Bradford Road, below the station and separated from the Sheds, were the working-class houses where many of his employees lived. This was the main road, described as such, which passed by Victoria Park and the exit point of Hard Ings Lane down to Stockbridge near where the Worth flowed into the Aire. Parallel to the Bradford Road was Lawkholme Lane, and Lawkholme was the name given to the substantial district of Keighley which at its end culminated in allotments and in the grounds of Keighley Rugby League football club. On summer Saturday afternoons Bradford League cricket (of a very high standard) was also played there.

Although Lawkholme was a socially stratified district, anyone living within it came to be dubbed a Lawkholmer. There was social stratification too in Utley along the road to Skipton. Much of it was obvious, some of it subtle. 'End houses', as Richard Hoggart explained in relation to south Leeds, were deemed superior to mid-street houses. So-called 'unoccupied' spaces, of which there were far more in Bradford than in Keighley, were treated as playgrounds. After I left Keighley the appearance of the whole district of Lawkholme, including its street and road system, as well as its social stratification, was completely to change, although not all at once. It was only after the arrival of Indians, Pakistanis and Bangladeshis that great changes took place, not least in Parson Street, a long street with smaller streets leading off it, which linked Bradford Road and Lawkholme Lane.

Before leaving behind a lost Keighley I should linger a little longer in Haworth. In the sixth form I studied as one of my examination set books in English Literature Mrs Gaskell's *Life of Charlotte Brontë*, and I cannot have been the only boy in the school who took full advantage when we were examined of the local knowledge of Haworth that we had acquired by living in Keighley. I felt then that the opening chapter of Mrs Gaskell's *Life*, which I have read again in the course of writing this book, did not get Keighley quite right. She felt that its 'aspect' promised well 'for future stateliness'. If so, it did not live up to the promise. Meanwhile, was the Aire 'a slow and sluggish stream'? What about the River Worth, which made its way behind the parish church through a part of the town which I would dream about, beside what was called Low Street, and where, despite one would-be imposing 'arcade', the town did not seem to be on display.

Mrs Gaskell was right, however, about the 'kind of solid grandeur' that she found in the rows of working-class houses built of grey stone. In the 1930s many of them were being pulled down as part of slum clearance schemes. Some should have been saved. The people who lived in them were moved to new housing estates which were cleaner but not necessarily more comfortable.

I was uneasy about Mrs Gaskell's description of the road from Keighley to Haworth which I knew so well. I did not consider that the town of Keighley ever quite 'melted into the country' on the way there. She herself did not quite think it to be real country. But did every object on the way have a 'grey neutral tint'? My own abiding memory of the Keighley road that joined up at a crossroads with the road towards Haworth was that of travelling in 1927 in a line of taxis to the funeral in Denholme of my mother's mother, called Emma, like my sister. There had certainly been nothing neutral about the smell emanating from the soap works on the way.

I knew Haworth well as a boy but not as well as Denholme. Arthur Holdsworth, a son of a Haworth butcher, was the cleverest boy in my Grammar School class before we took our 'matric' examination. He was one of the very few boys who got a good report for his Latin. Nevertheless, he left school at that point and stayed on in the butcher's shop for the whole of his working life, eventually taking charge of it. He had no opportunity, therefore, to study Mrs Gaskell, but later in his life he achieved first-class honours in the Open University, an institution which had not been thought of in the 1930s.

Studying Mrs Gaskell's *Life* myself, I learned little from Kenneth Preston, good teacher though he was, about Mrs Gaskell as a person or about the nature of biography and autobiography. I make this judgement in retrospect. At the time I felt, quite wrongly, that I did not need to be taught more about the Reverend Patrick Brontë, his son Branwell, or his three remarkable daughters as real-life persons. I thought that I knew enough about them from their books and from the stage, and I knew a little of their pictures. I already had an inkling, no more than an inkling, that Mrs Gaskell was underplaying the importance of the creative relationships between them. I liked best her descriptions of the hills above Haworth as 'sinuous wave-like hills . . . crowned with wild black moors'. She was herself somewhat uneasy inside Haworth parsonage and church. She noted what she called the 'dainty order' of the former, but she was unimpressed by the church. For her, its interior was 'commonplace'. It was neither 'old enough nor modern enough to compel notice'.

As a Unitarian she was bound to be somewhat superficially interested in Anglican and Methodist evangelism, and I felt in the mid-1930s that I knew more than she did of Haworth's eighteenth-century evangelical incumbent, the Revd William Grimshaw, Perpetual Curate from 1742 to 1763, who was a close friend both of John Wesley and George Whitefield, two evangelicals whose theology was quite different. Grimshaw used to preach twenty or thirty times a week in private houses in and around Haworth. I had been to a Grimshaw commemoration when I was a boy at school before I read Mrs Gaskell's biography, having no intimation then that half a century later, from 1989 to 1996, I would be President of the Brontë Society.

In that capacity I would read lessons in the parish church and attend Society meetings in the nearest of the rather forbidding Methodist chapels. My first chairman was an authority on Mrs Gaskell, but I felt that he did not make enough of her determination to honour Charlotte as a woman more than as an 'authoress'. 'Women's studies' have advanced far more quickly in my lifetime than almost any other branch of history and have affected my own reading and writing about the whole of history. Juliet Barker's *The Brontës* (1994), a remarkably comprehensive study, has the right approach to the whole family. She roots them in a village and a countryside that I have always known well.

That knowledge was my main qualification for becoming the society's longest-serving president. I welcomed the close associations between the Brontë Society and a Gaskell Society, and although at school we paid too little attention to Mrs Gaskell as a person I was impressed – and still am – when I read an old book, Mrs Ellis H. Chadwick's *Mrs Gaskell, Haunts, Homes and Stories* (1913). Among Mrs Gaskell's haunts was the small village of Silverdale on Morecambe Bay, a place that I loved as a boy.

On the occasion of the Grimshaw commemoration I went to Haworth Church with my school friend Leo White, and I can now reveal, having raised the issue of autobiography and biography, that in December 1937, when I won my Scholarship to Sidney Sussex College, Leo wrote in his own handwriting a little loose-leaf forward-looking biography called *Briggs by White* which he bound in stiff black covers and handed over to me. I learnt more about biography (and autobiography) as literary forms from Leo than from reading Mrs Gaskell's *Life* around the same time. In retrospect Leo's seems a remarkable production. It had a preface and an epilogue, and it consisted of four chapters – character; school life; religious life; and social life. Leo admitted (correctly) that he was only in a position to describe 'glimpses' of my life and to write upon 'those parts of that life' which concerned him. He had known me for 'some five years' –

Preface

These remarks must by their very nature be only glimpses of the life of Briggs, for I can only write upon those parts of his life which concerned me.

It has been my privelege to know Mr. Briggs for some five years, although the deeper roots of friendship were not sown until we entered the sixth form together after Mr. Briggs had matriculated brilliantly bringing to a close a General School life which had been devoid, niether of merriment nor sorrow

Briggs and I took Modern studies in the upper School so that we were cast together yet again, with fortunate results for both of us.

Part of the preface to Leo White's biography.

in fact it was a little longer – and that we had shared experiences that would have a 'lasting influence upon us'.

I like one of his judgements in his first chapter, particularly the last word in it. 'Briggs can easily hold the stage for long periods and whatever he is saying or doing his strong personality is unavoidable.' It would be embarrassing to quote too much from this to me fascinating adolescent study in biography except to note that in 1937 Leo found me 'without side or pride', that 'I was certainly better at criticism than at anything else', and that I extolled 'Liberty': 'the person who tried to crush the fair name of Liberty found Briggs a violent opponent'.

His chapter on 'Religious Life' was a subject which greatly appealed to Leo as a Wesleyan Methodist. He himself became an active local preacher and in later life one who was much in demand in a part of the country very different from that where we were born. Back in 1937, in the town where we were both born, he recorded his 'firm conviction' that in my own seventeen years of life I had 'crammed more religious experiences than many men of 30'. In retrospect the assessment is chastening. Leo added knowledgeably that I had not concerned myself exclusively with Nonconformist experiences. 'Who has explored so thoroughly the many religions of this world, Buddhism, Mormonism, "Rutherfordism" and many other theories of less pure breed.'

We had both experienced the pressures of the Oxford Group, 'the latest religion', although it did not consider itself to be such, that was 'sweeping through the Aire Valley' and had come to resist them. Frank Buchman had not then changed its name to Moral Rearmament. Nor were we offered free trips to Switzerland! As far as I know, local studies of the Oxford Group have never been collected and treated comparatively, although somewhere there may be an unpublished university thesis. (It is very difficult to keep track of these.)

I know from my own experience that Leo and I were never drawn into mutual confessions. We were never convinced Oxford Groupers. Instead we wrote essays on religion, even manifestoes of our own, urging Christian unity and condemning denominationalism as fiercely as in the future I was to condemn departmentalism. We left some of these in the letterbox of the patient head of Keighley's huge Wesleyan Methodist circuit church, fittingly called 'Temple Street'. Coincidentally Temple was part of his surname. We must have been a trial to him, particularly when he was preoccupied with the difficult enough problem of unifying different kinds of Methodists, each with their own history.

I sensibly sought no such access to the minister of Keighley's huge Congregationalist Church, located in almost equally fittingly named 'Devonshire Street'. Drawn as he was to politics, he was the minister who liked to think of himself as the outstanding spokesman of local Nonconformity. I thought of him at best as a pontificator. Looking back I recognize now that he did extremely valuable work when he welcomed to Keighley numbers of Basque children who had escaped from Spain during the Civil War.

I note too that, after that war ended and a few days before the Second World War began, he took them back home through Hendaye. I got to know some of the Basque children and, with difficulty, managed to keep in touch with them. I was amused, therefore, when my older son Daniel was sent by Lancing College to St Jean de Luz to help his French that he found himself staying with a family who at home spoke no French and only Basque. Sadly Daniel learned neither Basque nor French, but the family with whom he stayed owned what was said to be the best restaurant in St Jean de Luz. When Susan and I tried to get a lunch there years later we read the always forbidding words '*fermeture annuelle*'.

Back in the Britain of 1931 Leo and I had first got to know each other at the age of ten not in Keighley but in Kirkcudbright when we were placed together 'in camp' in the same tent with other boys, all very different by temperament, for ten weeks. Kirkcudbright was a revelation to me as it was to us all. We were drawn into the life not only of a town very different from ours but of a Galloway countryside very different from Rumbolds Moor. The camp was organized by Keighley Grammar School for the benefit of boys whom it felt required for health reasons a combination of good food and fresh air. We

My family of origin. My father, William Walker Briggs, was an only child.
So was his mother, Emma. My mother, born Jane Spencer, was the only girl
among six children. My sister Emmie, seldom called Emma, was four
and I was eight in this photograph.

Not far from home, the private Eastwood Park was re-named Victoria Park at the Queen's Golden Jubilee, when it became a public park. The house then became the Keighley Museum in 1892, famous for me as a boy not for its stuffed birds and geological specimens, but for its mysterious Egyptian mummy. It is seen here in a cricket score book of 1848.

I was a Wolf Cub but never a Boy Scout. This photograph was sent to me on my ninetieth birthday by Jack Taylor, who was born not far away from me on the same day, 7 May 1921. I am on the extreme right in the third row. Jack is second from the left in the front row. Our expressions are more diverse than our uniforms.

Victorian Keighley. A tranquil North Street and the Mechanics' Institute before the addition of Prince Smith's clock and the Public Library in 1892.

Keighley's first railway station, built in 1846. Well-known to the Brontës, the Worth Valley Line, now restored as a tourist attraction, linked with the London Midland and Scottish (LMS) Railway.

Keighley's gasworks, opened in 1876.

Praise the Lord and pass the ammunition. Keighley National Shell Factory in 1915, training its first women munitions workers. Many of them moved from the town's Victorian textile mills, some of them impressive buildings.

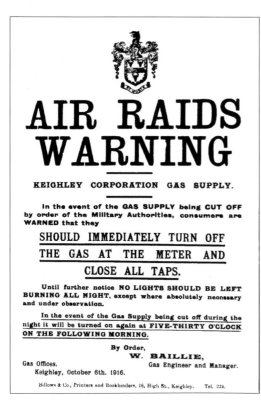

AIR RAIDS WARNING

KEIGHLEY CORPORATION GAS SUPPLY.

In the event of the GAS SUPPLY being CUT OFF by order of the Military Authorities, consumers are WARNED that they

SHOULD IMMEDIATELY TURN OFF THE GAS AT THE METER AND CLOSE ALL TAPS.

Until further notice NO LIGHTS SHOULD BE LEFT BURNING ALL NIGHT, except where absolutely necessary and under observation.

In the event of the Gas Supply being cut off during the night it will be turned on again at FIVE-THIRTY O'CLOCK ON THE FOLLOWING MORNING.

By Order,
W. BAILLIE,
Gas Offices,   Gas Engineer and Manager.
Keighley, October 6th. 1916.

Billows & Co., Printers and Bookbinders, 16, High St., Keighley.   Tel. 224.

The German Zeppelin *Hindenburg* over Westfield Crescent, Riddlesden, in 1936. I saw it pass over Keighley from the cemetery in which my father and mother were to be buried after the Second World War. Keighley, unlike Bradford, was not damaged by heavy bombing.

Keighley in danger? The Gas Works seemed particularly vulnerable in 1916.

Silence! The news-room of Keighley Public Library in its early days: it was endowed by Andrew Carnegie. This is the place where I learned not about a town, but about a world. Upstairs was the Philip Snowden Library, where I learned how to do my own historical research.

Henry Isaac Butterfield's imposing Cliffe Castle. I never went inside as a boy, but it was later bought for the town. It was in an honorary role as President of the Friends of the Castle, which I still am, that I kept my connection with Keighley before and after it became a part of Bradford.

Keighley Mechanics' Institute ablaze in 1962 in a photograph from the *Keighley News*. This was a landmark date in my own life as well as in the life of the town.

Ingledew Cottage, our Victorian home in Leeds.

Ashcombe House, our residence while I was Vice-Chancellor of Sussex.

Boundary House, Winchelsea, a holiday home, which had been damaged by the only bomb to fall on the town during the war.

The Provost's Lodgings, Worcester College, Oxford. Drawn by C. Maresco Pearce.

On parade in Leeds. History professors and lecturers join students on a graduation day in 1956. In the middle, to my left, is the co-head of the department, John Le Patourel, a medievalist. To his left is Austin Woolwych, who moved from Leeds after I left to take up a chair at the new University of Lancaster.

Old Keighlians. Meeting Sir Bracewell and Lady Smith at a party.

enjoyed both, quite unaccustomed to the way of life which we were now living. We ate lots of porridge, which I had never eaten before, and used to collect milk to accompany it on a rota basis from a farm not far away and carry it back to the camp in huge metal cans.

I kept a diary in Kirkcudbright in the first leather-bound commercial diary that I ever bought. My first entries in it were in plain English (not Scots!). Boringly I described the weather as 'excellent', and slightly more interestingly I mentioned being able one day to see Snaefell mountain – was I right? – in the Lake District. I did not refer in my diary to the frightening day when I and another boy slipped while bringing back the milk churn from the farm and in horror saw it all flow away. We were punished for our carelessness, but even with such provocation the Grammar School master in charge of us, Ernest Marsden, kept under firm control his formidable temper which used to terrify us at school in Keighley. All the camp suffered not quite in silence. We had to eat our porridge, which we never then came to like, without milk. I already preferred salt with it to sugar, and later in life got to like (good) porridge very much. I still eat it regularly in England as well as Scotland.

It was not only our eating habits that changed in Kirkcudbright. Even our sporting life changed. We abandoned 'rugger' for 'soccer', for instance, playing a lot of football, trained by an agile ex-Scottish League player who joined in our games and loved to score goals as much as we ourselves did. I also learned to swim in the Solway Firth. There was, of course, no Windscale, later to be called Sellafield, across the water.

On special occasions we went on expeditions and climbed mountains which seemed far away. We came to know the magnificent views of Galloway as intimately as we knew the views across the bleak moors around Haworth. On Sundays we went to church alternately in two rival kirks and listened to long Calvinist sermons. We sat through one inauguration of elders, at one of the longest religious services I have attended in my life. Even longer, years later, was the memorial service for Bernard, Duke of Norfolk in Brompton Oratory. I had come to know him better than any other duke I had met, although later –

and not too far from Kirkcudbright – I got to know even better the Duke of Buccleugh, one of whose homes was at Bowhill.

Back in 1931, when the only duke I had heard of was the Duke of Devonshire, all our weekday lessons, including science, were given us by Mr Marsden, who taught geography at the Grammar School. He did his job perfectly, switching easily from one subject to another and reading to us selected passages from Walter Scott's *Guy Mannering*, my first introduction to Scott, not the easiest of introductions. I was to find *Ivanhoe*, the next Scott novel that I read, relatively simple to interpret. It was because of its local resonances that we turned in Kirkcudbright to *Guy Mannering*. We visited Dick Hatterick's Cave, a very romantic place, and tried to interpret the mysterious personality of the gipsy Meg Merrilies. We were informed that William Marshal, to whom Meg was said to have been married, was buried in Kirkcudbright, and we were taken to see the memorial to him.

Marsden drew out memorably the drama of *Guy Mannering*. He loved drama, acting in the most successful amateur performances in Keighley. I was less interested in the drama than in other aspects of *Guy Mannering* that he conceivably may have liked but which did not interest my fellow campers, including Leo. Scott had given his novel the sub-title *The Astrologer*, and I felt something of the same kind of thrill in it that I was later to feel in science fiction. Scott insisted that *Guy Mannering* was fiction, but took as a compliment the observation that 'in detailing incidents purely imaginary' he had been 'so fortunate in approximating reality as to remind his readers of actual occurrences'. He made the most of mysteries.

I already loved mysteries, and on 12 June I switched my diary entries from English into Aotics, a private language which I invented and to which I referred in my *Secret Days*. At first it was a code, not a language. Later, however, I modified it, introducing grammatical rules. I returned to English on Saturday 25 June with the two unglamorous words, one of them mis-spelt, 'Muck Dutie'. Thereafter there was silence. I wrote no entries either in English or in Aotics.

Not surprisingly there was no reference in my diary or in our lessons to a novel very different from Scott's, *The Five Red Herrings* by Dorothy Sayers, which was first published in March 1931 just before we went to Kirkcudbright. (Had Marsden read it?) In her foreword to it Sayers pointed out that, while all the places she mentioned were real places, all the trains were real trains, and all the landscapes were 'correct', 'none of the people' in the novel were 'in the least like real people'. There was certainly no fictional element in the map of Galloway which was printed inside the stiff covers of her work, a map which clearly delineated roads and railways.

I used frequently to look at *The Five Red Herrings* between 1937, the year that I first read it in its twelfth impression, and May 1951 when I bought it in its twenty-third impression, the copy that I now own. It was the Lord Peter (Wimsey) novel of hers which I most read and which made me ask its author, daringly it then seemed to me, to address in 1939 a dinner in Sidney Sussex College at a club over which I then presided. Her visit made a great impression. She appeared in a huge black dress and talked less of fiction than of life. Her novel had made more use of genuine railway timetables than any person I encountered in 'real life' until I met John Manisty, who was in charge of the Watch in Hut Six while I was working at Bletchley Park.

Among the people Dorothy Sayers rightly thanked in her foreword to *The Five Red Herrings* were the booking clerks at Kirkcudbright station. In 1931 I saw little of them or of the painters who in her words formed a 'scattered constellation', 'radiating' brightness from Kirkcudbright's High Street as far as Gatehouse-of-Fleet. Nevertheless, I knew Gatehouse-of-Fleet well, and visited it again in 1937 and 1957, along with Creetown and Wigtown to the west of Kirkcudbright (I never got as far as Stranraer). I also knew Castle Douglas and Dumfries to the east. They, and not Glasgow or Edinburgh, were the places that introduced me to Scotland.

Neither in 1931 nor in 1937 did I have any intimation, a word that is beginning to figure far more in this book than in any book by Scott or Sayers (indeed did she ever use it?) that most of the railways she described would disappear long before my old age. Nor had I any intimation that from 1991, after I left Oxford, I would spend much of my time in what I never thought of as retirement on the other side of

Scotland in Tyninghame House, East Lothian. It had been built and lived in by another aristocratic family, the Haddingtons, who gave their name to the county town in what was then called not East Lothian but Haddingtonshire. The present Haddingtons, John and Jane, are very good friends. Haddington was the town where Jane Welch, Carlyle's future wife, was born – in a house beautifully restored by the Dowager Duchess of Hamilton, who wrote her sadly unpublished life.

Another person born in Haddington was Samuel Smiles, about whom I myself was to write much as an historian, bringing him back once more into public history not through Haddington but via Leeds, where he edited a radical paper and gave lectures to a mutual improvement class subsequently published in book form as *Self Help*. He became a prodigious and highly successful Victorian writer. He was also involved in railway management. The railway by-passed Haddington but Dunbar, a town with an even richer history than Haddington, was firmly placed on the main railway line from Edinburgh to London.

By 1991, when I moved into a very cleverly divided Tyninghame House, consisting of vertical, not horizontal, apartments, I had many links with both Edinburgh and Glasgow. Indeed, it was an invitation from Glasgow University to give two lectures on 'the cultures of cities', my title – I like plurals – as the University's contribution to Glasgow's City of Culture celebrations in 1991, that drew me after spending two days in Glasgow to (so far) twenty years in Tyninghame. I was invited by Timothy Clifford, Director of the National Gallery in Edinburgh, whom I had first met in Manchester, to stay with him in a section of Tyninghame that he had just acquired.

His first Tim-like words to me when I arrived were 'the middle section of the house is vacant. Why don't you buy it?' 'Sheer fantasy', I replied, but three days later we had bought it. I knew that I would be leaving Worcester College in 1991 and wanted to have a place to house all the books and furniture that I kept in Oxford. To pay for the Tower at Tyninghame, the oldest part of the house, which was still in the process of restoration after the departure of the Haddingtons, I sold a small house in Notting Hill Gate, London, which had originally been an 'artisan's dwelling'.

It was sad to have to sell it – and since we did its market value has unbelievably increased – but in the whole of my life I have never felt myself to be a Londoner. I have never lived for any length of time there, and although I have been to innumerable meetings in London, some of which I have chaired, I have never belonged to any London literary or political circle. I have always been a 'provincial', and my approach to history has reflected this, as I shall show in later chapters.

When I was a boy several trains from Glasgow and Edinburgh to London, some of which figured in *Five Red Herrings*, passed south through Keighley. One of them stopped at Keighley station at 2.15 a.m., less to despatch than to pick up passengers, and it was on that night express that I first travelled to London, though not in a sleeper, in 1934. My destination was not London, but Caudry, a small textile town not far from Cambrai in France.

On that first journey through London in 1934 I had time only to catch a glimpse of Buckingham Palace, Kensington Gardens and the River Thames before leaving Victoria, the railway station that after the war I came to know best. I walked most of the way to it, in the last stage, along a Victoria Street that looked very different then and was far more interesting than it was to become during the 1960s. When, in excellent weather à la Kirkcudbright, I arrived in Caudry via Calais, Lille and Cambrai, I met for the first time the Cordonniers, who treated me at once as a member of their family. While not rich, it was better off than my own in Keighley. This was the beginning of a very special relationship in my life. From the start my friendship with the only child in the family, Jacques, was closer than that with Leo in Keighley.

I learned more about France then and on two subsequent visits to France before 1939 than I had learnt about Scotland in 1931, for, besides the Cordonniers, I stayed with two other very different French families, sharply contrasting ones, before war broke out. One lived near Valenciennes, where I learned how to ride a bicycle – Keighley with its 'sinuous hills' had few of them – and where I might have learnt to fire a rifle. The son, a passionate socialist, was preparing for war. The other family, good Catholics, friendly and cultivated, wanted me to travel southwards with them by car through France to the Pyrenees, including Lourdes, and back again via Paris. I learned more about religion from them than politics. Their older son, Noël, was deeply interested in literature. The father, a tax inspector, took me round his office and showed me tax records dating back to the Revolution. When one regime changed to another the only way to note the change was to identify the handwriting of successive inspectors.

When I had first arrived in Caudry in 1934 at the age of thirteen I was very tired, hot and thirsty, and I made the silliest mistake in my schoolboy French that I think I ever made. Jacques' mother, who was to die before the war, asked me, having no knowledge of English, how I felt and whether I needed anything, to which I replied not '*J'ai soif*', which was how I wanted to reply, but '*J'ai froid*'. She immediately ordered blankets to be brought and a hot water bottle. I immediately realized my mistake and was cheerily given wine diluted with water instead. That was my introduction both to France and to wine.

From the start I loved France and I learned also to speak the French of northern France fluently, if with a Yorkshire accent. I read a lot too in French, poetry, fiction, history. My life was changed in the process. I could even argue intelligently about French as well as about British politics, knowing that Jacques' father was an active supporter and friend of Edouard Daladier, the radical Socialist politician who in 1933 had become prime minister. I once or twice went to the *lycée* in Cambrai which Jacques attended and years later a very different post-war French prime minister, the socialist Pierre Mauroy, an old pupil of the *lycée*, learning that I had gone there before the war, very thoughtfully and generously sent me a great parcel of books on Cambrai and its history.

The imaginative scheme that linked Keighley and Cambrai had been devised by a teacher of French at Keighley Boys' Grammar School, Harry Milton, whom I got to know well although he never actually taught me French. He was known on both sides of the Channel as a writer of textbooks, and he used me as an intermediary during the late 1930s when some of the boys from Keighley who were sent to Cambrai were frightened by the experience of living with French families who spoke no English. Likewise some of the English families who spoke no French could not cope with French schoolboys from Cambrai sent to stay with them in Keighley. *'J'ai peur'* was what one of the boys actually said, and he meant it.

The part of France where most boys from Keighley travelled during the 1930s, *le Nord*, or more precisely the Somme, had been devastated during the First World War, and Jacques and I explored some of the areas which had been in the thick of it. We were not ourselves frightened by what we saw. Curiously, indeed, at the age of thirteen I felt closer to the nightmare of the trenches when I was gazing at the cenotaph in Keighley's Town Hall Square, where I had sat on my father's shoulders when it was officially inaugurated. It was later in my life that I realized what wonderful work the War Graves Commission was doing in France not far from Arras. I recall a lunch which I had in 1934 with the Cordonnier family in a restaurant in the main square, far more impressive than Keighley's Town Hall Square, and after the Second World War, when we swapped memories, Jacques and I remembered best not the war graves but the aperitifs, the lobster and the champagne which we consumed at that lunch.

I also remember another great lunch in Lille with friends of the Cordonniers which went on for four hours. Lille was a very grim industrial city in those years, grimmer than Bradford or Leeds. I had no intimation of how it would change much later in my lifetime. I was to stay there often after the building of the railway through the Channel Tunnel. I had talked a lot about that to Nicholas Henderson, an ambassador to France, who wrote a book about it, and even more to Alistair Morton, an alumnus of Worcester College, whom I once mistakenly invited to respond to a toast at an Old Members' Dinner. His pro-European views went down badly with his fellow alumni as did his pro-Tunnel views. Indeed, there were, most unusually, ripples of dissent. I was strongly in favour of the Tunnel and told Alistair so. I often thought of him when in a renovated Lille I found delight in going round its well-stocked galleries and lunching at La Huitrière.

On his trips during the 1930s across the Channel in the opposite direction – and with no Tunnel to speed his journey – Jacques prepared himself for the north of England. We visited both Bradford and Leeds, each as industrial as Lille then was, but we also explored the Haworth moors – he loved the heather and the bilberries, then a speciality there – and the country and villages round Morecambe Bay, including Silverdale. Jacques got on well with my parents and taught my father to drink table wine. He came to love the north of England as much as I loved France, and he was staying with us in a friends' house in Morecambe, 'Bradford by the sea', just before the Second World War broke out. We were staying with friends of my grand-parents. Jacques's family had a holiday villa on the Channel coast at Ault near Le Tréport, and I remember well daily walks above its cliffs and one memorable visit to the Château d'Eu where Queen Victoria and Prince Albert had stayed with Napoleon III and the Empress Eugenie. I knew as much then about Napoleon III as about Queen Victoria.

There were short aeroplane flights that operated from near Eu, flying above the Channel, and Jacques and I begged to be allowed to take one. It showed the closeness of connection between our two families that Jacques' father, Victor, insisted that I should get my father's approval before climbing into the skies, and so I did with great difficulty not because my father objected but because we had no telephone in our home in Keighley. I have never forgotten the experience of that first flight of my life. I wish, looking back, that I had been keeping a diary in 1934 as I had done in Kirkcudbright in 1931. When years later I travelled by Concorde, an appositely Anglo-French venture, from London to New York and gazed out at the huge vistas of the Atlantic coast I thought back to the Channel vistas of 1934.

In that year Jacques and I used to compare the poems and plays that we were studying at school, though he was to acquire a doctorate in pharmacology not in literature or in history, and he was more curious about *The Decline and Fall of the Roman Empire* by Edward Gibbon than about *Jane Eyre* or *Wuthering Heights*. I studied a Gibbon set book for Higher Certificate, not the whole of his great work but for Gibbon a key part of it, 'the age of the Antonines', and along with his history his own memoirs. Neither Jacques nor I would have thought of comparing the latter with Mrs Gaskell's *Life of Charlotte Brontë*. We concentrated instead on Gibbon's compelling style which we liked to parody. The first half of his sentence 'I sighed as a lover, I obeyed as a son' meant little to either of us then. 'I obeyed as a son' did.

In *The Decline and Fall* Gibbon revealed his strong sense of place, including the associations surrounding places. 'I can never forget nor express the strong emotions which agitated my mind as I first approached and entered the eternal city', he wrote unforgettably for his readers as well as himself:

> After a sleepless night I trod, with a lofty step, the ruins of the Forum; each memorable spot where Romulus stood, or Tully spoke, or Caesar fell, was at once present to my eye; and several days of invocation were lost or enjoyed before I could descend to a cool and minute investigation.

It was in Rome itself that Gibbon conceived the idea of composing a history of the city, extended later to the entire empire. 'It was at Rome', on 15 October 1764, 'as I sat musing amidst the ruins of the Capitol, while the bare-footed figures were singing Vespers in the temple of Jupiter, that the idea of writing the decline and fall first started [in] my mind.'

Looking back after my long lifetime I know that I was not ready during the 1930s either for Gibbon or for Rome. Twenty-one years later, when I first visited, I was ready for both. Nevertheless, when I went up to Cambridge in 1938 the first essay that I had to write was on the decline of the Roman Empire. Was it due to internal or to external forces? My essay was far too long, far too derivative. How else could it have been? My excellent young supervisor, R. C. Smail, 'Otto', who just before the war was working on crusader castles in Syria, which eventually I was thrilled to see, tore it to pieces, a unique but necessary experience for me.

Soon Smail was to join the Army, returning to Sidney Sussex in 1945 where he became a pillar of the college. I don't think that I ever talked to him again about Rome, although the oldest undergraduate history society in Cambridge, the Confraternitas Historica in Sidney Sussex, whose centenary I attended in 2011 – Neville Hind attended its fiftieth anniversary – endowed those undergraduates running it with Roman titles. For a time I was Magister Rotulorum, then Princeps. We sat proudly on a Senatorial couch and wore red socks. There was also, I should add, a Tribune of the Plebs.

I made my own first visit to Rome, but not to Italy, on my honeymoon, which began in Sicily, in 1955. On our return north Susan and I spent three happy days in the city of Rome exploring both its ancient and modern sights. The Colosseum and the Catacombs were on our itinerary as were the Piazza da Roma, the Spanish Steps and the expensive shops on the Via Veneto, and we stayed in a hotel not far from the wonderful railway station then recently opened. I had been impressed by the story of how Henri Pirenne, the Belgian economic historian whom I heard reading a paper when I was an undergraduate in Cambridge, told his companion, the great historian Marc Bloch, on a visit to Stockholm, that the first building they should see there was not the old palace but the great new city hall. It was a great tragedy that Bloch was killed by the Nazis during the war.

After Rome Susan and I spent several more relaxing days in France with Jacques and his family, who were now living in Compiègne, a city with its own rich history. We also took time to go to Paris, parts of which I had already got to know well, street by street, on post-war trips there. Slightly older than me, Jacques had married earlier, and Susan and I enjoyed meeting his wife and their twin boys. Twins had played – and were to play – an important part in the life of my own family. My grandfather had twin brothers and my daughter Judith has twin sons. My father's mother had been an only child as he was. So was Susan. Generations were succeeding each other and we were defying demographic trends in our own family. In 1955 my father was already dead. So was Jacques' father to whom I owed so much.

An English historian, whom I have already mentioned but whom I did not meet until 1961, Richard Cobb, four years older than me, had already through his love of France – and of Paris in particular –

become fascinated not only by particular places but by the very 'sense of place'. I was so impressed by what I had already heard of his unorthodox approach to history that when I left the University of Leeds for the University of Sussex in 1961 I used professorial privilege at Leeds, as I very seldom had done, to have Richard appointed to a vacant history post left by the move to Sussex with me of one of my colleagues in Leeds, Maurice Hutt. Normally such an appointment would have been left to my successor. I broke the rules.

This was the start of a special relationship with Richard. While at Leeds he met one of my students there, Margaret Tennant, whom he married in 1963. They had three sons and one daughter. In 1963 he moved to Balliol College, Oxford, as Fellow and Tutor, and I was an external member of the Oxford committee which appointed him Professor of Modern History at Oxford in 1973. This was a chair 'attached' to Worcester College, and when I returned to Worcester three years later as Provost, a return that I had never contemplated, I saw a great deal of him.

Richard's first book to appeal to a large audience, *Second Identity*, had appeared in 1969 before he became an Oxford professor; it had a long autobiographical preface, and its title referred to his own double identity as an Englishman and Frenchman. Eleven years later, his *Streets of Paris* dealt in meticulous detail with four *arrondissements* in the city in which he brought back to life both wartime collaborators and members of resistance movements. *Still Life* (1983) consisted of sketches of his childhood in Tunbridge Wells where there were neither collaborators nor resisters.

Some of Richard's most remarkable books appeared during his professorship, which ended with his retirement in 1984, but was followed by a further three years as a Senior Research Fellow in Worcester College. He became as deeply loyal to it as his pupils were to him, and he willingly accepted my invitation to him to become Dean of Degrees, which no one expected him to accept. That particular deanship involved no meetings. He detested them, but he loved leading processions in cap and gown to the degree ceremonies in the Sheldonian or the Examination Schools some distance away.

Free from statistics and from ideology, Richard by choice dealt in his writings with forgotten people, the first of them the *sans-culottes* of revolutionary Paris. Clothes for him could be the key to history. His 'home town' Tunbridge Wells was 'a place where clothes called to clothes, cutting out words and greetings'.

In writing this chapter I might have followed in relation to Keighley – or tried to follow – the approach that Richard used in writing about Tunbridge Wells, describing all the people who lived in the *arrondissement* of Lawkholme. I would never have been happy, however, focusing on any Yorkshire *sans-culottes*. I was more interested than he was in industrialization, taking it in my stride in a way that the other great historian whom I have already mentioned, W. G. Hoskins, never could do in his pioneering books on local history, among them *The Midland Peasant: The Economic and Social History of a Leicestershire Village*, which traced the archetypal history of a single place, Wigston Magna. Hoskins, in advancing the study of local history more than any other single historian, particularly disliked the nineteenth and twentieth centuries.

He had an even stronger visual sense of place than Cobb. 'As the sun sets behind the crumpled outline of the Charnwood Hills', he wrote in an article which appeared as early as 1946, 'the evening light throws long shadows across the pastures of east and south Leicestershire, revealing in many places the presence of shallow ditches and banks that form a distinct pattern.' This was a landscape of deserted medieval villages. I liked Hoskins's way of describing it and the way he introduced the term 'pattern', one of my favourite words, which I used in the title of my first co-authored book, dealing not with local history but with international relations, *Patterns of Peacemaking*.

I first heard of deserted villages when I was studying medieval history as an undergraduate at Cambridge and, wearing wellington boots, tramped along ditches and banks, exploring the remains of lost ploughed fields with John Saltmarsh, who was as much of a pioneer as Hoskins. Agreeably he was something of an eccentric too, and appropriately he spent part of the war years in Hut Three at Bletchley Park. The notes he sent me were invariably typed, and since he did not bother to use the typewriter properly, though he preferred it to his own handwriting, the signature at the end of them always read 'JohnxSaltmarsh'.

One of my fellow troopers across the fields with him was Maurice Beresford, whom I was to meet again at Leeds University in 1955. He worked very much on his own and was never associated with the history department – School it was called – in Leeds, but he wrote about working-class streets in Leeds with as much meticulous care as he wrote about deserted villages. One of his books (1959) was called *History on the Ground*.

Unlike him, and unlike Hoskins, I looked at my own historical research in a different way. I began by writing the second of the two volumes on the history of Birmingham which the city of Birmingham had commissioned before the war to celebrate the centenary of the incorporation of Birmingham in 1838. It was a volume which was to have been written by the then Vice-Chancellor of Birmingham University, Sir Charles Grant Robertson, but he died before Volume I, written by Conrad Gill, was finished. No one in the history department at Birmingham wanted to take over the task and so, encouraged by Philip Styles, a member of the department, who was an alumnus of Worcester College, I told the powerful Town Clerk of Birmingham, who asked me to take it on, that I would do so. My sole question to him was 'Could I look at any notes Sir Charles had left?' 'Of course', he replied, but three weeks later he wrote to me and said that Sir Charles had left none.

It was as well that he had not, for he had never made any claims to be interested in local history nor had he any sense of place. Left to my own devices, I approached representatives of Birmingham's great families, the Kenricks, the Marriotts and the Cadburys. They were as interested as I was. They transformed my own work as a young and developing historian. I must add here, however, that I could not have written my *History of Birmingham* without the help of Valerie Norris who was in charge of the superb Birmingham collection in the City Library. I was to realize as I wrote more and more history just how indispensable good archivists and librarians are.

It was from novelists even more than from historians that I had realized in my twenties how important a sense of place is whether the place being written about is attractive or not. My model was (Enoch) Arnold Bennett, born at Hanley in the Staffordshire Potteries in 1867. I noted in my first chapter how R. H. Tawney gave WEA tutorial classes there without paying much attention to what the potters were doing themselves. They doubtless told him. In *Anna of the Five Towns* (1903), his first main literary achievement, Arnold Bennett did not romanticize the local environment that he knew so well or the local characters who figure in his 'plot'. What could be more compelling, however, than his description of 'the north end of an extensive valley which must have been one of the fairest spots in Alfred's England':

> [Five continuous towns] united by a single winding thoroughfare some eight miles in length have inundated the valley like a succession of great lakes . . .
>
> They are mean and forbidding of aspect – sombre, hard-featured – uncouth, and the vaporous poison of their ovens and chimneys has soiled and shrivelled the surrounding country till there is no village lane within a league but what offers a gaunt and ludicrous travesty of rural charms.

Viewed from a terrace above 'the snake-girt amphitheatre' provides the setting for an 'unending warfare of man and nature':

> Here, indeed, is nature repaid for some of her notorious cruelties. She imperiously bids man sustain and reproduce himself and this is one of the places where in the very act of obedience he wounds and maltreats her.

What's in a place could never be better demonstrated. History, however, is about more than places and people. Fascinated as I have been with both, I have been just as fascinated with time. In my next chapter I turn to an equally fundamental question about the past, 'What's in a date?'

Chapter 4

What's in a Date?

One of the complaints of people who are put off by history is that it is all about dates – '1066 and All That'. Some school history still is. The best school history never has been. Behind every historical date there is what journalists call a 'story'; and in order to tell a story you have to consider what happened first – there may be a prelude – and what happened next. You need not, of course, choose to tell the story in that order. Writers of fiction can play with time, offering alternative endings, or none, while journalists, under the control of their editors, necessarily drop stories before they are completed. They may or may not pick them up again at a later point. Film-makers can, like television directors, use flash-backs. They can also introduce documentary material from older stories.

I myself have learnt most about dates from detective story writers, who have to think very carefully about chronology. The year 1921, when I was born, does not figure prominently in history textbooks. It was, however, the year when Agatha Christie produced her first published novel, written in longhand, *The Mysterious Affair at Styles*. In it she introduced to the world her Belgian detective Hercule Poirot who has outlived all the politicians of 1921. This was the year also when Lytton Strachey published his *Queen Victoria*, four years after *Eminent Victorians*, the book for which he is best known. Strachey attached little importance to dates; Christie attached much. There is one scholarly book, published in New York in 1976, called *The Agatha*

Christie Chronology. She was as much concerned with times of the day as with days on the calendar.

Historians and biographers are bound to be as selective in their choice of dates as in their choice of themes. They are forced by the nature of their endeavours to ponder on the special relationships between private and public events. I bring in Queen Victoria and Lytton Strachey, for instance, for personal as well as public reasons and I introduce a lecture into the list of dates which I cover in this chapter. When I gave it at the Victoria University in western Canada, a half century after Victoria's death, I was surprised to be introduced by my chairman, who seemed to me quite aged, with the words 'We greatly welcome Professor Briggs because he was born only twenty years after the death of Queen Victoria.'

I was only in my early forties then. I was not a great admirer of Strachey's *Queen Victoria*, but I was enthusiastic about his *Eminent Victorians*. I quickly knew, of course, after I first read him, how different we were as people and as historians, but I had had Strachey in mind when in *Victorian People* (1954) I chose characters who had links between them through whom I could explore what was then a neglected period in Victorian history.

The mid-Victorian years, beginning for me with the Crystal Palace in 1851, were, I thought, a kind of plateau with mountains and abysses on each side. My metaphors were geographical. Strachey's never were. Instead he thought that his *Eminent Victorians* resembled a musical quartet. He chose his four characters from all parts of Victoria's reign, not bothering much about when they were born and when they died. He did not divide Victorian England into phases. I thought that to be essential. Like Julius Caesar's Gaul I divided it into three parts. I was profoundly interested in when my characters were born and when they died. Since Strachey was not, one of his characters, Thomas Arnold, died before the Victorian age had really begun. Strachey himself did not die until 1932. No one could ever describe him as a Victorian. I often have been.

As I now look back as an aged historian to my birth year, twenty years after Victoria's death, two institutional dates stand out for me, the founding of the Musicians' Union and the founding of the British Legion. I note too a non-institutional date. In January 1921 Chequers was presented to the nation as a country residence for the prime minister of the day, whatever party he led. He could invite anyone he wished. I was invited to a lunch there by Ted Heath because he wanted to separate himself at the lunch table from Indira Gandhi whom he knew that I knew. It was neither an historic nor a happy occasion. And for me it was a once-and-for-all event.

'The Great War' (1914–18), with necessary capitals, is usually thought of as the great divide of the twentieth century – or as the end of a 'long nineteenth century'? Even in the twenty-first century Armistice Day, 11 November, remains a great occasion, thanks in the first instance to what is now the Royal British Legion. It transcends party politics. Each year it reminds the whole country not only of the First World War but of all the twentieth- and twenty-first-century wars in which this country has been involved. In 2011 the rituals at the Cenotaph in London were better organized and even more moving than any that I can remember. There is a War Memorial Trust, too, which monitors the condition of war memorials in Britain and encourages protection and conservation, and I was glad when one of the most able postgraduates I have ever supervised, the Australian historian Ken Inglis, chose as his subject for an essay in my *Festschrift* in 1990 the war memorials of Melbourne and Sydney, without knowing of my great interest in monumental remembrance.

As a schoolboy in my teens I had to be reminded of what my family regarded as my own oldest memory, for me a very vague memory, that of sitting on my father's shoulders at the opening of Keighley War Memorial, also called the Cenotaph, in a new Town Hall Square in 1924. As late as 1900 the site had been a rubbish dump. By 1921 there were shrubs growing. In 1924 when the Cenotaph was unveiled there were 28,000 people present, more than half the total population of the town. The British Legion was as prominent locally as it was nationally. I do not know what the Town Hall Square looks like now.

It was in that same Square, in August 1939, when the Square was probably at its best, that I heard newsboys shouting the news of the signing of the Nazi–Soviet Non-Aggression Pact. That for me was a genuine private and public memory with a date attached to it. It remains vivid in my mind. I shall never forget it. On 1 September the Germans were to invade Poland. That was the biggest of public dates, although I had seen the war coming when in 1938 I went up to Cambridge. So also had E. J. (Jim) Passant, the Senior History Fellow in Sidney Sussex. When he interviewed me for a scholarship in 1937 he told me, 'You are only a baby, but a war is coming and I am recommending you for a scholarship because I would like you to get your degree before you go into uniform.' I did. December 1937 was a crucial date in my life. I owe an immense debt to Jim. No other date in my own life down to that point is worth comparing with it.

I knew in 1937, of course, of many public dates that mattered even more in the nation's life, the most important of which seemed at the time to be the Abdication of Edward VIII. There was certainly a story behind that. Because the woman whom Edward loved and for whom he gave up the throne was American, however, it was bound to figure in American as well as British chronology. I had met no Americans before 1939, but I knew that they had their own chronology. In the year of my birth, 1921, the newly inaugurated President of the United States, Warren G. Harding, who left behind him little to remember, reiterated his pre-election promise that the United States would never join the League of Nations, and it did not join what then became known as World War II until Pearl Harbor, their biggest of public dates, 7 December 1941. Long before then, indeed long before Strachey died in 1932, I had already accumulated many dates to remember in my short life that I still remember, some of which figure in the history books, and some of which were American. A few were fixed in my private memory. Thus, during the short-lived General Strike of May 1926 I remember going up with my father to coal piles by the Leeds and Liverpool Canal to collect coal for our fireplaces. I also remember a very different event in 1927, that of being awakened in the night and sitting on my father's shoulders to watch (did I actually see it?) a much heralded eclipse. I remember, too, without knowing the date, my father installing electricity in our house. I do not remember the Wall Street Crash, however, although I remember photographs of the Governor of the Bank of England, Montagu Norman, from the 1920s onwards.

I have noted already how I watched – and did see, this time without my father – Al Jolson in the first talkie, *The Jazz Singer*, made in 1927. though Keighlians probably did not see it until 1928. Keighley then had two cinemas – one, the Cosy Corner, tucked away down a side street, the other far more imposing, the Regent. I went to both as Hollywood arrived in Keighley. I was interested only in the products of that distant 'factory of dreams', for it was not until I went up to Cambridge that I saw early films from Germany and France. Even then the main film on display, French, German and American, interested me far more than the newsreels which were part of the daily programme.

It was only after the war that I started visiting regularly the news cinema outside Victoria Station in London where there were no main films on offer. I became fascinated then with watching what the editors of newsreels, like Movietone, made of history in the making. I was to encourage the academic study of newsreels when I was Professor of History at Leeds. I even examined one pioneering doctoral thesis devoted to them. Yet I had not needed newsreels in May 1929 to inform me of the general election which brought the Labour Party into uncomfortable power – Philip Snowden was Ramsay MacDonald's Chancellor of the Exchequer. Two years later I was more aware and far better informed about the general election of August 1931. I followed day by day the formation of what was called the 'National Government', even speculating as to what King George V as well as his prime minister was 'up to'. It was of local as well as national interest. MacDonald kept Snowden as Chancellor only until November 1932. Snowden's almost religious belief in free trade made their continued association impossible. Before the break came I remember an active member of Keighley's Independent Labour Party stopping me in the street in 1931 and calling Snowden a traitor. That was news from below. By then I was reading newspapers to add to the information that I needed in order to follow not necessarily intelligently the course of events. (I do not think that I then understood, let alone used, the word chronology.) At home we took none of the national newspapers, however, only the *Yorkshire Observer*, published in Bradford, the *Keighley News*, published not far from my school, and the *Yorkshire Post*, published in Leeds.

In Cambridge, by contrast, I read all the newspapers I could get through in the reading room of the Cambridge Union of which I became a life member. Possibly for social reasons, I never spoke in a debate. I also read periodicals – *The Spectator* was the first; but I read *Tribune* also and *Granta*. *The Times* and the *Manchester Guardian*, as it was then, were the newspapers on which I depended most. I looked too at the *Daily Mail* and the *Daily Express*. In the *Express* Lord Beaverbrook insisted day by day for as long as he possibly dared to do that there would be no war. His foresight was as faulty as Jim Passant's had been prescient. Beaverbrook served as a member of Churchill's wartime government. Another historian who had been active before the war was E. H. Carr, whose 'leaders' were to engage and provoke readers of the wartime *Times*. He was one of my examiners in 1941.

I leave out of this book Second World War dates, personal and public. I had to study them more carefully than I had done before, using works of reference about the Soviets and Japanese as well as British and American dates, when two years ago I set out to write *Secret Days*. It was not only at Bletchley Park that days mattered more than years during the Second World War. In writing about them my personal dates proved extremely difficult to remember and establish except birthdays and, tragically, the deaths of friends in uniform at sea and on land. I kept diaries bound in cardboard rather than mock-leather, for two of the war years, leaving out all that I was doing as a cryptographer. They reveal the diversity and intensity of my special relationships in what, looking at the whole of my life, were unique circumstances.

My unrecorded memories are still vivid, but also fallible, and, as Julian Barnes points out on the first page of his Booker Prize-winning novel, *The Sense of an Ending* (2011), like all memories 'what you end up remembering isn't always the same as what you have witnessed'.

I shall return to that novel and to Penelope Lively's *How It All Began* (2011) in the last chapter of this book. In the rest of this chapter I will pick out only the dates that in retrospect matter most to me in any examination of my special relationships.

I start the list of my own post-war dates as I would have picked them out at the time with 1948 when I went to Paris to study a centenary year of revolution, and with 1951, the centenary year of the Crystal Palace in Hyde Park. The prefix 'post' was to become one of the most overworked of all prefixes during the 1990s, but it was not much used during the 1950s. 'Revolution' and 'crisis' were the most overworked of words then. It was then that I celebrated my thirtieth birthday, what Dylan Thomas, born in 1914, had called his 'thirtieth year to heaven'.

Dylan, whom I read avidly at Bletchley, was to die in 1953. I was introduced to him for the first time in 1951 at an open-air performance of a Shakespeare play produced by Nevill Coghill in Exeter College gardens. Coghill was to go on to produce an unforgettable *Tempest* in Worcester College garden before I left the college for Leeds in 1955. After I returned to Worcester as Provost in 1976 I gave what was said to be an also unforgettable party near the lake. Coghill had made good use of it for Caliban to climb in and out of, and some of the people who had acted under his direction declaimed some of their lines again. Some of the audience had seen the original performance. Time had turned round.

The 1950s was a decade when open-air amateur drama flourished in Oxford with Ken Tynan standing in as an actor in OUDS (Oxford University Dramatic Society). His style was easy to parody, but I felt that I was in the right place at the right time when I had the chance of talking to him in Oxford's Examination Schools both before and after he took his viva. The oral examination was of vital importance both for candidates fearing a failure or those hoping for a first. I just happened that day to be in the Examination Schools as an examiner in my own subject and had been required to withdraw from the vivas when one of the undergraduates whom I had taught in my own college was being examined. He did not get the first he much coveted and in my view deserved. I am not sure what grade of degree Tynan got. In retrospect – and even at the time – Oxford examinations could often go wrong because of a badly chosen group of examiners, chosen 'from above'.

There was no such 'happenstance' in the two biggest public events of 1951 – the Festival of Britain, which opened on 1 May and was conceived of by its Director, Gerald Barry, former editor of the *News Chronicle*, as a 'tonic for the nation', and the general election of 25 October as a result of which, after six years in office, the Labour government lost power to the Conservatives led by Winston Churchill. During the election the Labour politician Herbert Morrison, who had become known by then as 'Lord Festival' for his skilful handling of every kind of festival problem from finance to personnel, was a particular target of Winston Churchill, who hated the very idea of the Festival. This was of particular concern to Morrison, who had greatly admired Churchill when he was Home Secretary in the wartime coalition government and preferred him to Attlee. After the illness and resignation of Ernest Bevin in 1951 Morrison had for a very brief time taken over the Foreign Office, for which he seemed to me – and not only to me – quite unsuited, and it was a consolation for many that in October Eden returned to the Foreign Office with Churchill.

Between 1955 and 1960, when I was in the University of Leeds, I got to know very well (feeling like an insider) all the main characters involved in the Festival of Britain, but I knew very few of them in 1951 itself, except Paul Reilly, whom I had met through the 'Britain Can Make It' exhibition of 1946, and Max Nicholson, Morrison's Permanent Secretary. I went to the Festival of Britain as a visitor, broadcasting about it then and later for the Schools service of the BBC. Reilly, whom I liked, was to become Director of the Design Council of which I was for a short time a member.

What I was most interested in and knowledgeable about in 1951 were not the preparations for the Festival of Britain but the experiences of the Great Exhibition of 1851 held in Hyde Park. I had written a pamphlet about it, *1851*, for the Historical Association, which was my first attempt at singling out one particular year for special attention. In it I covered domestic politics and international relations as much as the Great Exhibition itself. I was to concentrate on the Exhibition itself, however, in *Victorian People* (1954) and in the first chapter of *Victorian Things* (1988), which I called 'The Great Victorian Collection'. Between writing the two books I had found out far more about the Great Exhibition than I had known in 1951.

The political and economic events of 1951, though not the religious events, were even more varied than the events of 1851, and it was entirely appropriate that in 1951 the magazine *History Today* was founded. I was associated with it from the start through Garret Drogheda, Brendan Bracken, wartime Minister of Information, and Alan Hodge, who had been a leader of the team helping Churchill to take through the press his *History of the English-Speaking Peoples*. Again in the light of what was to come later, it was interesting that the new magazine was to be published by Longman, the oldest publisher in the country, with whom I was to have a long and very special relationship and whose history I was to write. The sub-title of that history, chosen by me, was *A Study of Longevity*. This was institutional longevity. It seems curious to me, looking back, that my interest in institutional – and individual – longevity goes back to a year when I was celebrating my thirtieth birthday.

It also seems more clear to me, but only in retrospect, that some of the most memorable dates in 1951 were concerned not with Britain but with the world. On 2 March there was a purge of the Czechoslovak communist party. On 11 April the President of the United States, Harry S. Truman, relieved General MacArthur of his Far Eastern Command and replaced him with General Matthew Ridgway. Attlee had his part to play in that story. On 23 June Guy Burgess and Donald Maclean, the 'missing diplomats', fled to Moscow. On 20 July King Abdullah of Jordan was assassinated in Jerusalem. That directly affected my plans for visiting the Middle East in 1952. On a different plane *The Archers* serial on radio began in 1951 on the BBC's Light Programme and the American musical *South Pacific* was staged in London. For me one of the new books of 1951 which I bought with pleasure was the *Complete Poems* of Robert Frost. He had far more to say to me then than Dylan Thomas, not least about partings of the ways. Such partings were figuring in my experience as much as in my dreams.

The next date that I pick out in reviewing my own life and work during the 1950s, 1957, is not a year that figures as prominently in national and international history as 1956, the year of the Suez and Hungarian crises. Yet 1957 was the year of Sputnik and the year when life peerages were created in Britain. Across the Atlantic Fidel Castro began 'total war' in Cuba against the government of General Batista, and, in what was still described as 'the Far East', Khrushchev, after a visit to Beijing (still called Peking by most Westerners), declared that any United States attack on China would be regarded as an attack on the Soviet Union. Also in 1957 J. K. Galbraith published his book *The Affluent Society*.

In 1957 the institutional date of greatest importance to me in the shaping of my own future was the creation of the Victorian Society. Yet this was the year when I became President of the Workers' Educational Association, when I first joined the University Grants Committee, and when I accepted an invitation from General Sir Ian Jacob, then Director-General of the BBC, to write a history of broadcasting in the United Kingdom. Three paths converged.

The convergence had something in common with future convergences of events in my life, for example, in 1991, when I was seventy years old, and in 2011, the vantage point from which I am writing this book after my ninetieth birthday. All the connections cross time: they are not lateral. In 1958 I wrote a long centre-page article about Galbraith's book in the *Observer*, I was to become a life peer in 1976, and I took over the Presidency of the Victorian Society in 1983, succeeding Nikolaus Pevsner. The declared purpose of the Victorian Society was initially to safeguard Victorian (and Edwardian) buildings threatened by demolition. It was a worthy purpose in itself, following a protest that failed against the destruction of the great Euston Arch, but I wanted a Victorian Society with more to do than safeguard buildings. I wanted it to explore and promote Victorian studies. In that I was closer in my outlook to John Betjeman, poet and later a good friend, than I was to Pevsner whom I never knew really well. I feel that it is historically right that Betjeman should figure so centrally in the magnificently restored St Pancras Station which was successfully preserved. It was to St Pancras that in my boyhood I usually travelled to London, mainly on my way to France.

Moving ahead in time from 1957 I have to pick out another key date only three years later. I had been invited by the Australian historian Keith Hancock, whom I had known at Birmingham and in Oxford, who at the same time as starting to work on a biography of Field Marshal Smuts in 1957 had become Director of the Research School of Social Sciences at the Australian National University (ANU) in Canberra to become a visiting professor. My immediate predecessor was Alexander Carr-Saunders, who had just retired from the Director-Generalship of the London School of Economics. I was expected as part of my duties to travel round Australia and visit all the universities that I could, and through these visits I learned all I possibly could about what I realized at once was a continent not a country, a continent of legends. Most Australians lived in great cities; the legends gathered round the millions of square miles of 'bush'. The Aborigine native Australians scarcely came into the reckoning.

Most immediately important for me, I had time in Australia to think quietly but intensively about what it would be like to be involved in creating a new university. Hancock, having returned to England, placed his Canberra house at my disposal for my family to live in. He hoped to get me to stay in Australia, but just before I left Southampton to travel to Australia in a long voyage by sea I had told John Fulton, first Vice-Chancellor of Sussex, that I would join him there as his deputy and ultimately his successor.

Keith's in no way attractive house, which had been designed by his first wife Theadin, who was herself something of a legend, copied a house that they had built in England and was totally unsuited to the Australian climate. I had to get my friend Noel Butlin, later a Professor of Economic History at the ANU, to bring in huge electric heaters. I used to work not at home but in the Australian National Library, then housed in wartime Nissen huts, or in nearby University House, almost always attacked on my way there by ferocious magpies. The classicist Dale Trendall, co-founder of a Dante Society, used to congratulate me sardonically for always fighting back with a stick, the first that I ever owned. In Keith's absence his wonderful secretary Marjorie Brockle-bank, who was to become his second wife, looked after us well and became godmother to one of my children.

The range of my Australian friends was wide. I got to know well John La Nauze, who seemed to know how Keith's mind worked, and Manning Clark, from whom I learned of the curious ways in which religion and politics, including Roman Catholicism and Communism, were entangled with each other.

I also got to know students, among them would-be professors, and it was on Australian soil that I delivered what, looking back, seems to me the most important lecture that I have given in my life. It certainly has been the most influential. I was asked by the Research Students' Association of the ANU to deliver in Canberra the first of a series of annual lectures designed to enable members of the university to discover the ideas of distinguished Australian and visiting scholars on 'the present state and future prospects of investigation and education in their own and related disciplines'.

That was a comprehensive remit. I do not know who drafted it, but I particularly liked two phrases in it – 'present state and future prospects' and 'their own and related disciplines'. Another word in the same remit I was less sure about – 'investigation' – seemed to suggest an enquiry carried out by a detective, and much as I liked detective stories I had no desire to write one. I had not then heard the term 'investigative journalism'. Had it been coined? The word 'map' in the title that I myself chose for the lecture, 'The Map of Learning', had long been one of my favourite words, as had the word 'boundary'. I have noted earlier that I like employing geographical metaphors.

Behind that was a personal history covering three universities. I had chaired the sub-faculty of geography, anthropology and archae-ology in Oxford when I was a young don only because geographers, anthropologists and archaeologists did not want the sub-faculty to be chaired by a representative of either of the two 'disciplines' other than their own. With Bletchley between, I was fascinated by geopolitics in the years before and after the beginning of the Cold War and my interest in all three subjects was as great as Cole's in the three subjects of PPE. After all, before I had gone to Bletchley, I had listened to archeological lectures in Cambridge and studied aerial photography of open fields. In post-war Oxford I had been invited to serve as a young and enthusiastic advisor to a group producing a new Oxford University atlas which presented physical geography in an entirely new way, and while at Leeds I ensured that the historical geographers in the geography department should work closely with historians in the school of history.

Nevertheless, while making the most of the metaphor of the map in my 'Map of Learning' lecture, I stated in its second sentence that, despite my title, my lecture would be a journey without maps. I was greatly taken at the time by the writings of Michael Polanyi. His book *The Study of Man* had just appeared in 1959. I quoted his persuasive words:

> The personal contribution by which the knower shapes his own knowledge manifestly predominates both at the lowest levels of knowing and in the loftiest achievements of the human intelligence.

Another writer I had in mind was the Swiss psychologist Jean Piaget, and through him I felt that how and what children learned was highly relevant to how and what university students learned. I conceived of a great arc linking the first years of primary school and the last years at a university. They were years of finding out through exploration.

I stated clearly in my lecture that I would formulate a number of ideas that I would try to implement in a new university at Brighton, one of the scores of new universities which were being created in the middle of the twentieth century throughout the world. I then brought in as an illustrative local example what an Australian journalist, writing in the *Sun-Herald* had recently said about modes of university learning in England. The great Australian runner Herb Elliott was about to go to England to study in Cambridge. His likely education would be different, the journalist wrote, from the usual kind of Australian university education. 'Lectures in Cambridge are not compulsory', the journalist went on, 'but each week students are closely "quizzed" by tutors at "supervision" sessions on what they have learnt during the previous week.'

Quizzes, like spelling bees, were becoming popular both in England and in Australia during the 1950s but I had never thought of university students being quizzed in either country. Later in my lecture I expressed the hope that Herb Elliott would not be 'quizzed' by tutors at supervision sessions in Cambridge but that he would 'argue and discuss with them problems' which were of mutual interest to them both and where they could both learn in the process. I kept it in the back of my mind, but did not mention in my lecture, that I had a vivid memory of formidable Australian headmistresses playing slot machines after I had just given a WEA lecture

Years later, I was thrilled to meet Herb when he invited me to give two lectures in 1999, one in Sydney, one in Melbourne, as part of a cultural contribution to the Olympics which were to be held in Australia the following year. I chose to lecture on the culture of sport, which by then had generated more quizzes and attracted more gamblers than almost any other subject. It had also collected more statistics. I had already worked on the history of sport in Britain and America. It was one sturdy strand in my writing on leisure history, a subject I feel that I pioneered. I had lectured on it in Adelaide in 1960, but I had had no intimation then that I would choose the history of sport for two lectures on Australian soil at the end of the century, or indeed that Herb Elliott would be my wonderful host. I had no intimation either that students at the new university in Brighton I was helping to found in 1960 would win *University Challenge*, a highly superior television quiz, only eight years later. I still have a magnum bottle of champagne, empty alas, that we drank after the victory. Not a drop of it was wasted, as it always is when new liners are named before taking to the ocean or after Grand Prix victories.

I have so far left out of this account of my 'Map of Learning' lecture what I said about Francis Bacon, who was far more prominent in my

Canberra lecture than he was to be in other versions of the lecture which I later delivered in Britain and the United States and were widely reported, usually in greatly abridged form, in the press. I had first read Bacon's book *The Advancement of Learning* (1605) in an edited 1868 popular edition which I owned, knowing that in 1868 Bacon was at the height of his influence in Britain. It was recognized by Victorians that he was one of the greatest English prophets of material advance through technology.

Bacon had written *The Advancement of Learning*, however, in the light of the far-reaching changes in the map of the world in the sixteenth-century age of discovery and in the spread through printing of what was called 'new learning'. He was inspired to turn from the exploration of the earth to the exploration of the 'whole universe of nature' and foresaw 'the world of inventions and sciences as yet unknown.'

In other parts of my Canberra lecture I looked more closely at Victorian Britain. 'Our times too have their new learning, like the Renascence [*sic*] Age' A. W. Ward, a Cambridge graduate, had written in a paper published in 1878 with the very pertinent title, 'Is it Expedient to Increase the Number of Universities in England?' Ward answered plainly in the affirmative. 'Existing national means in university education are insufficient to meet our existing needs.' Nevertheless, he added, as I would add in 2012, that 'a reckless or haphazard increase in the number of universities is inexpedient in any age or country'.

Ward appreciated clearly that most of the subjects that would figure in the twentieth-century university curriculum, not least history, then a new academic subject, were nevertheless academic products of the nineteenth century, each furnished by 1878 with journals, societies and institutes. They would become 'professionalized' and would be treated as 'disciplines' as they planned symposia and conferences. Each discipline had its own date-line. 'Progress' was faster in Germany and in France than in Britain. *Historiche Zeitung* and the *Revue Historique* preceded the *English Historical Review*.

History, which was Ward's own subject, became a separate department in Manchester well before it did so in Oxford and in

Cambridge. For a time Ward himself held simultaneously the chair of English Language and Literature. He dropped the English Language component in 1880, but not the English Literature. In 1890 he was succeeded as Professor of History by T. F. Tout, who established a remarkable partnership restricted to history with a second professor, James Tait, at his side. 'While Tout took the lead, Tait kept the balance.' The Tout–Tait partnership took its place in history, while the study of history itself became very differently organized from the history Ward had studied in Cambridge.

In my Canberra lecture I devoted a substantial section to my own views on the study of history, which I had elaborated on in my inaugural lecture at Leeds on 'History and its Neighbours' which curiously I published in an Anglo-Italian magazine, *Occidente*, on the editorial board of which I sat:

> I want historians to devote more time not only to people in society (with proper concern for people) but to the study of societies [I should now add and cultures] both in themselves and comparatively.

I placed particular stress on the word comparatively, and in addition quoted R. H. Tawney's observation that 'if research requires a division of forces, a humane rendition requires a synthesis, however provisional, of the results of their labours'. Finally I attached great importance, as I was to do in Sussex, to bridging the huge gap between the humanities and the sciences with the social sciences helping to link the two. I argued this case also in the *Scientific American*, which in that phase of its illustrious history liked consulting me and from time to time printing pieces by me.

I did not refer in Canberra to the influence on my thinking of recent developments in the biological sciences or mention the term 'interdisciplinarity', which I was to stress at Sussex. I had been fascinated by the methodology of Francis Crick, James Watson, Maurice Wilkins and Rosalind Franklin when they worked on the structure of DNA. Nevertheless, I quoted a dictum from Eric Ashby's admirable *Technology and the Academics* (1958), which was to guide me at Sussex.

'The path to culture should be through a man's specialism, not by by-passing it.' I refused to contrast general and specialist education. Nor, for that matter, did Keith Hancock. He did not wish the Research School of Social Sciences to become 'an aggregate of departments'. He tried to work more closely with scientists whom he regarded as real humanists. He even thought of adding the words 'and Humanities' to the name of his School.

When I got back from Australia to England by air through India, I was not plunged immediately into the affairs of the new university I had been contemplating in my Canberra lecture. I returned to Leeds to deal with the affairs of the big department, which I headed solely for the rest of the academic year. My co-head, the medievalist Professor John Le Patourel, rightly felt that, since he had shouldered alone the responsibilities of the department in my absence, it was time for him to have a quieter period before I moved down to Sussex. We did not know quite when that would be. John Le Patourel was not in an easy position. Despite the differences in our interests and experience we had got on perfectly as a pair. He knew that it would be difficult to replace me and, unlike me, he did not have an ally in the Vice-Chancellor whom he knew had encouraged me to move to Sussex to join his closest friend John Fulton.

John Le Patourel, who had become a good friend, cared little for travel outside Europe, never having been to the Middle East, India, the United States or Australia. A Channel Islander by birth and by loyalties, he concentrated on European history. It was not that he and his wife did not like travel. They loved to go to France by caravan. He was better known as an historian in France than I then was and he had a much-cherished honorary degree from the University of Caen. He knew that I had decided on my way to Australia not to become Dean of the School of European Studies of Sussex but Dean of the School of Social Studies instead. I am sure, though we never discussed the change, that he believed me to be right.

Europe was a somewhat different continent when I returned to it at Christmas 1960 from what it had been in the early summer of 1960 when I left. The Berlin Wall was shortly to be built, but on its west side the economy was booming. Western Europe accounted for 58 per cent of world trade and manufactures and over two-thirds of global gross national income. Britain was being left behind, and although EFTA, the European Free Trade Association, was brought into existence just before we left for Australia, during the 1960s Germany and Italy increased their exports six times faster than Britain. I was drawn around this time to the writings of Andrew Shonfield, an able, imaginative and persuasive non-academic, a journalist by profession, who from 1961 to 1968 was Director of Studies at the Royal Institute of International Affairs. In 1961 there was to be a Cold War 'crisis', a real crisis. Nikita Khrushchev, who had taken control of the Kremlin within four years of the death of Stalin in 1953, was at the centre of the stage during the Cuban missile crisis, which brought the world nearer to general war than at any time since 1945. The young American President, John F. Kennedy, forced him not to build nuclear missile bases there. There was no real alternative way of stopping him, but Kennedy's Cuban policies, which always took account of Cuban refugees from Castro in Miami, never appealed to me.

While we were in Australia there had been another turn in the Cold War and in 1961 the split between China and the Soviet Union hit the headlines. Khrushchev was to be removed from power in 1964. I was not so busy when installed in Sussex to ignore international politics. Indeed, I used to argue about them with Barry Supple who succeeded me as Dean of Social Studies after I became Vice-Chancellor in 1967. I had brought him from Canada to Sussex very early in the new university's history, using the telephone as our main instrument of communication, and Susan and I regarded him as one of our closest friends.

By a coincidence I was in Australia again the following year, 1968, the year of biggest change in Europe. This was the year of '*les évenements*' in France. However much historians, not only in France, were spurning events as the main units of historical time, neither politicians nor journalists could dispense with them in considering historical time day-by-day. In May 1968 France was brought to a virtual halt as angry students and young workers went on strike in protest against authority. The protest spread to Germany and to Italy before reaching England. As Vice-Chancellor of Sussex I sometimes felt that the winds of protest were blowing at gale force mainly from France, but sometimes just as powerfully they blew in from the United States where student protest was associated with civil rights campaigns and, at the end of the 1960s, with opposition to the Vietnam War. I shared their views when we had our own *évenements*.

I never feared radical protest on the Sussex campus, but I disliked some of its manifestations, particularly the shouting-down of speakers even when they were deliberately provocative. I regarded myself not as a liberal but as a radical, and I knew that if anybody could make the campus situation intolerable for everyone living on it, it was I. I knew too, more fundamentally, that most students would change their opinions, even their values, later in their lives. Because we had a higher proportion of foreign students than most universities and a higher proportion of journalists and media practitioners in Brighton than in most towns or cities in Britain I also knew that what happened at Sussex University would be widely reported. In fact, there were other university institutions torn more by protest than Sussex, notably Essex and the London School of Economics. Militant ideologies were canvassed, demonstrations were organized, often not efficiently, and sit-ins lasted for weeks. There would be some members of what was then a divided Sussex faculty who did not realize that without common sense, good intelligence and above all courage we might have gone the same way. I knew too that while my own 'intelligence' had to be efficient, I would hate to have to rely on my own personal characteristics in dealing with 'situations'.

Some people in the local community, and indeed in the press, were to me infuriating. One Brighton councillor called for an end to the town's annual grant to the university: it was, he said, quite erroneously, 'a hotbed of communism'. Another outraged councillor suggested that we needed a team of psychiatrists in order to investigate what he thought was our 'sickness of the mind'. I was sometimes more nervous about the behaviour of councillors – and MPs – than of students.

Four Sussex *évenements* linger in my mind. Having been appointed Vice-Chancellor, I was leaving my house in Lewes to move into the Vice-Chancellor's official residence when an official from the American embassy in London had red paint foolishly thrown at him. I did not know that the official was in the university or who had invited him, but I got an urgent telephone call from the university telling me what had happened. I took the call in the oddest of circumstances. All the furniture had been moved out of our house and only the telephone was left. I listened in silence. A few minutes later I had a second telephone message from the headmistress of a well-known girls' independent school. She was a good friend of mine, but her message was almost as disturbing. Her head girl had eloped with one of 'my students'. It proved not to be quite the case. A third call came from the American Ambassador, David Bruce, also a friend of mine. 'Don't worry, Asa, about the red paint', he told me. 'I know that you know how to handle it. Worse things are happening in every American university every day.'

There was a sequel soon afterwards. I met the Duke of Edinburgh, by a coincidence my own age, at a reception which had nothing to do with universities. He came up to me, pulled back my ear and asked me 'Any red paint?' There was a sequel for him to that story. The next time I met him a year or two later I was a guest at the degree day of the University of Edinburgh, where he was Chancellor, and got a message from him asking me if I could kindly come and talk to him at the back of the platform. He had had a message from Cambridge University of which he was also Chancellor, about violent trouble there. 'What should I do about it?' I told him quietly 'Nothing.'

My second *évenement* relates to Scotland also. I got back by train from a meeting in London to find three or four reporters waiting for me at Lewes railway station. I was asked almost the same question that the Duke of Edinburgh had asked me. 'What are you going to do about it?' This time I had a different answer. 'About what?' 'Stirling' was the reply. There had been trouble there at the new university on the occasion of a visit by the Queen, and I had not received the news by telephone, or, indeed, by the post that I was the only person that the

Vice-Chancellor and the Stirling students could agree upon to carry out an independent inquiry. I decided, without immediately telling the reporters, that I would help Stirling. I got very little thanks for my trouble.

In Sussex, by contrast, I had the support of a majority of students for the actions that I took after the red paint incident. I saw 'in the presence of witnesses' the two students who admitted that they had thrown the red paint, one an American pursuing research in Sussex in medieval literature, and suspended them both from the university for the rest of the academic year. (We did not use the Oxford or Cambridge term for this – 'rustication'.) The President of the Students' Union, a future British ambassador, wrote to Godfrey Smith of the *Sunday Times*, who was preparing a profile of me:

> Student disciplinary officers were involved with the case throughout. The punishment (suspension of the ringleaders) was fair and was accepted by a meeting of the Students' Union unparalleled in size. Had the hand of the Vice-Chancellor on the tiller been heavier or tighter, I am sure that the outcome would have been much less happy for all concerned.

I feel this long after the event and students like to tell me so. Yet, the second student involved in the event, the non-American, did not agree with my action and even years later failed to recognize the Union's endorsement of it.

My third *évenement* was very different, and unfortunately I was not in a position to take action. It was instigated from outside the university and only two student groups at Sussex took any part in it. It was my first real introduction to a 'rent-a-crowd'. The Indian High Commissioner, Appa Pant, a distinguished and highly cultivated person, came to the university at my invitation – this had not been the case in any previous 'troubles', a wonderful euphemism. I did not know, because no one in the Indian High Commission told me, that he was a regular target for Maoist groups in British universities. Later Dorothy Woodburn, partner of the former editor of the *New States-man*, Kingsley Martin, with an impeccable and high-powered left-wing background, sent me documentary proof that this was so. Appa Pant found it impossible to complete his lecture which I subsequently had published. Relations between India and China were almost at their worst at this time. I love both countries, however, and subsequently at the invitation of the great Joseph Needham I succeeded him as Honorary President of the Society for Anglo-Chinese Understanding. I travelled many times to both countries until Tiananmen Square.

The fourth *évenement* concerned me personally and directly. I did not give many public lectures outside the university, although I spoke regularly to students without any problems at least once a term. I had a high profile. However, I decided that in 1970, the centenary of the first national education act, that because of both student and public interest I would lecture about it. I had a very large audience, with local councillors, teachers and senior educational administrators prominent in the front rows. Unfortunately or perhaps fortunately – I was not sure – the lecture coincided with one of the most difficult periods of student unrest in almost all universities, a few of which had not experienced it before.

The issue was access to student files, and a group of militant students at Sussex decided to join a protest that they knew little about and to stage a demonstration in the rather wonderful molecular science lecture theatre where I was lecturing. The first ten minutes were chaotic, but I succeeded in making myself heard, told the protesters that I would give the lecture and at the end listen to the demands and talk to them for as long as they liked. I went on to give the lecture in attentive silence. It referred almost entirely to a past long before those listening or their parents, even their grandparents, were born and was warmly applauded at the end, mainly, I add, by the visitors in the front rows. Then to everyone's surprise I took off my jacket and, an unprompted gesture, said sharply 'and now down to business'. Most but not all of the guests left and I now myself listened in silence while the protesters listed their demands. Eventually they agreed to leave me to talk in private about their demands with the officers of the Students' Union.

We did, and by the next morning had hammered out an acceptable arrangement which was based on the principle that no one would have access to any individual student's file except the student and his or her personal tutor. This kept lawyers or would-be lawyers out of the picture – and incidentally me! The decision was ratified the following morning almost unanimously. In many universities the dispute went on for months, involving sit-ins, ransacking of offices and even both legal and police intervention. The Sussex outcome was as satisfactory to me as Vice-Chancellor as it was to the students.

A few students rushed to examine their files without consulting their tutors, but the rush stopped quickly. We thereafter kept no secret student files in the university. There was a sequel, however, for in 1978 I published an edition with a long and scholarly introduction of *The History of the Elementary School Contest in England* by Francis Adams, who was relying on parental memories. My publisher, founder of the Harvester Press, was an old Sussex student of mine, John Spiers.

The year 1973 was not a good year for me. My mother died, always a landmark date in personal histories, and for the first time since I was a child I suffered from a serious life-threatening illness. This began during a visit to the meeting of Commonwealth Vice-Chancellors in Accra in 1972, a very different Accra from the city I had confronted on previous visits. I saw far too little of the city on this occasion, but somewhere within it I caught malignant malaria, which Ghanaians proudly proclaimed had been eliminated from the old Gold Coast. I realized that something was wrong soon after I got back to England and was having an open-air family picnic at a remote Sussex pub. I had a temperature and my head was in a whirl. I went to bed at home and not in hospital and had strange hallucinations.

I made a foolish effort to address the freshers of 1971 at Sussex soon after their arrival, as I always did, and had suddenly felt that they were swimming away from me. I knew that I had to go on leave, but quite uncharacteristically in the condition in which I was I was afraid of people outside my own family whether I knew them or not. I stayed in bed for what seemed an eternity. Yet it was not until I felt strong enough to cross the Atlantic that I suddenly realized I was well once more.

The country as a whole was not well when I returned. The 1970s were a different decade from what far too glibly were being called the 'Swinging Sixties'. It was during this 'sobering' decade that my personal dates became interlocked most firmly with public dates. There were two general elections in 1974. In 1973 there had been an international oil crisis which had hit the country hard as it hit the United States. Back at home, however, it was the coalminers, who brought Heath down.

No generally agreed labels have been attached to the 1980s and 1990s. I know, however, which personal dates figure most prominently in what I regard as the *fin-de-siècle* years of my life. One of the greatest dates in my own life, 1991, came two years after one of the greatest dates in world history, 1989, the bicentenary of the French Revolution. The collapse of communist regimes in central and Eastern Europe brought with it what seemed at the time an unprecedented sense of drama. Just before the great wall separating two Berlins and two Germanys, what the German communist leader Walter Ulbricht had called the 'anti-fascist protection barrier', was breached and pulled down, I had been present at an Anglo-American conference at Ditchley Park where some of the best informed and most intelligent participants suggested in discussing shapes of the future that the destruction of the Wall was imminent. I longed to go to Berlin to watch it being destroyed but because of imperative college commitments I could not do so. I wish now that I had defied them. I did manage, however, to acquire through a friend a small piece of the Wall. I treasure it as much as I treasure a fragment of one of the wooden chips collected at Hawarden when Gladstone was engaged in a favourite occupation, chopping down trees.

In 1991, having reached the age of seventy, I ceased to be Provost of Worcester and, anxious to cause no problems for my successor, I rarely returned to Oxford during the last decade of the twentieth century. It was then, in 1991, that I moved all my books, paintings and furniture from Oxford to Tyninghame House in Scotland. It was a strange but exciting experience to watch all of our Oxford possessions being loaded into a huge furniture van marked Shore Porters,

Aberdeen, in the back yard behind the Provost's Lodgings. This was the biggest break so far in my life, but I never regarded it as retirement. Our possessions were moved with great skill, but I discovered one thing, a formidable one for me, was wrong. My passport, which had been on my desk, was missing.

My last year in Oxford had been a very busy one. On a brief sabbatical in the United States in 1990 – for all my travels I have been granted few of these in my life – I received a telephone call from Michael Howard, then Regius Professor of History in Oxford, inviting me to deliver the Ford Lectures in my last year. Perhaps wrongly, I regarded the invitation as an honour that I could not refuse, although it involved changing all my American plans and adding an exceptional academic burden for me to carry during what was likely to be the busiest of all my years in Oxford. Nevertheless, I recognized the magnitude of my opportunity. I was completely free to choose the subject of my lectures and in settling on 'Culture and Communications in Victorian England', I was in a position to link the two fields that I had concentrated on most in my academic work – the Victorians and the communications media. There were few historians in 1991 who did or indeed could link them.

As is customary the lectures would be held in the Examination Schools and were likely to be well-attended. They would also be published. I was glad that, because of my own record, a number of Open University students would be present. I was glad too that I had the full support of the group of senior historians that I had gathered together in Oxford. Nevertheless, I was not entirely happy about some of the arrangements. I had to fight to be allowed to have the lectures recorded and I had to pay the cost. A few years later I got this refunded by the University without pressing. In 1991 I was uneasy also that the Ford lecturer was required to confine his subject matter to England. That too was soon to be changed. I would have liked to have been able to introduce more comparative analysis, across countries and periods.

Sadly my lectures were never published. In the first instance that was my own fault. I was very busy during the 1990s on matters concerned with current and future trends in communications on both sides of the Atlantic and I came to the conclusion that I should modify the content of my lectures in the light of further reading. I had had less time to prepare them than most Ford lecturers. Then new complications arose during the first decade of the twenty-first century. I was dogged by so many illnesses, beginning with deep-vein thrombosis, followed by prostate problems and later by macular degeneration of one of my eyes, that I found it impossible to prepare them for belated publication. I regarded my complaints, some physical, as being somewhat like those of Job. They all greatly reduced my physical mobility but not my mental activity.

Unfortunately, I felt the Oxford University Press, operating in quite new circumstances, treated my lectures, when at last I offered what I hoped was a final version of them, as if they were a completely new work that should be reviewed and judged by new referees. The fact that they were delivered in 1991 and then had been well received was irrelevant to the people in charge of the OUP's history publishing, none of whom I knew. Some of the suggestions these new reviewers made about their publishable form were helpful and some were contradictory. After considering them all I made significant changes in the contents of the lectures I had sent to them, and added footnotes, difficult and painstaking; however, I did not change the titles that I had given to the lectures. The shape of the new book was not different from the old. I have a strong belief in the autonomy of a Ford lecturer, and regard OUP's decision not to publish them as a big mistake.

What I said about culture in my lectures as delivered and as re-written owed much to G. M. Young who, looking back in time, was the biggest single influence on my work as an historian. He had immense curiosity, a necessary attribute of a cultural historian, yet he was aware of his limitations. He had very little interest in what had come to be called during the 1950s – long before I delivered my lectures – popular culture. In rewriting my lectures I began to think of some of them as strategic, a term I did not employ in 1991, when I was exploring the contours (note the geographical metaphor) of culture. I wanted my publication to influence future research by other historians. One of my strategic titles was 'How Many Cultures?'

I concluded certainly far more than two. If I had been allowed more than six lectures I would have called one 'Blackpool and Bohemia'.

My most provocative lecture in 1991, which I substantially rewrote, was called 'Culture versus Communications'. I had Matthew Arnold very much in mind when I delivered it in its 1991 form. I read as much then as I could of Arnold's prolific prose as I did of Ruskin's, which was even more voluminous. I also rewrote what I had said about him. There were many personal associations. I remembered my schooldays when I had been drawn to Arnold's poetry and had enjoyed walking and climbing in Ruskin's Lake District. My last Ford lecture I called 'Markets and Institutions', a subject that now interests me even more in the strange circumstances of 2011–12 than it did in 1991 – and earlier. In a profound sense it seems 'relevant' to all human motivation and action.

One underlying theme in my lectures and in a preface I wrote for my publication was the nature of lectures themselves as a favourite Victorian mode of communication. Far too little had been written earlier about their appeal, their variety and their limitations. T. H. Huxley, therefore, received as much attention in the for-publication version of my own lectures as Arnold or Ruskin. Important books had been written about him since.

Another underlying theme in my preface was my conviction that the history of communications before the rise of broadcasting should be explored as adventurously as history since the advent of the BBC. I was to find it immensely stimulating to work with Peter Burke, whom I had appointed to Sussex to teach sociology as well as history and who was to become a distinguished professor in Cambridge. Our *A Social History of the Media: from Gutenberg to the Internet* first appeared in 2002. It has subsequently appeared in three editions, all of them examining social and cultural matters as well as technological and economic changes. It has been translated into fourteen languages.

In 2002 we had passed the great date 2000, long-anticipated, which marked the end not only of a century but of a millennium. The words 'Towards 2000' had begun to be used as a kind of slogan during the 1960s, although as early as 1946 Aldous Huxley had written of 'futurology'. I myself associated that 'coming into its own' largely with the American sociologist Daniel Bell during the 1960s. Bell, two years older than me, was a good friend whom I often met, for the first time at the University of Chicago when he was an instructor in social sciences. In 1987 he was Pitt Professor of American History and Institutions at the University of Cambridge. He died in January 2011.

In 1968 in *Daedalus*, the lively periodical produced by the American Academy of Arts and Sciences under the direction of Stephen Grab, he announced a collective research programme that would look ahead to the year 2000. There were problems – and dangers – in looking ahead which were explored in D. Kumar's *Prophecy and Progress: the Sociology of Industrial and Post-Industrial Society* (1978). For me that was essential reading.

I finish rewriting this chapter for the press at 5.30 a.m. on the first day of a new calendar year, 2012. I saw on television the wonderful fireworks that ushered the year in. One hundred and twenty-five days to my ninety-first birthday. 2012 is a leap year. Rightly, given the title of this chapter, I am thinking about time. Summer time starts on 25 March. The last birthday card for my wife, which arrived this morning, bore the comforting words 'Better late than never'. Her birthday which we celebrated happily with the family on 27 December, without fireworks, has already passed into our personal history.

Most of the words that accompanied the end of the old year and the coming of the new were not comforting. The front cover of the *New Statesman*, dated 2 January 2012, states 'And you thought 2011 was bad . . . A guide to the political and economic crisis to come'. On the late afternoon of 31 December I listened to the football results, among them the rather surprising score Barnsley 4 Leeds United 1. With abiding memories of the former Leeds player and manager Don Revie in mind I found the score superstitiously ominous. Barnsley is the home town of my publishers.

In my next chapter, the draft of which has already been written, I leave dates behind and turn to individuals and institutions. I am not sure, however, that in doing so I abandon omens, I know too that even after I have finished revising my next chapter there are still five chapters to go. A distinguished American historian, Walter Prescott Webb, author of a pioneering book, *The Great Plains*, that linked geology, geography, anthropology, history and psychology, told the American Historical Association in its seventy-second presidential address in 1958:

> Though it takes resolution to begin a book it takes more to complete it. There are dark moments when the struggling author wonders why he began it, and if it is worthwhile anyway. There are times when he is lost in the dark forest of alternatives. He can't go forward and he can't go back.

In going forward I am encouraged, if not comforted, by the fact that Webb called his address to the Historical Association 'History as High Adventure' and that his first book, published in 1935, bore the title *The Texas Rangers*.

Chapter 5

Institutions and Individuals

The institutions that I have known best in my own life have been universities, most of them far older than I am. I knew virtually nothing about them when I was a boy but I knew almost more than I wanted to know about them by 1961 when the new University of Sussex took in its first undergraduates.

Public interest in them was not then a new phenomenon. Whenever there was talk about reforming them, as there was during the 1850s, the talk spilled over into a broader discussion about institutions of all kinds. I recall one article of October 1889 in the *Edinburgh Review* which focused on old universities. 'Few institutions are so generally interesting as the historic universities,' the writer began. 'Few appeal to so many sections of modern society.'

> It is not only in the upper ranks of the people that Oxford and Cambridge are believed in, but also among the masses of the artisan population, and this is the more surprising when it is remembered that the degree in which the universities affect the lives of those masses is exceedingly small. 'University men' are really very few and far between in the great centres of population.

There were other institutions, of course, notably the workhouse, which locally was often described as *the* institution. It did not need Dickens to bring out all its horrors. I have written a lot about both universities and workhouses as a social historian interested in 'education' and 'welfare', but the British institution about which I have written most words is the BBC, founded in the twentieth century in the year after I was born, 1922. Throughout my life I have listened to and watched its programmes in totally changing circumstances, more, I confess, for entertainment than for instruction. In writing about the history of broadcasting I have had to examine the history of countless other institutions, religious, philanthropic, economic, theatrical, cinematic and sporting. Some of the institutions were far older than the BBC; some came into existence because the BBC was there. I was thus drawn into 'total history' even more than I was when I wrote the second volume of *History of Birmingham*.

How to relate those individuals who are described as founders to the institutions that they founded raises at once, in the case of the BBC, the name of John Walsham Charles Reith, an Aberdonian born in 1889. In 1922, knowing nothing about broadcasting, Reith, one of the few founders of an institution to give his name to an adjective, 'Reithian', had been appointed first general manager of a commercial company, albeit an unusual one. 'There were no sealed orders to open,' he wrote soon after he was appointed. 'The commission was of the scantiest nature. Very few knew what broadcasting meant: none knew what it might become.' His company with a staff of three was certainly not conceived of then as an institution. By 1927 when the number of staff had risen to 989, it already was. From the start it had stressed the concept of public service.

In 1927, however, with no change in its initials, the company became a public corporation based on a royal charter not on an act of parliament, with Reith as its first Director-General and the sixth Earl of Clarendon as its first Chairman of Governors. The favourite image of the new BBC during the late 1920s and the 1930s was not that of a great corporation but of a great British institution. The Archbishop of Canterbury, who probably knew more about institutions than anyone else in the country, including the monarchy, was one of the first people to describe the BBC as one. The image of the institution and the image of the Director-General became blurred, however, even after Reith had left the BBC in 1938. I explained in my last chapter why 1938 was an important date for me. It was a far more important date to Reith – in that year he ceased to be Director-General. He never again felt that he was 'fully stretched' and 'in command'.

If Reith had no sealed orders in 1922, I had none in 1957 when I accepted the invitation of the Governors and Director-General of the BBC, then Sir Ian Jacob, to write 'a history of broadcasting in the United Kingdom'. I laid down three conditions. I insisted first, that it should be called *A* history, not *The* history; second, that it should not be regarded as an official history; and third, that I could only write it if I had the co-operation of Reith, who thought that Jacob should never have been appointed to the post of Director-General in 1952. I did not then know how many volumes, if more than one, would be required, but I decided very quickly to devote my first volume to the *Birth of Broadcasting, 1922–7*. I wanted to complete it before too many BBC veterans died. My book appeared equally quickly in 1961.

I won Reith's approval, which I was asked to do, in Reithian fashion. I invited him to lunch in my club, appropriately the Oxford and Cambridge, at my expense, before he decided, in his own words, whether or not 'to co-operate with me'. On leaving lunch, towering over me even though he stood below me on the club's steps, he told me solemnly that he had decided to do so. He added even more solemnly that if I had written my lunch invitation to him on BBC headed notepaper he would have 'torn it up and cast it into the flames'. And so began our co-operation, genuine and for me indispensable.

My special personal relationship with Reith was crucial to the writing not only of my first volume, but, still more so, of my second *The Golden Age of Wireless*, published in 1965. From the moment of our parting on the steps of the Oxford and Cambridge Club he gave me full access to his handwritten diaries which I read at his then home in Lollard's Tower, at the entrance to the Archbishop of Canterbury's London house and offices. I felt that Reith (I found it difficult to address him face-to-face as John) would often deliberately leave the diaries open near to a passage in them that would particularly interest me. No secrets were to be hidden from me.

It was essential for me, however, to relate passages in the diaries to other archival sources inside the BBC. I knew that during the 1920s Reith had had many enemies both inside and outside it. Two of them had strong Keighley links. Philip Snowden's widow, Ethel, described by Emmanuel Shinwell as 'the would-be Sarah Bernhardt of the Party', was a governor from 1927 to 1932. She infuriated Reith as much as she infuriated Clarendon. I never met her as a boy. M. B. Lees-Smith, Labour MP for Keighley, whom I did meet, was Postmaster-General, the minister in charge of BBC affairs, when Ramsay MacDonald, to Reith's relief, appointed Clarendon Governor-General of South Africa. Lees-Smith thought that Reith was a neurotic megalomaniac.

Because of the strength of feelings on the part both of Reith's critics and of Reith himself it was essential for me to draw on versions of broadcasting history other than his. I found a manuscript history, *Early Life in the BBC* by Ralph Wade, particularly interesting. Later I was to benefit from private papers lent to me by Oliver Whitley, son of J. H. Whitley, Clarendon's successor, and the unpublished memoirs of Robert Foot, a wartime Director-General. The foundations of the BBC's archives had been laid in 1927, when the Central Registry was formed, and Miss M. S. Hodgson had been designated Archivist. She was very helpful to me when I started my history, but we both agreed that an internal reorganization of BBC archives, which constituted the finest collection of broadcasting archives in the world, was necessary not only for an historian but for the staff of the BBC. I insisted above all, then and later, that they were public records.

I have always been deeply interested throughout my life in 'national archives', how they have been stored and how they have been resourced, sharing the opinion of Sir Arthur Doughty, who for a whole generation was Dominion Archivist in Canada, that of all national assets they are 'the most precious'. 'They are', Doughty maintained, 'the gift of one generation to another,' and how they are selected, retained and cared for 'marks the extent of our civilisation'. Canada has pioneered the collection of film archives which are as essential for historians as documentary archives.

I was to be chairman of a BBC committee on archives, very diverse archives, written, broadcast and musical, set up in 1976, long after I had started to write my history, which published a report in 1979 after a series of regular meetings and considerable research. The then Chairman of the Governors of the BBC was Michael Swann, whom I had first met as the Principal of the University of Edinburgh. The secretary of the committee was the historian Norman Longmate, an alumnus of Worcester College, and the members, all distinguished in their own fields, were drawn from the whole domain of communications. Some I knew, among them David Francis, Curator of the National Film Archive, David Jenkins, Librarian of the National Library of Wales, Randolph Quirk, the great lexicographer – and much else – of University College London, and Margaret Gowing, Professor of the History of Science in Oxford University and a close colleague of Keith Hancock in preparing and publishing the wartime civil service official histories.

Others whom I did not then know well included Marius Goring, actor, producer and television scriptwriter, Benny Green, freelance writer and broadcaster, Michael Tilmouth, Professor of Music in the University of Edinburgh, and Michael Holroyd. I knew Goring's voice, of course, and Holroyd's books. Donald Sinden, actor and chairman of the Theatre Museum Advisory Council, and Anthony Hobson, bibliographical consultant and historian, became new friends. Susan and I stayed several times with Anthony in his beautiful house and went with him to opera and to orchestral concerts in Southampton. Donald Sinden I still see when I am writing this book.

After the Archives Committee had finished its work I discussed with senior members of the government our recommendation that in any future BBC charter there should be a formal reference to the archives. I ensured that this was done in the course of interesting talks with Merlyn Rees, then Home Secretary, whose offices were located in a building which I knew from my Bletchley Park days. I did not find it easy to convince future chairmen and directors-general of the BBC that the insertion of a reference to archives in the charter constituted an obligation. There was a continuing belief in Broadcasting House and in Television that the main value of the archives was financial, and there was a reluctance too to open them up to greater access. Personally I benefitted immensely, and sometimes I felt uniquely, from being what the governors thought of as the historian of the BBC. I thought it essential to catalogue them properly, and I was able in consequence to establish a happy personal relationship with Jacqueline Kavanagh, head of the Caversham archives. I was not properly informed about what was happening in music and script archives, however. Much that was valuable continued to be quietly destroyed. Thanks to Jacqueline I could study BBC papers not at Caversham but in my own office and, indeed, in my home.

I now have my own alarmingly huge personal archive of broadcasting history, British and foreign. It was envied by my American friend Eric Barnouw who brought broadcasting history to life in the United States. I fear that no one in future will be able to build up a personal archive as rich as mine. I have worked closely with Barnouw in the Annenberg Archive in Philadelphia, and with Elihu Katz in the Annenberg Archive in Los Angeles. I regarded Walter Annenberg as a great benefactor who liked archives and collected Victorian narrative paintings. So do I.

With the Internet, mobile phones, email, Facebook, Google, Twitter and other devices, the employment of which we did not foresee then, the communications system is very different from what it was in 1979. As I have confronted change, not all of it technological, I have tried – and it is not easy – to keep myself up-to-date. I have been motivated by co-authoring with Peter Burke several editions of our book *A Social History of the Media: from Gutenberg to the Internet.* In a further edition we may have to substitute Twitter for the Internet in our title. The vocabulary changes with the technology. Words like 'blogging' – an activity which I never participate in – have now entered the general language. Digitalization has opened up endless possibilities.

In co-authoring *A Social History of the Media* and in writing my many books before *Special Relationships*, I have relied on visual and oral history as much as on documents and books. The pictures that I study in writing my own books include cartoons and comics, prints and portraits. Selecting them is a delight for me: I never leave the selecting to others. Visual history now thrives, particularly on the television screen.

Before I met Paul Thompson, whose contribution to oral history in this country is unique, I had already talked across the Atlantic to Alan Nevins, founder of founders, both about oral history and business history four years before I accepted the BBC invitation to write my history of broadcasting. As for oral history, it was not until 1969, the year when the first men landed on the moon, that a meeting was held in the British Institute of Recorded Sound, a body with which I was directly involved, to set up the Oral History Society. Yet, as long ago as 1773, Samuel Johnson told his readers to note that 'all history was at first oral'. One of the people present at the meeting in December 1969 was George Ewart Evans, not 'an academic', who was beginning to realize that the fieldwork that he had been engaged in for years could be called oral history. It was like learning for the first time that you were talking prose.

I was to work closely with Paul Thompson in the founding of the National Life Story Collection in 1987, two years before the twentieth birthday of the Oral History Society *Journal*. The National Life Story Collection is itself now older than the Oral History Society was then, and, working from within the British Library, it has published several detailed studies of urban and city life very different from the rural life recorded by Ewart Evans. In recording social change it continues to benefit from technical change. When I was carrying out regular research for my first two volumes on broadcasting history I found it difficult for technical reasons to record any interview even if the person being interviewed was willing to be recorded – and most were not. New forms of recording have revolutionized historical research.

My own special contribution to oral history in the 1950s and 1960s had nothing to do with technology. I used to bring together a group of people, preferably in a place outside a studio, who trusting to their memories were willing to talk over old arguments and re-create old atmospheres, as have been the people participating in Sue Mac-Gregor's *Reunion* programmes. Reith himself would not participate in such 'games' as he called them, but he loved to listen to the recordings of the symposia arranged by me, which I myself treated very critically as sources of information. The BBC made my work easier by giving me an assistant of seniority inside the BBC hierarchy who helped me to select the participants and introduced me to those whom I did not know. I also did a number of formal interviews, not all of which could be described as conversations. One was with Frank Gillard who, after he retired as Director of Radio in 1969, carried out a large number of interviews with BBC employees for the BBC archives. Gillard, strongest advocate of local radio in Broadcasting House, had a long and distinguished career as a broadcaster, including a period as a wartime reporter.

Another interview which lingers in my mind was with R. H. S. Crossman, whom I knew in many capacities and who, in 1936, was picked out by a gossipy journalist as a future chairman of the governors. In 1969, when he was Secretary of State for Health and Social Security, he was to invite me to chair a departmental committee on nursing. My radio interview with him was on a totally different subject, 'black broadcasting' – wartime stations pretending to be German but actually operated by Britons. Dick, who during the war had worked at Woburn Sands, not far from Bletchley, was an even more versatile person than I was. Before the war he had been an Oxford don. With this in mind I got him to read the proofs of the third volume of my history, *The War of Words* (1970), which covered broadcasting in the Second World War. One of his gifts was that he left to the world *The Crossman Diaries*, which, unlike Wilson's *Diaries*, were frank. They were not as lively and informative as Barbara Castle's, however.

The first of my special assistants within the BBC was Douglas Clarke, who spoke and typed notes to me that were as authoritative as Reith's handwritten letters about the early years. Clarke was loyal as well as helpful, able not only to share confidences but to keep secret what I was writing about. He was followed by three very different 'helpers' or, to use a term which I prefer, co-operators. I got on well with all of them, better, I think, than they would have got on with Clarke or, indeed, with each other. They had diverse BBC experience of their own. Denis Wolferstan, colleague, guide and friend, was a perfect choice to succeed Clarke. He was the only one of the three who travelled with me at home and abroad. When I was writing *The War of Words* we had one memorable visit to France, where we met the survivors of a remarkable *équipe* of French broadcasters who combined spontaneity with professionalism. *Les Français parlent aux Français* was a programme which should never be left out of history books. I also got to know and like Darsie Gillie, head of the French section of the BBC, and his wife, whose obituary I wrote for the *Guardian*, and through them met many members of the Resistance. With Denis I investigated the curious history of the V for Victory campaigns, which deserves a monograph, and of the liberation of Paris, well described by journalists at the time. I learnt many secrets that I had not learnt at Bletchley.

My third co-operator, Leonard Miall, had himself been a participant in the stories and I had met him several times before he started working for me. As he pointed out, his greatest claim to fame was that in June 1940 he had escorted General de Gaulle to a BBC studio for the first time. The BBC had been informed simply that an unnamed French general would take the microphone: his talk was not trailed. Nor was it recorded. Miall loved telling the story. He also edited a book *Richard Dimbleby, Broadcaster, by his Colleagues* (1966). Miall was essentially an anecdotalist, and when, years later, he wrote a book of his own on BBC history it was not very well received.

His successor as my helper, John Cain, had a quite different BBC background from Miall's, but we were able with the indispensable help of Pat Spencer to create a small history unit which survived until the regime of John Birt, the first Director-General to move over to the BBC from independent television. Then in my view the whole nature of the BBC as a national institution was transformed as was the language in which its mission was proclaimed, 'Birtspeak'.

John Cain wrote a well-received book to celebrate its seventieth anniversary, *The BBC: 70 Years of Broadcasting* in 1992. I had written *The BBC, The First Fifty Years* in 1972. John's interests overlapped with mine, for he had become Head of Further Education also in 1972, and we had many friends in common. He went on to carry out independent research of his own on the important contribution of broadcasting to philanthropy and the humanitarian causes which it supported and for which it raised funds.

In recalling the years that I devoted to the history of broadcasting, far more years than I would ever have expected when I talked to Jacob in 1957, I remember that I never entirely won the goodwill of many of my fellow professional historians, some of whom, like George Kitson Clark, ensconced in memorable rooms in Trinity Great Court, thought that I was wasting my time and talents in writing about broadcasting. They believed I should have used my energies in writing about the Victorians or about twentieth-century British history as a whole. I was and am sure that they were wrong. It is impossible to understand the political, social and cultural history of the United Kingdom, or indeed of any country, without examining the evolution and influence of what has come to be called its media system, with newspapers long preceding broadcasting. Institutional history has connections with all other kinds of history. Nor can it be divorced from world history.

I devoted almost as much time to the study of broadcasting in other countries as in the United Kingdom, first through the International Institute of Communications (ICC, originally called the International Broadcasting Institute), founded in Rome in 1967 with the support of the Ford Foundation. Through it I travelled to conferences in locations as different as Cyprus, Mexico, and (still undivided) Yugoslavia, meeting local broadcasting dignitaries, a class in themselves. As unpaid Research Officer of the International Institute I also published a series of monographs on broadcasting in different countries. They covered all its different aspects and they required protracted critical editing. I remember the one on Lebanon most vividly. Lebanon was hailed by its author as a model of toleration. Second, through the Aspen Institute in Colorado, which produced and continues to produce monographs on all kinds of media operations, I kept in close touch with the always-changing media world.

It was through the Aspen Institute that I was awarded the Marconi Medal for my work on the history of communications. This enabled me to acquire research assistance, something that had never been provided for me by Oxford, Leeds or Sussex universities. More important, it strengthened my links with MIT, the Massachusetts Institute of Technology, a powerhouse of ideas. In the ICC I became close friends with its director, Eddi Ploman, who moved from Swedish Television. In Aspen I came to know Charlie Firestone. He ensured that whoever was in charge of the Institute, dependent as it was on outside finance, communications would be an essential part of its programme. We talked in a wide variety of places about everything, not just communications developments and policies, but particularly science fiction which Eddi knew even more about than I did. Eddi and Charlie, who never worked closely together, introduced me to a wide range of interesting and important people, whom I would not otherwise have met. They included managers and critics, technologists and performers, editors and politicians. A few of them might have been labelled celebrities.

I worked closely also in both these international settings with people I knew already in Britain, particularly women. The first was Hilde Himmelweit, like me an academic, whose influential *Television and the Child*, a pioneering work, appeared in 1958. Attractive and lively, she made an impression on everyone she met. The second, quite different in attitudes and experience, was Joanna Spicer, who had risen as high inside the BBC hierarchy as any woman then could. Only Mary Somerville had risen higher in an earlier period. Joanna remained in post with different titles until 1972. Inside the BBC people were known by initials more than by names, and from 1964 to 1972 her initials ACTD disguised the title Assistant Controller, Television Development. There were other 'BBC women' who figured in my life. I did not know or work with Hilda Matheson, whom I have written about in my books, but I became a friend of Grace Wyndham Goldie, who wrote some of the first reviews of BBC television for the pre-war *Listener*.

After Joanna left the BBC to join the Independent Television Companies Association, ITCA, which had its offices in Mortimer Street not far from Broadcasting House, I was to co-author a book with her, *The Franchise Affair*. The title was borrowed from a novel of 1948 that I had greatly enjoyed, by Josephine Tey. It fitted our contents better than her absorbing medieval narrative. We began on Sunday 28 December 1980 when leading representatives of thirty-four commercial television companies reported for interview at the Independent Broadcasting Authority (IBA), which by then covered both television and radio, at 70 Brompton Road. It was a building that I knew well. My own relations with the IBA were excellent. I shared the view of Brian Young, its Director-General, former headmaster of Charterhouse, who had succeeded Robert Fraser, a personal friend, that the IBA was best regarded simply as an 'additional public broadcasting service', distinguishable from the BBC by its mode of finance, commercial advertising. He was on more difficult ground, however, when he referred to a 'paternal tradition, reaching back to Reith and now needing to be defended'.

There is a particular fascination about the events of Sunday 28 December in that the rituals of the IBA, which had an element of absurdity about them, got mixed up with the rituals of Christmas and more especially of Holy Innocents' Day. Separate messages in sealed envelopes were carried by dispatch riders from Brompton Road to Whitehall. The details of which groups had been awarded franchises were deemed secret. I do not think that press comment referred at any point to institutions. I shared the judgement of the *Spectator* that 'it is difficult to think of anything quite as preposterous as the pantomime last Sunday'.

I confess that in any case I was rather more than the member of a pantomime audience. I was not an uninterested party. I had been a director of Southern Television, one of the two companies, it seemed to me arbitrarily, to lose its franchise in that year. The Chairman of the IBA, Bridget Plowden, had been Vice-Chairman of the BBC from 1970 to 1975, when, like Charles Hill before her (moving, however in the opposite direction) she 'changed sides'. Unusually, but not uniquely, she had strong links with education. In 1967 she had been chairman of the Central Advisory Council for Education which produced a major national report 'Children and their Primary

Schools'. It was not easy during the 1960s to separate educational and broadcasting issues. Nor could you leave out politics. The problem was when personal likes and dislikes influenced judgement as they did for Lady Plowden.

Joanna Spicer followed up our book, which was rich in detail and divulged many secrets, with a thorough study of the first direct elections for a European Parliament following Britain's entry into what was then called the European Economic Community on 1 January 1973. They were first held in June 1979 and were to be held every five years. The European Parliament was to meet both in Strasbourg and in Brussels, but there was to be little sense of creating a 'citizen's Europe'. It seemed to me, as it still does, that while the language of 'federalism' is full of pitfalls, if Europe were to establish itself it would have to be a 'Europe from below'.

In 1976 I had returned to Oxford from Sussex, becoming Provost of the college where I had once been a young Fellow. It was a move I never expected. It was still an all-male college, but it was to go mixed far earlier than I or my distinguished predecessor, Oliver Franks, had expected. In a decade very different from the 1960s, it was a time to reflect as much on the future of 'Oxbridge' colleges as on their past. Numbers and finance had to be taken into account as well as past institutional reputations. Very little interest was taken in universities outside 'Oxbridge', except by undergraduates and some alumni. No Fellow in the college asked me about what it had been like to be vice-chancellor of a new university. Like them I had to preoccupy myself with money. In my first Worcester conversation in 1976 with my friend and former colleague, David Mitchell, the Vice-Provost, I went over with him the recent Worcester College accounts and we agreed that they revealed a far worse situation than Oliver Franks had suggested.

I was asked nothing in Oxford about the process of the creation of new universities in the 1960s. Now I can see the process in retrospect and, I believe, at least in part in perspective. I had become directly involved in the process as a result of being appointed a member of the University Grants Committee (UGC), under the chairmanship of Sir

Keith Murray. Murray knew me well in Oxford when he was Rector of Lincoln College, and I saw him informally on a regular basis before I went to Leeds. He wanted to include me, not because of anything to do with new universities, but as a professor in an arts subject from an important civic university, whose Vice-Chancellor, Sir Charles Morris, he had also known in Oxford. He was aware that Morris was one of the few vice-chancellors who believed strongly in increasing total student numbers. It was doubtless he who suggested to Murray that I should become a member.

When I moved from Leeds to Sussex in 1961 I was placed in a unique position inside the UGC. I became the only voice of a new university and was expected to explain to my fellow members what being in a new university was like. If I had not been there I very much doubt whether Murray would have appointed any member directly from a new university. As it was he made me a member of its small new universities sub-committee which considered applications from local bodies anxious to acquire a university.

In 1957 the UGC had advised the Chancellor of the Exchequer that 'places in the universities should be made available for 124,000 students by the late-1960s', adding that this number might have to be increased by 10 per cent to 135,000. In a memorandum of 1960, written by Murray, '48–60', all this, including a reference to the higher target, was set out. The target would become as high as 168,000, the memorandum continued, had it not been for two additional considerations. First, it was unlikely because of a lack of physical resources that the universities could have carried out the larger building programme that this higher target would have entailed. Second, since it was evident that in some universities there was a 'tail of students' who were academically incapable of completing their degree courses, 'an increase in competition for entry for these places was desirable'. In the light of this UGC advice, the Chancellor authorised a building programme of £15 million a year for each of the four years 1960 to 1963.

During the summer of 1959, after I had joined the UGC, it reviewed the situation in the light of fresh evidence which had been supplied by the Ministry of Education and the Scottish Education Department. More children than had been expected were staying on at school to seventeen years and over. 'It was clear', Murray's memorandum concluded,

> . . . that the potential student population in the late 1960s or early 1970s might rise as high as 200,000 . . . We also considered the position in the universities and concluded that their experience in handling the larger building programme in the years following 1957 could now enable the building programme to be increased. We therefore sought and obtained authority from the Chancellor to enter into discussions with the universities in order to ascertain whether as a first stage a further expansion of 35,000 to 40,000 places beyond the previous target of 135,000 would be practicable and what the capital cost would be. This expansion we regarded as a minimum first instalment, fully justifiable as a matter of urgency.

When Murray wrote round to the universities and tried to find out what their answers would be, he discovered that many universities were completely unwilling to do anything to increase their numbers. In particular, some of the larger provincial universities, having reached a figure of 5,000–7,000 students, were reluctant to increase numbers. They were not worried that acquiring land near to their premises would be exorbitantly expensive but they feared that a greater increase would 'destroy their cohesion'. Meanwhile, it was the view of the UGC itself that the small universities, 'which' they believed, had 'great potentialities, while in some cases really anxious to expand, should not force the pace unduly'. It was also the UGC's view – and here there was an explicit theory of growth and scale – that a university should not double its numbers in less than ten years if it were 'to preserve its characteristics and retain the essentials of a university education. It must also have regard to the need for preserving a balance with the community, sometimes a small one, which surrounds it.' The conclusion was logical:

We have no hesitation in affirming that some further new institutions are needed and we recommend that immediate steps should be taken to encourage their establishment so that they can make their contribution to the national need of the moment. Plans must be discussed and laid, buildings designed, curricula decided if we are going to start in the early 1960s. All of these things take time.

This was a clear recommendation with a clarion cry element in it.

I remember well the 1959 discussions that led up to the memorandum. Lionel Russell, the UGC member who could inform us most about what was happening inside the schools – he was Director of Education in Birmingham – focused on the 'trend' in the sixth forms. A few members were more worried about 'the tail'. Geoffrey Heyworth supported expansion in the name of business. Murray himself had enlightened views about the need for qualitative as well as quantitative change in curricula and modes of teaching.

Those who were worried about the 'tail' were confused in their thinking. It was not to be the new universities that were to cater for it; they were at or near the head of the queue for able students. Where they were to be situated would influence their attractiveness to applicants.

That was far from the end of memorandum '48–60'. In the past, Murray went on, neither the government nor the UGC had ever, 'as it were', sought to say 'where universities in this country should be'. No official British map of universities of any kind had ever been produced with a few flags flying on it, as was the case in some foreign countries. 'Most of the existing universities had been brought into existence as a result of local enthusiasm and enterprise, supported by local finance and may only later have attracted financial assistance from the state.' Admittedly, Murray added, the picture was very different from 'that which it was' in the nineteenth century when most of the provincial universities were founded, and different even from what it had been in the early twentieth century. Universities cost more to build and to operate. 'The number of private benefactors is smaller. The government contribution is very much larger.'

Nevertheless, we assume that it would still be the view of the government that, generally speaking, locally interested efforts are essential pre-conditions to the establishment of a new institution and that it should be for those concerned in a given area, not for the government, to take the effective steps to that end. The government's role as we see it is to encourage the sponsors if they, the government, are satisfied that there is a need for a new institution.

That was how the UGC interpreted history, and its interpretation also contained within it an interpretation of economics. There was too much stress in the thinking, I believe, on the economic aspect of the acquisition of free or nearly free sites, though it was right to treat this issue as a test of the intentions and commitment of local authorities.

In '48–60' Murray then turned last to 'publicity', a theme which it was impossible to avoid throughout the 1960s but which was less discussed in 1960 than it was to be in the 1970s when national rather than local publicity, particularly through television, had strongly influenced public attitudes. The question of the need for new university institutions had 'excited considerable public interest over the past two years', Murray maintained,

> partly, no doubt, because of the Sussex project, but mainly because of the growing public concern about the need to find more places in the universities in order to cope with the growing numbers of qualified students coming from the schools. Not only have such bodies as the Association of University Teachers, as well as private individuals, expressed their views and stimulated discussion, but people in various areas up and down England have been discussing the desirability and possibility of setting up their own university.

In these two years, the UGC had received many approaches, including from Norwich, York, Gloucester, Cheltenham, Coventry, Kent, Essex, Stevenage, Hereford, Lancaster, Whitby, Bournemouth, Hereford and

Stamford. Some of these, like Norwich and York, were revivals of previous approaches. Others, such as Stevenage and Essex, were new initiatives.

The effort to set up a university generated considerable local publicity. Because of the large number of applications, the UGC appointed a small sub-committee to examine them. I was a founder member of it and very soon we had made our first enquiries. Two of the local 'bids', which in retrospect is the right way to describe them, from Norwich and York, had looked strong and had met necessary criteria. Each city was rich in history, tradition and culture. Each, it seemed, could be supported by other university cities, Cambridge in the one case, Leeds, Sheffield and Hull in the other. (This argument, which I never liked, was soon to lose its force.) Each was,

> the centre of good communications and was well served internally. Each has assured the UGC that it could find houses and schools for staff and lodgings for students until such time as halls of residence can be provided. [Note that such a time was envisaged.] In each case the sponsors claimed that they had secured the goodwill and active support 'of the local authority, the Church, industry, local notables, etc.', and requested to bring before the sub-committee a deputation representing a wide variety of interests.

It had been difficult for the UGC 'to estimate the precise financial implications of new provision in places like these'. 'Little guidance' could be obtained from 'comparison with University College of North Staffordshire, which was a very special case, or the proposed University College of Sussex which is still in the planning stage'. Was this entirely true? Would it not have been possible to have offered a few further observations? Computers were not in use then, of course, in relation to projection or model building. The guru of university computing was Brian Flowers, who proved to be a good friend of the University of Sussex. The financial argument that followed was brief, in retrospect too brief. Yet it was the final conclusion of memorandum '48–60', which was sent directly to the Chancellor of the Exchequer, who was still then responsible for university policy, and not to the Secretary of State for Education, that stands out:

> we submit that there is a need to encourage the establishment of some new university institutions and we seek the authority of the Chancellor to enter into discussions for this purpose with those who have already been considering the possibility in Norwich and in York.

This conclusion won the unanimous support of the members of the UGC. Indeed, it was received with acclamation.

In March 1960, the month that the UGC memorandum appeared, I found myself by a coincidence in Brighton for the annual WEA conference, always a very difficult conference to chair, and before I went down to Sussex I had received – and had been forced to decline – an invitation to stay with John Fulton, who had been appointed Principal of what was still called a university college. I had to decline because I knew that I would be too busy and preoccupied at my conference, where from the chair I had to follow trade-union rules and where I had to be present in late-night smoke-filled rooms fixing deals, to avoid staying in a conference hotel. Fulton pressed me very hard, however, and added that 'if you can't stay with me, I'd like to see you at the end of your meetings'. And this I did.

In consequence, we went out in wellington boots to see the site of the proposed university college not in the town but on the Downs, a totally unspoilt site, with large numbers of sheep on it and no people. Being interested in urban life I felt that it was beautiful but 'far out' and that a site in Brighton, an attractive urban place, would have been better. I was already interested in towns and cities, and I felt that it was to them that universities really belonged. The idea of a 'campus university' was to come later when new universities were actually in existence.

On returning to Brighton station to catch my train, Fulton called out along the platform as my train was leaving 'Why don't you come down and join me? As my deputy, you would deal with the planning side of the University and with its academic build up.' It was a flattering invitation, but I found it difficult to make up my mind about how to respond. I had no real reason for wishing to leave Leeds. I was a northerner who had chosen to leave Oxford for industrial Leeds, not rural Sussex. I knew virtually nothing about Sussex. I had been to Brighton beach only on two previous occasions, on one of them drinking champagne with Sir Robert Adam, Adjutant-General during the war, and his daughter Barbara.

What actually made Susan and I move south is worth considering, for the psychology of new university creation was of crucial importance and has sometimes been misleadingly interpreted. Wives count in all moves. Little though I knew of it, Brighton seemed an attractive place likely to make a good university centre. In the circumstances, the first thing I did was to consult Morris, my own Vice-Chancellor in Leeds. Somewhat to my surprise, he encouraged me to accept Fulton's offer, not, I know, because he wanted to get rid of me, but because he himself envied the opportunity. He was also a close friend of Fulton! They had been at Balliol together. Charles Morris and his brother Philip were then powerful figures in what was undoubtedly a kind of 'university establishment'. Philip, who did not share his brother's views, was Vice-Chancellor of Bristol. The fact that Charles approved the creation of new universities – without ever quite understanding what they might be – was of national importance.

Having listened to his weighty advice and having discussed the offer with some of my friends and colleagues, including friends on the UGC, I still could not make up my mind. As I have explained in the last chapter, I was about to go to Australia in June to teach at the Australian National University during the summer vacation, and we were to travel out there by sea from Southampton. I still had not made up my mind when, with my wife and family, I got on to the ocean-bound liner on a bright and sunny June day. It was the thought of the journey that settled the matter. My wife and I, who had spent hours pondering on Fulton's offer, suddenly agreed that it would be a terrible journey if we were to go on agonizing about what to do for several weeks at sea. 'Why don't I get off the boat and ring up from that telephone kiosk down there and say that we will go?' I asked Susan, who perhaps had been waiting for me to ask this question. And so, I got off the boat just as the announcement had been made on the microphone that we were due to sail in ten minutes' time. Fortunately, Fulton was in his office, and I told him at last that I would join him as a professor, as a dean and as his deputy. (Little, if anything, had been put into writing.) 'I'll come to Sussex' I said. And that was how I reached my own decision.

I have told this anecdote, an interesting and an amusing one, I think, not because it is an anecdote but because it throws light on current attitudes in 1960. There was no tremendous feeling in 1960 that even Sussex, for all its backing, was going to be an absolutely safe new university proposition. Fulton had immense enthusiasm, but he had no academic staff at that time, and he still had Swansea in the forefront of his thoughts. For him, as for Morris, Balliol College was also never far from his mind. Further back for John was Scotland.

A powerful personal incentive to move south for me was that since I was the first academic to be appointed I would have a major part in the appointment of others. Already I was thinking not so much of individuals as of a team. I felt strongly that while it was essential to form some kind of institutional conception of what a university should be, you should not be too much influenced by what already existed. You should think afresh. Gimmicks were not important; getting back to fundamentals was. And I felt that the first academics at Sussex should do this for themselves.

For that reason, I confess that I was never very happy about the UGC's idea of an Advisory Committee for each new university. Not surprisingly, therefore, because of my distrust of these committees, not shared by John, it was to work out that the Advisory Committee in the University of Sussex was to play a very minor role in the development of the university, a lesser role certainly than Fulton would have allowed it. The views of some, but not all, of its members I thought were ill-informed, even wrong, although I liked its chairman, the Vice-Chancellor of Durham, Sir James Duff, with whom I could talk freely. I could discuss with him my own conception of what Sussex should be and not be. I did not want it to be a liberal arts college on

Portrait of Asa Briggs by Trevor Stubley, 1979. This fine portrait was commissioned by the magazine *The Dalesman* for a series on Yorkshire 'celebrities', although by that time we were living in Oxford. We liked it so much that we bought the original.

Myself in the garden of
Worcester College (*right*),
with the lake and the
Provost's Lodgings in the
background, *c.* 1980.
*(Photograph by Matthew
Briggs)*

Portraits of Susan and
myself *(left and below)* by
our great friend Derek Hill,
painted in the Provost's
Lodgings at Worcester
College, Oxford, in 1988.

The wall-hanging (*right*) commissioned by us from two primary schools in Oxfordshire, Langford and Kelmscott (home of William Morris), each motif designed by a different ten- or eleven-year-old child under the inspired guidance of art teacher and textile designer Sue Rangeley. Two mini-bus loads of children came twice and the children explored Worcester College, the gardens and the lake. This wall-hanging was a fitting farewell to the College in the year of my retirement, 1991.

A watercolour of Falmer House, painted by Mona Hoddell in 1968. Designed by Basil Spence, this was the first building on the University of Sussex campus to be completed.

An aerial photograph of the University of Sussex campus in 2010, showing its enormous increase in size.

With Lord (Richard) Attenborough, then Chancellor of the University of Sussex, on my eightieth birthday in May 2001.

I am seen here on a graduation day in July 2010 with the actor and comedian Sanjeev Bhaskar, Chancellor of the University of Sussex since 2009.

We have lived only intermittently in our eighteenth-century Lewes home,
The Caprons, since we bought the house in 1972. The cellars, said to be medieval,
are now full of filing boxes reflecting my work over seventy years.

(Photograph by Susan Briggs)

Two panels (*right*) from our painted room in The Caprons, commissioned by us in 1985
from Julia Rushbury, another artist friend and close neighbour in Lewes, to celebrate our
thirtieth wedding anniversary. The room is an autobiography in pictures. These panels
show books by me and some symbols of my interests.

A sixtieth birthday card from our friend and near-neighbour Walter Hodges, whose name will always be associated with the Globe Theatre.

The South Bank in 1951 (*right*) during the festival of Britain. Hugh Casson was Director of Architecture for the Festival.

Hugh Casson sent congratulations at important times in my life.

(1) On becoming Provost of Worcester College, Oxford, and being made a peer, in 1976.

(2) On leaving Oxford in 1991 and buying our part of Tyninghame House, which he turned into a fantasy castle.

Bigg Castle

A memento of the Great Exhibition of 1851 (*right*).

Was this the ultimate 'Special Relationship'? A photograph taken by Susan of me with President Bill Clinton in Silicon Valley in California.

Part of our collection of American souvenirs. Note the ping-pong bats which commemorate Nixon's visit to China in 1972.

Portraits of me away from home. Sunbathing in Corfu on a holiday with Frank and Kitty Giles, painted by Susan c. 1990.

Sitting by the fire during a winter holiday at our home in Portugal, painted by Susan.

At work in the garden, as seen in a letter from Susan Lasdun.

how well it looks in our home, when you come on January 22nd. Meanwhile a thousand thanks from us both for everything and much love
Susan.

Susan and I are born collectors, even magpies but have always been less interested in the aesthetics of objects than in the themes they display. Between us we assembled a remarkable collection of Victorian Staffordshire figures. But almost all of these that we kept at The Caprons were stolen in the most professional manner in 2005: none were recovered. We moved on to Maoist figures: Mao looks across at me in my study.

A temperance plate (*left*).

A Staffordshire figure of Louis Napoleon, later Napoleon III.

A stoneware figure of the leading Liberal and reformer Henry Brougham.

My favourite Chinese figures: Chairman Mao and Madame Mao.

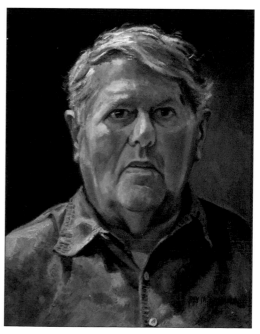

Objects communicate. There were mobile objects long before there were mobile phones. We bought these in Cape Verde. Had they been brought in from Ghana?

This portrait of me does not look 'foreign' but it was painted during a cruise by Susan's excellent art teacher on the ship, Tony Paul. I sat as a model for the class.

Anyone for tennis, cricket, football? Some sporting mementoes from our collection.

Château Haut-Brion, the vineyard I know best. The château is near Bordeaux and can be reached by tram.

My ninetieth birthday party, 7 May 2011.
The party was held in the garden of our
son Daniel and his wife Anabel. Eleven of
our fourteen grandchildren were there and
many friends of all ages.

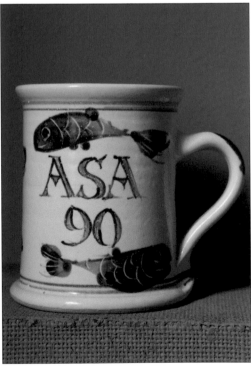

A birthday reminder, a present from a
friend, given to me at the party.

the American model, which I already knew at first hand. I wanted it to be a fully fledged university from the start with an equal place for science and for the arts, and, equally important to me, there should be technology too.

I had been just as strongly influenced in my thinking about the map of learning before I went to Australia by developments in the biological sciences as I had been by developments in history, and as far as technology was concerned I had been strongly influenced also by two very different fellow members of the UGC, Eric Ashby, whom I have already introduced, and Sir Willis Jackson from Imperial College. Even before that, however, I had been interested in technology as an historian, and as an economist I was deeply concerned about Britain's engineering future. On the UGC itself I had already made a special point of getting to know what went on in the engineering departments of the universities which we visited. Marine engineering in Glasgow wasted public funds with nothing in return. Civil and electrical engineering were everywhere neglected.

I emphasize this point because it is sometimes suggested that those of us who were interested in new universities were disturbed by the sight of industrial plant. I did not believe that the study of technology should be restricted to places where there was smoke – and there was still plenty of that in 1960.

The ideas that I put into my 'Map of Learning' lecture and a number of my other writings at the time were guiding ideas for the nine academics who encountered the first Sussex students in 1961, although I realized clearly that all these ideas and others needed to be thrashed out by the nine of us. I knew that I had no monopoly of knowledge or experience, but I believed that, like John Fulton, I had 'vision', a quality that always matters. At the time I maintained, and I still maintain in retrospect, that the most important phase in the creation of a new university is the selection and assembly of a small team of people who are willing to think things out afresh and who, untutelaged, having argued with each other, set out to produce some kind of pattern that will both develop and inspire. At Brighton I did not just want to assemble a collection of distinguished academics, as

Jack Butterworth did at Warwick University, and leave them to get on with it as individuals. Nevertheless, looking years ahead, I foresaw that Warwick, having got through its early troubles, would flourish as an alternative model to Sussex.

In Sussex we worked in our first year not behind what came to be called 'plate glass' but in two converted nineteenth-century houses in Brighton – it was like living in a kibbutz – and we all knew each other very well indeed during that first year when we set out to explore together just what the new University of Sussex was about –and what it might be. The discussions took little account of age or status. One of our number had had no previous university experience. One had already known more universities than almost any academic in the country. We argued on equal terms. The students in Brighton argued too in what were flatteringly called common rooms.

Neither I nor Fulton nor anybody else imposed a pattern on the University of Sussex. There was only one shared idea on paper which was there when we started our discussions in 1961. That was that we would get rid of departments altogether at Sussex and have 'schools' in their place. The main reason why that idea was taken for granted was a curious one. Before we had any discussions at all, the Director of Education for Brighton, W. G. (always known as Bill) Stone, who had played a very important part in the local initiative to create a university, had reached the conclusion, if only because Brighton was relatively near to the continent of Europe, that it should have a School of European Studies. This was a term that he was the first to use and a term that seemed to us all to be the right one. It was the idea of that school, which I had considered a few years earlier in a radio discussion with Stone and others, that encouraged us to think in terms of a pattern of schools rather than departments, a pattern that some other new universities would be quick to adopt.

We might have reached the same answer, however, I believe, had there been no such discussion. At Leeds the history department under Le Patourel and myself had been called the School of History and not the Department of History. Yet inside the University it was treated as a department. While at Leeds that I became thoroughly dissatisfied

116

with 'departmentalism' as it operated there. It inhibited academic discussion and generated bureaucracy. If, for example, I as a joint head of a very big department wanted to work out staffing arrangements – or details of academic organization – with another department I had to sign bilateral treaties with its head. These took an enormous amount of time and those involved were often as much concerned with *amour propre* as with academic issues. It was particularly difficult to get permission for people to lecture across departmental boundaries even when they wished, sometimes desperately, to do so.

I had been used to a very different pattern in Oxford, but my own critique of departmentalism – for me it had become an *ism* – took shape in Leeds, where for the first time in my life I became fully aware of its consequences. I had known from my time as an external examiner at Birmingham that departmentalism was by no means confined to Leeds. I started at Sussex, therefore, with this one strong bias. I felt that departments ought to go, abolished for ever.

More interesting, however, was how to answer the question of what to replace them with. What schools and how many should there be? We thought about answers to these questions very carefully in 1961. We did not want schools to be super-departments. We wanted a flexible system that would enable us to create new schools in the future. That was an essential point. I personally attached a great deal of importance to a future School of Applied Sciences for reasons that I have explained: it came in very quickly in 1966 with no encourage-ment from the UGC. I also thought we ought to have a school of what were to be called Cultural and Community Studies. It would have to be more than a School of Education. That evolved over time.

In devising the school pattern, we were not entirely self-reliant, a point that I must emphasize given what I said earlier about the role of the Academic Advisory Committee. We found ourselves talking to consultants and advisers. For example, in relation to the School of Applied Sciences, I had a great deal of talk with Sir Willis Jackson and in relation to the School of Biological Sciences we all had a great deal of talk with Jim Danielli, then in University College, London, a biologist who was invited to join us but went instead to the United States.

During the course of our first year we also worked out one or two other policies. We thought that it would be a very good idea if everyone at the beginning of his or her university career in either arts or sciences should spend a certain amount of time doing something in common with people in other arts or science disciplines before beginning to specialize, within the less rigidly departmentalized Sussex curriculum. We introduced, therefore, preliminary first year courses which did not go as far as Keele had done, but in the same spirit as Keele set out to provide some sort of 'foundation'.

We went on to have protracted discussions about what such common courses would be. To my mind, a university is really a genuine university only if there is something which brings together the people inside it. That may be a prejudice, but like Ernest Bevin I do not like passports or visas either for academics or for students before they can cross the boundaries of disciplines. Alas, for security reasons alone – and these did not bother us in the 1960s – they now seem to be necessary.

The way in which we would carry out our teaching and learning patterns also preoccupied us in the course of our first year. The UGC was itself giving a strong lead at the time, for Murray at the top attached an enormous amount of importance to qualitative change. We were expected to deal with teaching seriously, and to break new ground, and in consequence, with the recommendations of the Hale Report on teaching in mind, we devised our own pattern which laid considerable emphasis not only upon tutorials but on seminars and small groups, more emphasis than was common in most places at that time.

Lectures were treated as ancillary. No academic who came to Sussex to teach in our first few years was obliged to give lectures. I knew perfectly well, however, from the nature of the people we were appointing to our first deanships that many of them would do so – who could have stilled David Daiches? I knew, too, that our science colleagues might feel them indispensable. We were never short of a sizeable lecture programme from the very beginning of the university.

I am trying to get at the aspirations of that very first year. It was an extraordinary year – we still had no science colleagues – but it was a key year, during which we established the proposition – or thought that we had done so – that there should be no gulf whatsoever in Sussex between professors and the rest. I said 'thought that we had done so', for that pattern did not persist in its entirety in the future as faculty numbers grew. I should add that the year was extraordinary for another reason. We had no buildings, we had no labs, we were not then in any sense a campus university, although the campus figured prominently in our minds. And we had very few students, only fifty-one of them, thirty-seven women and fourteen men. I remember talking to one woman student after a dance which was held in 1961 for the first time in Falmer House, a striking Basil Spence building on the university site. She said to me simply 'Professor Briggs, the place will never be the same again.' I entirely agreed.

And this is not the least of my reflections. Sussex was never the same again: indeed, at least until the 1970s it was never the same place in any two years. For every year that I was in Sussex, from 1961 to 1976, we had the sense of new experience. You could not settle into routines. There were changes of various kinds each year as we proudly defied the notion expressed in the UGC's memorandum '48–60' that you cannot double size in a short period. Our actual growth pattern was an interesting one. We went up from 51 to 450 students in our second year and reached the 1,000 stage two years earlier than the UGC had expected us to do. We found that this expansion in itself was extremely exciting. Such experience of growth is rare in this country outside universities. We did not use the term, which belongs to a later period, but what we were enjoying was 'enterprise culture'.

Some of us even enjoyed the talk about buildings – and the planning of them. Our architect, Sir Basil Spence, who produced an overall plan for the future university in 1959, was a great talker, not least to visitors to the campus. Although academics had had nothing to do with choosing him as architect he liked to feel that he was one of us. The problems of the physical development of the site were not, I think, fully understood by the UGC, nor were we generously treated. I was shocked by the amount of money being spent on new buildings in Oxford as compared with ours, and we were, I fear, to pay the price.

If Spence, who was mistrusted by the UGC, had had his way, the university would have looked better then – and far better now. Sadly perhaps, costs did not figure at all in his vision, as it had to do in ours and in that of the UGC.

Another point should be made about the mood of 1961 and later. If you bring together academics from different university backgrounds, they will introduce quite different elements into the mix. In the first mix, for example, there was the University of Wales, Oxford, Cambridge, Leeds; and very soon we had brought in academics from most universities in the country. Through my UGC experience I could detect in the early years at Sussex that there was a bit of Edinburgh here, a bit of Newcastle there, and many bits of somewhere else almost everywhere. There were also some academics whom we deliberately attracted from outside the university world altogether, like John Roselli from the *Manchester Guardian*. They were lively voices and they had no sympathy with bureaucracy.

What united us was a determination to make the best of our own university. We were keen to think about what it was that we were doing. I can see – indeed I saw at the time – that there was a quite different way of conceiving how to develop a new university. Bring reputable professors in and leave them free to get on with it. That was not our way, although I could see certain practical advantages in following that course, and when we had shared long hours of discussion I found relief in contemplating alternative models. I realized quickly that there were aspects of our system that might create difficulties. An enormous responsibility lay on the deans. They were appointed on grounds of ability. What if they were to become elected? Would students feel as much 'at home' in schools as they did in the best departments in other universities? Who would be responsible for the social life of schools? How would we make 'administrative' arrangements for academics who were teaching in more than one school?

In answering the last of these questions we had to develop the quasi-feudal conception of 'school of first allegiance'. An academic could choose to teach in any school, but only one of them was responsible for the management of his salary. The school secretaries acquired extra power through this process. Then a related question arose: how would waves of new academics respond to the distinctive pattern of our university with which they would be unfamiliar? I must confess that by 1966 the pattern of schools at Sussex was already extremely complicated as far as teaching was concerned and needed a good deal of understanding on the part of any newcomer, since its full implications were difficult to appreciate. The UGC, under a new chairman, John Wolfenden, found it all too difficult to cope with. Sussex did not fit into its routines.

I realized from the start that each new group in our mix in the future would find it increasingly difficult to contribute to decision-making through the kind of shared joint experience that we had made the most of in the first year. As the academics who made their way to Sussex became more specialized – and we had to look for specialists – some of them would have little desire to contribute to general discussion even if they had the chance. Like all academics elsewhere, they might look to their peer group in other universities rather than to the special opportunities of Sussex.

We also knew that the public was interested in what universities were and might be and in consequence an 'image question' as well as structural and curricular questions came up. At the beginning of the 1960s, Brighton's proximity to London meant that we caught something of the 'swinging London' mood. As a result we were actively monitored by the media from the start. This was the only time in my life that I appeared in both *Vogue* and *Reader's Digest*, within a short period of three months. We were all conscious of the regular presence of cameras; we were all concerned that we were in danger of being over-glamorized. No 'redbrick university' had ever been in this position.

Nonetheless, some images were backed by statistics. We had a great appeal for would-be undergraduates, particularly perhaps, but by no means exclusively, women undergraduates, and we were backed by unconventional schools as well as by fashionable media. I wrote several little pieces at the time in one of the many manuals that were then being produced on 'How to choose a University' in which I emphasized how important it was in making a choice to be concerned not with images, but with what the structures, the curricula, the modes of teaching and real merits or demerits of the place might be.

During the 1960s there was a strong sense that students should make choices and that they should not take anything for granted. I must emphasize, however, that the particular curricular pattern that we devised at Sussex was not designed to meet already proclaimed student wishes. Indeed, students played no part in the initial preparation of the Sussex curriculum and relatively little, except by way of feedback, in its development during the later 1960s. It was we, not they, who explicitly set out to ensure that Sussex would provide a distinctive educational experience. We were also interested, of course, in their own earlier experience and in the experience that would follow their university education. Indeed, we wished to draw on the former and use it within the educational process.

We related our concerns more generally to the national problem of access – with all its social implications – and because of this and not in order to get round our glamour image – we introduced the first scheme to admit students to a university who had no A-levels and students from deprived homes. Happily the success of our scheme produced a new element in the student mix. I myself had always been interested in adult education, and the 'mature students' received a good deal of my own personal attention. So, too, indeed, did continuing education, which at that time was of little concern to most vice-chancellors and professors.

I watched the process of the creation of other new universities with great interest and knew some of the people who were involved in their creation and development. I worked, too, I believe, on their behalf inside the UGC. I recall, nonetheless, that at no point in the process of their coming into existence did they ever have all that much to do with each other. They did not operate in any kind of way as a bloc. I cannot over-emphasize the point, which was not appreciated at the time by outsiders or even by most people in 'traditional' universities. It is true that one member of the University of Sussex, Martin Wight, was on the planning committee of the University of Kent – there were a few cross-linkages of that kind – but there was very little cross-talk.

I myself had some of it, however, with the first Vice-Chancellor of the University of East Anglia about the role of schools, but the schools pattern that emerged in East Anglia was different from the Sussex pattern: only the use of the term 'school' was common. I also spoke to sociologists at Essex, whose Vice-Chancellor, Albert Sloman, became a personal friend, but their curricular pattern was even more different from ours than East Anglia's. Yet, for all my contacts, I do not think that I was unique in feeling that I had enough to do in my own place without concerning myself too much about others. I may have felt more strongly than most of my colleagues that every new institution had to work out things for itself. It should not be derivative. I was not involved in a Sussex export trade, except trade in ideas about specialization, interdisciplinarity and departmentalism.

There was a place, of course, for association with other universities that were far away. York did not stretch out to me. Lancaster did. Its Vice-Chancellor, Charles Carter, whom I knew and admired, drew me into discussions both of national educational policy and research, and we developed together one of the rare examples of collaboration between two universities, in this case in the field of operational research. We talked of a Northwest/Southeast axis, and brought to Sussex the then head of operational research in Lancaster.

The consequences of each of the new universities following its own course of action are interesting and important. If we had been brought into existence by a quite different mode, nationally dictated with no local bidding and free from local pressures influencing the way in which things worked or might work – or, indeed, if there had been not different advisory committees, but one, we might have produced duplicated institutions or institutions that if they were not quite duplicated, would have been very similar to each other. In fact, we were more different from each other than 'redbrick universities' were – although there were significant differences, for example, between Nottingham and Leicester, that I fully recognized. I am deeply grateful, in retrospect, as I was at the time, for the fact that we were different, that there was great variety. Nor were we graded in the minds of the UGC. We all got off to the same start.

Variety carried with it responsibility, and it was certainly the role of any central funding body to ensure that funds were well spent and that within the system as a whole there was the minimum of waste and no unnecessary duplication. I recognize clearly in retrospect that if we had not been able to work within a national quinquennial planning system, we would have found it impossible to plan as we did, but at Sussex we developed planning procedures of our own. Our planning committee was the first planning committee in the country to deal at the same time with academic planning and with the resource implications of planning: indeed, we had no separate finance committee in the university after our first few years. Our new-style planning committee also included members of Council so that in a sense we broke the dividing lines that separate academics from others. From the start we also found it essential to take undergraduates and graduate students completely into our confidence about the shape of the university accounts. It would have been quite absurd in a new university for people to have felt that things were being hidden away from them.

We were never lavishly treated financially. Lord Annan was wrong when he argued in more than one place that the new universities were given too much money during the 1960s. Indeed, in one particular respect – new buildings – we were treated extremely toughly in that we were forced to obey norms which took very little account of what I would now call 'campus' infrastructure. We were, in fact, producing new communities on often challenging sites, and it was very difficult to get the officers of the UGC to think in terms not of individual buildings, but of the relationships between buildings and the site as a whole.

University finance began to be a topic of discussion everywhere in 1961, the first year of Sussex, when the UGC was given a warning from a Treasury minister, the first such to come to a UGC meeting: he talked to us in the crudest language possible about cakes and shares. (I saw Heyworth, the Chairman of Unilever, cringe.) That was before the Robbins Committee was appointed, and in my view the main role of that committee, which did not produce the new universities, was first to assemble the best statistics that had ever been produced and, second, to underline the importance of providing adequate national resources if educational targets were to be met.

I have now abandoned the idea of writing a short monograph on the seven new universities of the 1960s. The most innovative and radical of all new university institutions, the Open University, with which I was associated almost from the start, has been the subject of several of them. First talked of in 1963 by Harold Wilson, then leader of the Labour opposition, in what became a famous Glasgow speech, as the University of the Air, the project quickly became something else. This was largely because of the taking over of the policy-making of a new distance-learning institution by Jennie Lee, widow of Aneurin Bevan. Through her I became one of the most active members of an energetic planning committee set up in 1967, just after I had become Vice-Chancellor of Sussex. Jennie, who by then had become Minister of State for the Arts, gave a press conference on 18 September to mark the establishment of the committee, which was to be chaired by Sir Peter Venables, Vice-Chancellor of the University of Aston in Birmingham. (Peter Venables's son became a very valuable early member of the University of Sussex.) Its terms of reference were to work out a comprehensive plan for the establishment of an Open University as outlined in the White Paper of February 1966, 'A University of the Air', and to prepare a draft charter and statutes. The committee would get down to work in October, and, in the words of a press release, it was 'expected' that the university 'will be launched by autumn 1970'.

I was proud to be able to be directly involved in the creation of another new university, most special of the universities, and glad that it would be grant-aided directly by the Department of Education and Science outside the aegis of the University Grants Committee. This was not because, having become a vice-chancellor, I had had to leave the UGC but because it no longer had a chairman of the calibre and vision of Keith Murray. I was glad on the whole too that 'by agreement with the BBC' the television programmes would be broadcast on

BBC2. There was a long history behind this. I would not have objected, however, to some of them being broadcast by commercial companies. I thought too that radio should have been given more attention in the White Paper – television was the glamour technology.

By October 1967 I was well used to reading between the lines in all official statements, and I had been aware through my WEA contacts, which continued after I became Vice-Chancellor, and my knowledge of what went on in Broadcasting House, that there had been a long and complicated prelude to the White Paper of 1966 and to Jennie's statement of 1967. Nevertheless, my main object, as Jennie's was, was to get to work as quickly as possible. I approached our common tasks with optimism and enthusiasm, and I was delighted to be given the vitally important task of chairing the curriculum sub-committee. That, I felt, had a real team job to do, not dissimilar to the job the first nine members of the faculty in Sussex had done in 1961.

Peter Venables was a perfect chairman of the whole planning committee, which included representatives who wasted no time and always listened. I myself did not want our committee to try to do too much. I wanted us to leave to the University's first Vice-Chancellor and his colleagues the task of really creating the University which in the 'outside world' – and not least in Wilson's Cabinet – had more critics than friends. The *Economist* was on its side and, after the committee had reported, Geoffrey Crowther, a former editor, was rightly chosen as the OU's first Chancellor. The *Times Higher Education Supplement* was against the whole idea of it. Michael Young, who had proclaimed the idea of an Open University in the very beginning, was not happy about what was happening or would happen, wanting as he did a 'less pretentious' college devoted to flexi-learning, much, perhaps most, of it at a sub-university level. He never won the confidence of Jennie Lee. She wanted a real university, and so did I.

By far the best account of the prelude to the story of the Open University, which was to be told in some detail by its first Vice-Chancellor, Walter Perry, was written by Ralph Toomey, a very wise civil servant, whose backstairs role was as important as Wilson's. His account was not published, but he gave me a copy which I treasure. It emphasized what to me were two extremely important points. First, government departments were even worse in their dealings with each other than university departments. They obstructed rather than assisted necessary change. Second, there was no agreement behind the scenes on what an Open University would be. Michael Young's was only one of several alternative visions.

A point of my own that I have always stressed was that the Open University could not have been brought into existence had there not been a conjunction of rising educational demand and new communications technology. White papers on broadcasting were as significant in the story as white papers on education. I gave my own interpretation of the early history in the first Ritchie Calder Memorial Lecture on 'The Role of the Open University' in November 1985.

Ritchie Calder was a link man in many of my own stories. He was a Vice-President of the WEA when I was President, a member of the OU Planning Committee and, not least, the father of my extremely able and knowledgeable research student Angus, who wrote *The People's War*, and of Nigel, editor of the *New Scientist*, for which I wrote many articles, some forecasting the shape of things to come. The organ that I was then using most for my own writing was *New Society*.

Chapter 6

Business, Labour, Politics, The Arts

At first glance ironically, I have made most of my connections with businessmen through universities. In the Oxford University of the 1950s, when the idea of a business school would have been anathema to most dons, I took part in short courses (and discussions planned by my close friend Neville Ward-Perkins, Fellow of Pembroke College, and Norman Leyland, Economics Fellow of Brasenose College). Many of the businessmen attending them were Oxford alumni, a description not much in use in Britain at the time. A few of them had studied at the Harvard Business School.

In my own college I was tutor to a number of undergraduates who later in their lives became well-known businessmen, among them Ronnie Utiger, who told me that he was more interested in moving into industry than into commerce, Julian Ogilvie Thompson, a South African, who from 1985 to 1997 was chairman of De Beers, and two Sainsburys, John and Tim, who were to be among the biggest benefactors to my Oxford college after I became Provost in 1976. They set up their own Linbury Family Trust. John's wife Anya was a beautiful ballet dancer. For me there were to be other chains of connection with the Sainsburys. As an undergraduate in Cambridge I was a regular customer at the wonderful Sainsbury's shop, not far from my college – with the crowded Dorothy Café in between – where you could choose excellent cheeses and buy tasty 'titbits' that were available nowhere else in the town.

When I turned seriously to retail history in the early 1950s and wrote the history of Lewis's of Liverpool, I reflected on the life of John and Tim's father, who also became a baron: he remained a supporter of the Labour Party in his old age. By then we had moved into the age of supermarkets. Over the years the Sainsburys straddled the parties, with one branch becoming fervently Liberal. John, who at that time may have been less interested in politics than his father, was conservative to the core. Tim became a Conservative MP, for Hove, a key part of the Sussex University territory. He, more than any other member of the family, cared rather for politics than for business. They were united through their philanthropy and their support of the arts. Their cousin David, who was a trustee of the Social Democratic Party between 1982 and 1990, became a Labour minister under Blair in 1998. He has recently been elected Chancellor of Cambridge University.

Just before I was married and moved to Leeds in 1955 I took up seriously the history of retailing. This was not in order to explore the history of Sainsbury's, although I would like to have done so, or to examine the history of one of Britain's great chain stores like Lipton's or Maypole, but to write a book on the history of perhaps the oldest British department store, David Lewis of Liverpool, founded in 1856. A great showman, Lewis had served his apprenticeship not with one of the large merchant houses of Liverpool but with a firm of tailors and outfitters, Benjamin Hyam and Company. The company which he founded acquired a chain of department stores in the shopping areas of provincial cities – Leeds, Manchester, Birmingham, Bristol, Hanley and Glasgow – where it had set up stores at various times. In Leeds, its Headrow store was a local landmark. The chain was not as well known to economic historians as John Spedan Lewis's pioneering organization, which, incidentally was to figure prominently in the history of code-breaking at Bletchley which I wrote about in *Secret Days*. The chess player, Hugh Alexander, prominent as a cryptographer at Bletchley, was its Research Director before the war, while Gordon Welchman, a key figure at Bletchley, held the same post just after the war.

I enjoyed writing my history of David Lewis's which, reflecting his philosophy, I called *Friends of the People*. I was still putting it through the press when I married Susan. I describe in my book how David Lewis, born in 1823, began what was a dramatic career as a retailer in 1856 when he acquired a small shop in Ranelagh Street, Liverpool, the first step in a career which was to transform the story of the British department store. He died in 1885, only a few weeks after his Birmingham store was opened, in the carefully chosen words of the *Birmingham Daily Post* 'an event rather of public than of private or business significance'. I could have had no intimation that thirty years later I would attend a ceremony to commemorate its closure. I was invited to speak then by the Provost of Birmingham. In 1885 there had been no Birmingham Cathedral.

There had been no thought either that, under a quite different chairman, Lewis's would acquire a store in London more palatial than John Lewis's. It was the store which Gordon Selfridge, a former partner of the great American retailer Marshall Field, had opened triumphantly in 1909. Twenty years later, in 1929, a year of national economic depression, when the future of Selfridge's was uncertain, Frederick Marquis, later Lord Woolton, who had joined Lewis in 1920 and became chairman and managing director of Lewis Ltd in 1928, had told Selfridge that 'the day will come when we will buy your business, but not until you have finished with it'.

When I was writing my Lewis's centenary history, I got on well with Woolton, who liked me as an historian and even more as a northerner. Our relationship was not unlike that between my friend Charles Wilson, Professor of Modern History at Cambridge from 1945 to 1979, and Geoffrey Heyworth, the Chairman of Unilever, who in 1947 invited Wilson to write a history of Unilever. The scale was not specified; Unilever imposed no restraints on Wilson, a friend with whom I was to stay on post-war visits to Cambridge.

Heyworth of Unilever was the first really big businessman whom I met. I was to have many dealings with him on many fronts, and to become a good, if not a close, friend. He had few of these. I knew as soon as I met Heyworth that, for all the wide range of his public activities, he was essentially a private person who gave little away. I remember one of my first encounters with him, during the early 1950s on the tarmac of Madras airport in India, when I was struck by the way he triumphed over physical disability. While in India on this early trip there I met other big businessmen, notably members of the Parsee Tata family, whose subsequent business history was to extend its range and scope and draw it into a global empire of its own, which included many distant countries.

I was aware when I talked about corporate management in India as in West Africa, that I was on the same wavelength as Heyworth. He gave me a copy of a 1956 annual report of his, which Unilever published – all its annual reports had titles – which he called *The Managers*, in which he insisted that 'without good managers neither this nor any business could thrive'. At the time I related such lectures to the mainly American literature of 'managerial revolution' and 'organization man', highly controversial, which I had first come across on the American side of the Atlantic when I read James Burnham and Peter Drucker. Heyworth himself avoided generalization and controversy as much as possible. In private he was quite a good listener, but the Unilever board meeting held in London on Thursday mornings at eleven o'clock rarely lasted longer than an hour. In the concise words of the second Viscount Leverhulme, son of the founder of Lever Brothers, 'there was not a great deal of discussion'.

One person on this side of the Atlantic who believed in the importance of business management was Noel Hall, who in 1943 had been selected by Heyworth from a highly diverse field to be the first Principal at the new Administrative College (note that the word management was not used in its designation) in Henley and who in 1960 became Principal of Brasenose College where Ward-Perkins, Leyland and myself had organized our business symposia. Heyworth does not appear to have had much to say about the subjects that interested him either in Henley, with which I was later to become considerably involved as a governor, or at weekend conferences of businessmen, politicians and academics at Nuffield College, Oxford, which made him a visiting fellow in 1947 (it made Morrison one at the same time) and an honorary fellow in 1960. He always refused to 'lead off' for the college. He could not be provoked.

The Warden of Nuffield College from 1944 to 1955, Henry Clay, the first academic economist to become a junior adviser to the Bank of England, had written Heyworth a very persuasive letter asking him to become a Fellow:

> I am most anxious to get you into a position in which you could gradually interest yourself first in the studies, and then in the wider questions of the University . . .
>
> There is a good deal of guesswork in the Economics and Politics taught in universities [the subjects that I was teaching in Worcester College before I got my Readership]: you have [by contrast] whether by nature or training, the habit of insisting on the facts of the problem before generalising.

I saw very little of Heyworth before I left Oxford for Leeds, and even when I was in Oxford the businessman I knew best in Nuffield, where I was a Faculty Fellow, was not Heyworth but Raymond Street, a fellow northerner as I then thought of myself. I liked talking to him not only about the textile industry but about the sequence of well-prepared working party reports that came out regularly under the Attlee government. They dealt informatively with different sectors of the British economy, many of them recording not the rise of British industry but its contraction.

The word 'sector' was much in use at the time, although it did not figure in Anthony Sampson's vocabulary in his *Anatomy of Britain* (1962), a book which I discussed with the author in detail, chapter by chapter. I loved the circles of institutions that adorned the back of the hard covers of his book. That was my vocabulary too. I used to stay in London with Anthony when I was visiting the metropolis from Leeds during the years between 1955 and 1961 and did not want to use the railway night sleeper, which had the best attendants in the country, one or two of whom I got to know well. They were good gossips.

I did not meet as many businessmen in Leeds itself as I had expected to do. They kept to themselves. I was never entertained by the Tetleys, for example, although they were prominent in the management of the university, nor by any of the Keighley businessmen who had been names to me in my boyhood. I did become a friend, however, of Stanley Burton, who taught me much about clothes retailing, and of Bernard Gillinson, also in the clothing industry on a small scale. Gillinson's business premises were near the great Leeds market, one of my favourite places in Leeds, particularly on late Saturday afternoons when prices at the market stalls, particularly those selling fruit and vegetables, were often dramatically reduced.

Bernard, an academic manqué more than an entrepreneur, was a frequent host to Hugh Gaitskell, the Labour leader, whom I had got to know a little before I had moved from Oxford to Leeds; his lively stepson, Raymond Frost, had been a pupil of mine in Worcester. Gaitskell took a great interest in me and made me several offers of public jobs which would now perhaps be labelled 'patronage'. I hasten to write that money was never mentioned. I preferred Aneurin Bevan to him, as I believe Attlee did. It was always instructive to chat with him about topics as different as coal and steel nationalization and the fortunes of the Co-operative movement, which had direct links with the Labour Party. I had already been invited more than once to the Co-operative College in Loughborough, sometimes to talk about Robert Owen. Above all Gaitskell wanted to talk to me about the University of Leeds, where he felt that he lacked good friends. There were, he believed, too many Trotskyites there (some of whom I knew personally). I saw a lot also of Hugh's wife, Dora, mother of Raymond, and of Bernard's highly talented wife, Rose, born in Riga, with no children of her own but a friend to all young artists in Leeds. She was also, more than incidentally, the best cook that Susan and I had ever met. The Gillinsons lived just above Roundhay Park and had the Roman Catholic Bishop of Leeds, a future cardinal, as a neighbour.

While I was talking Labour politics to Gaitskell in Leeds I was writing a book about a zealous Liberal politician, Seebohm Rowntree, who had died in 1954 just before I travelled north. Born in 1871, he should have been honoured in the 140th celebration of his birth in this the year of my ninetieth birthday. It was in 1947 that I was asked by the Rowntree Trust to write what I insisted should be called *a* study of his work, and not a biography of him. While writing it I spent a lot of time as a guest of Peter and Eve Rowntree in their comfortable house, The Homestead, where Seebohm himself had lived. He had certainly left his mark on it. Indeed, he still seemed to be around in the house when I carried out my research among his hitherto unsorted papers. I had a young assistant, Ian Smart, who performed an indispensable task in initially sorting them out.

No two Rowntrees could have been more different in outlook and behaviour than Seebohm and Peter, father and son, but there was a very powerful family sense similar to that of the Cadburys which I had observed in Birmingham when I was writing the history of the city. Like the Cadburys, the Rowntrees were pioneers of the chocolate industry. They were Quakers who believed in temperance as much as in chocolate. I loved to visit the Cocoa Works in York and the nearby community where many of his workers had lived, as I had enjoyed visiting Bournville in Birmingham. No two cities could have been more different than York and Birmingham, one ancient with Roman walls and a Minster. No two businesses could have been more similar. It seems as strange to me that both were to be taken over by foreigners as it did when Keighley was swallowed up in Bradford.

Within a York context it would be a bad mistake to treat either Seebohm or his father Joseph solely or, even worse, simply, as philanthropists. Living in quite different times, they were both pioneers in industrial management. 'Industry', Seebohm told an American audience of employers and trade unionists in 1937, 'is the Atlas which bears the world on its shoulders.' One of my necessary tasks in writing my study of Seebohm was visiting the United States and getting to know particular businessmen there with whom he co-operated. It had been Henry Denniston, whom he described as his oldest and dearest American friend, who developed the idea of management research groups. The relationship between the two men was reciprocal. It was under Seebohm's guidance that Denniston set up a Works Council in Framingham, Massachusetts. I like to know that it was in 1921, the year of my birth, that Seebohm, in an address to the American Academy of Political and Social Sciences, treated 'betterment' as a process. It could not simply be 'installed'. It had to grow. People should approach the study of society with the same care for investigation and experiment as when they approached the study of the natural world.

I had learned much about business and about psychology when I set out the results of my own study in 1961, the year I went from Leeds to Sussex. Again dates are interesting and the conjunctions that went with them. *A Study of the Life and Work of Seebohm Rowntree*, which gave equal attention to his many writings and to his political concerns, was the first book of mine to be published by Longman. His own first book *Poverty, a Study of Town Life* (1901), a 'grand inquest', also published by Longman, was waved aloft on Liberal platforms between its date of publication and the general election of 1906, which the Liberal Party won with a huge majority. An alliance between Seebohm and David Lloyd George, which did not mean quite the same for the two of them, followed. The book and the alliance must be examined critically. What I wrote about it so long ago was not hagiography. Both men were capable of making serious mistakes.

In retrospect, the main effect of my being drawn into the world of the Rowntrees was that it gave depth to what I wrote about the welfare state. A by-product, however, was that I met in York some of the local dignitaries, journalists and clergy who, in unlikely alliances between Quakers and Anglicans, were pushing for a new university in York. J. Bowes Morrell, who as a very young man was the only non-Rowntree on the board of the Cocoa Works in the year when the first volume of *Poverty* appeared, was now working in association with Canon Purviss of the Minster to press for a University of York when I was completing my book on Seebohm.

I was then a member of the University Grants Committee and I have a vivid visual memory of the two of them, one short, one tall (or so it seemed), walking side by side up the path to the house where I lived in Leeds, a house beautifully named Ingledew Cottage. (It had been the builders' house when the Roundhay Park estate was developed in the nineteenth century.) They had thought of my becoming York's first vice-chancellor: I had the proper birth qualification, and I had even contemplated living in York when I moved from Oxford to Leeds in 1955. They were too late. Already I had been approached by Sussex, and as it was I had very little to do with York University, except for its music, after I completed my *Seebohm Rowntree*.

Ironically my closest association with the new university, which took in its first students three years after Sussex, was through a Leeds Jewish business friend, Jack Lyons, who did everything that he could to establish music in York. He not only invited Susan and me to concerts in York, but gave us a bedroom to stay in when we were together in London. It was in his home, complete with large heated swimming pool, that I first met the promising young Conservative politician Edward Heath. Sadly Jack's involvement in the legal entanglements of the Guinness affair, ludicrously still untried when he died (I was completely on his side), made his life burdensome. Fortunately York University stood by him. It continued with the full support of a few people, particularly myself, to continue to call him Sir Jack Lyons when a stupid government stripped him of his title. The Royal Academy of Music in London continued to call him so also.

It was at the meetings of the UGC in London that I saw almost face-to-face my great businessman friend Geoffrey Heyworth. When I wrote about his work as a member of the UGC in a chapter in a collected book of memories published in 1984. I began not with a university or with universities but with his *Report of the Committee on Social Studies* which had appeared in 1965. It roused my enthusiasm. Heyworth was appalled, as I was, by the slow development of social studies in Britain. I wrote of him in 1984 that 'when in full flight, though his language was not always as floral as his facial expressions, he was capable of commanding not assent but enthusiasm'. The Chairman of the UGC, Keith Murray, a friend, depended on him totally.

Whenever the UGC was involved in a 'visitation', a pompous term, to a university, old or new, Geoffrey, as I now always called him, enjoyed drawing out young members of staff who were engaged in teaching and research in the widest possible range of disciplines, particularly social studies (few observers then called them social sciences). He was not the only businessman on the UGC, but all his fellow members thought of him as the most genuinely representative of them. He was, of course, far more besides. In 1961 he invited me to join the Leverhulme Trust Research Awards Committee, which distributed research funds to academics (and at that time to artists too). The committee was chaired by James Mountford, Vice-Chancellor of Liverpool University, the university of the city where Heyworth's father had been a businessman. In the year when Heyworth retired from the chairmanship of the Leverhulme Trust at the age of seventy-four I took over the chairmanship of the Research Awards Committee from Mountford, who had taught me as much about universities as Morris, my own Vice-Chancellor at Leeds. He also wrote an informative Penguin about them.

One of Heyworth's public activities, which I know little about, was his chairmanship, which he took up in 1960, of the Council on Prices, Productivity and Incomes, founded by Harold Macmillan three years before. The press described him at that time as one of 'the three wise men', but the Council was as highly controversial as the National Incomes Commission set up in 1961 along with the National Economic Development Council. Given trade-union power at that time, which the press and large sections of the public considered inordinate, neither of them was able to achieve its purpose. Nevertheless, when I look back on a radio series that I presented on industrial relations and strikes, I am struck by the fact that both high-powered employers and high-powered trade unionists called each other by their first names. There was a tacit, largely unacknowledged, collusion between business and labour. Its existence had been recognized by the great French historian of England, Éric Halévy.

Macmillan, who also acknowledged the collusion, was the first prime minister whom I got to know well, not through broadcasting but through my publishing connections. I also had a local connection, with him, I lived in Sussex. I had known one previous prime minister, Clement Attlee almost as well, however, and had seen much of him in private long after the war when we and the Attlees sat together at the captain's table on one of the first cruises we ever paid for. It was an Italian ship, the *Romantica*, sailing from Venice to Istanbul and back. It was the first time that I had met Attlee's wife, Violet, a keen if somewhat erratic clay pigeon shooter. When we went on trips from the ship the Attlees were always given the two front seats in the coach, and although nine out of ten passengers on the cruise would have voted Conservative, they approved of this. Indeed, they rebelled when in Istanbul a self-important Turkish guide launched an attack on Attlee and bawled out 'I support Winston Churchill.' Unanimously we demanded that our guide be changed. I still regard Attlee as Britain's best post-war prime minister.

The tangled interconnections between business, politics and education had become clearly apparent to me in Oxford, particularly through Nuffield College. I knew Henry Clay and his wife, Rosaline, who was a member of the remarkable Smith family and had every kind of family teaching connection within what the Americans called 'academia'. She is one of the remarkable women behind the scenes in this chapter, if less remarkable, perhaps, than Rose Gillinson, who loved meeting artists, of whom there were many in Leeds.

I met more young artists in Leeds than I had done in Oxford, for the University of Leeds had been favoured by a rich benefactor who offered it the opportunity of appointing on a three-, four- or five-year basis Gregory Fellows in music, poetry, painting and sculpture. I got to know some of the Fellows very well and Susan and I entertained them in Ingledew Cottage and within a very limited income bought paintings and sculptures from them. 'Nibs' Dalwood, the sculptor, was a worthy successor to a previous well-known Fellow, Kenneth Armitage, although he would have hated my using the word 'worthy' to describe him years after I had known him extremely well. We had great arguments, particularly about politics, and he and his wife Mary entertained us in their home as much as we entertained them. Sadly he died before he was anywhere near his prime.

The painter Terry Fox, another very good friend, lived on and is recognized as one of England's best twentieth-century artists. We have several of his pictures which we treasure. Kenneth Leighton, the musician, was one of the people who introduced us to 'contemporary music' before we went to Aldeburgh. I am glad that Huddersfield puts on festivals of contemporary music in the twenty-first century.

The words 'entertain' and 'entertainment', carrying with them a variety of meanings, meant quite different things to me in Leeds than they had done in Oxford. In Leeds entertainment was informal and I used to meet Gregory Fellows in their favourite pub near the back of the great town hall where wonderful concerts were put on. Apart from the Fellows, I met Fanny Waterman, a determined and dynamic musician who was to found the Leeds International Pianoforte Competition in 1963. There was a stuffy side to some Leeds life, including at the university, but, like the Gregory Fellows, Susan and I were largely outside it.

Entertainment in Oxford had become more sober in more than one sense of the word when we returned there in 1976 than it had been in 1955, when we left it. In both periods, however, there were two formal guest nights a week in Worcester College, one of them on Sunday nights, by 1976 exceptional, when Fellows and their male guests wore dinner jackets and their female guests usually long dresses. White ties, once *de rigueur*, had not survived the war. Most of the Fellows' guests were dons in other colleges. Very few indeed were businessmen or politicians. After dining 'in hall', not particularly well, they would retire after dinner to the Senior Common Room, where the senior fellow present, never the Provost, was in charge. As an honorary Fellow before becoming Provost, an unprecedented circumstance, I raised problems of protocol which I disposed of immediately by pretending that I was not an honorary Fellow.

I realized at once that the most important figure in the background on these occasions was not a Fellow at all but the member of the college staff who bore the title of Common Room Steward. It was one of his most important tasks to look after the wines, particularly the port, although less port was being consumed in 1976 than had been when I was a Fellow of the college from 1945 to 1955. In 1976 I was not only an honorary Fellow but the Senior Fellow. Sensibly I only behaved as such when there were no Fellows present, only lecturers and their guests. Susan was not granted personal dining rights until three years after I became Provost. Fellows' wives had none. Until 1978, when the college went mixed, as my immediate predecessor Oliver Franks said to me that it would not do, she had to be escorted into hall by a male Fellow. She had no place in any college hierarchy.

I was determined, therefore, in 1976 not to rely solely on this traditional mode of entertainment, although I made full use of it – I knew that some businessmen and all politicians, Conservative or Labour, liked to participate in the rituals. So, too, did ambassadors. By then, through Sussex, I knew many of them. My object was to open up the College to the outside world, an object that few of the College Fellows fully shared. Susan and I started to give Sunday lunch parties in the beautiful Provost's Lodge where the quality of the food (and drink) was guaranteed. None of it came from the College kitchens.

We were blessed with an admirable cook, Mrs Cox (we never called her by her first name, Peggy). Sadly the College did not retain her after we left the Lodge. I was glad that while I was Provost an old member of the college, whom I had taught when I was a young Fellow, provided me with an anonymous but extremely generous benefaction provided that I, and not the Fellows, could use it in what I personally judged to be in the interest of undergraduates. I employed it to improve college food, and when I left the College in 1991 we were serving some of the best undergraduate meals in Oxford.

I had sometimes invited undergraduates to our Sunday lunches. I wanted them to meet people different from dons. Most of them, of course, already had, particularly those from major public schools. Many of those who were invited were from grammar schools or from 'comprehensives'. Some were foreign, and they were at the centre of our parties at Christmas when formally the College was closed. Our guests at the term-time parties were deliberately diverse, and very soon the parties came to be regarded as a distinctive feature of the College. Wives wrote of them as well as husbands. Roy Jenkins was the politician who captured most admiringly their spirit. There was a difficulty, however, in maintaining security, not least when he came to lunch. Ambassadors had their own entourage. Others had security forced upon them. I remember policemen in plain clothes looking carefully around the Lodge before any guests arrived. On one occasion, when I had invited Geoffrey and Elspeth Howe and also the scientist Colin Blakemore, a real academic, two separate lots of policemen arrived. Colin was under threat from animal rights protestors.

Our businessmen, like Win Bischoff, then head of Schroeder's, along with his wife Rosemary, were usually left alone. So too was Jim Sherwood, an American business friend who often came with his wife Shirley. He owned Sea Containers and later the Orient Express and the eastern railway line connecting London and Edinburgh. Shirley, a contemporary of Susan at St Anne's, who was not only a botanist but became an expert on contemporary botanical paining, had the dubious advantage of being born a Briggs. She helped young artists in many countries and, through exhibitions that she planned herself, established her own special relationship with Kew. Simon Hornby then of W. H. Smith, and his wife Sheran, a member of the P. G. Wodehouse family, were 'regulars'. So was Gordon Richardson, who had been frequently entertained by Oliver Franks.

Most of the businessmen whom we invited, a few from Cowley, more from abroad, were from the communications field (Robert Maxwell was never on our lists), but they were as diverse a group as the guests as a whole. I often had the experience of introducing one well-known businessman to another, equally well-known, whom he had not met before. I nearly always invited scientists, technologists and, not least, historians. (Keith Thomas was my first guest in hall when I arrived back in Oxford.) Denys Lasdun and his wife Susan were friends who played a big part in my later life. So was Drue Heinz, who became a benefactor of the college, endowing a Hawthornden Fellowship in English Literature at a time when the University was not able (or willing) to pay for such a Fellowship.

In general, I showed no interest in inviting 'celebrities', a term that was coming increasingly into use. They have not figured in this chapter. Celebrity has little to do with renown or fame, and fully developed celebrity culture is one of the horrors of the twenty-first century. I confess, nonetheless, that before I moved from Brighton, where local celebrities were abundant. I had greatly enjoyed meeting Marlene Dietrich when she appeared in a concert in the Theatre Royal on Monday 2 August 1965. I know the precise date because I kept the programme which, regretfully I now feel, I did not ask her to autograph. A note 'About Marlene Dietrich' in the programme describes her as 'brave, beautiful, loyal, kind and generous', but does not use the word celebrity. The programme included a 'salutation' to her from Jean Cocteau: 'your beauty is its own praise'.

At our Worcester lunches I did not exclude Fellows of the College, some of whom were good friends; so too were several heads of other colleges, particularly Tony Quinton at Trinity. He and his sculptor wife, Marcel, used to try to co-ordinate the timing of their parties with ours. Tony Hall, whom I had known when I was a young Fellow, was one of the most distinguished of our guests. He combined archaeology, care for the disabled and a detailed knowledge of Chinese art. We each had our own favourite ambassadors to invite to lunch, in our case the Spanish ambassador Puig Bella Casa, the Swiss ambassador to Austria, François Pictet, member of an old Geneva family, and the Italian ambassador, Paolo Galli, whose father too had been a distinguished and learned diplomat, and Kingman Brewster, one-time American ambassador, who was to come to Oxford as head of University College, where Arnold Goodman was Master in our time. I had known him in many different capacities, but not as Harold Wilson did as a solicitor. Our children were always welcome at Goodman parties.

When we left Oxford for Scotland I greatly missed both undergraduates and college entertaining. I was more than lucky, however, to meet as a neighbour in Tyninghame House the businessman among all businessmen who was to matter to me most in the whole of my life, Alistair Grant, who had been the first person to move (with his wife Judy, christened Judith) into Tyninghame House after the Haddingtons had left it and its contents had been sold by auction. Alistair was born in 1937 in the town of Haddington and, with no family advantages, went on to carve out a remarkable business career starting with a spell in Unilever from 1958. That was one personal link between us. Another was that he was educated at a Methodist school in Yorkshire, Woodhouse Grove, which was not far from Keighley and which I knew as a boy.

Having left Unilever, he was associated with a businessman very different in temperament and background from himself, James Gulliver, and when Gulliver's Argyll Group failed to find a way into the Guinness empire, which I knew well from visits to Dublin before the Distillers Group took it over, he moved into retailing, becoming in 1986 Deputy Chairman and Chief Executive and subsequently in 1993 Chairman of Safeway. He was an enterprising and innovative business-man who liked to find out for himself what Safeway's very diverse stores were like from the inside. They were diverse in scale, in their range of customers and in their profitability, and he learned much by visiting them without notice and taking his local managers by surprise. I enjoyed accompanying him on some of these visits, including that to his store in Orkney, as I had enjoyed visiting Marks and Spencer's equally diverse stores in less high-powered company when I was writing my *Marks and Spencer: A Centenary History* in 1984.

There was no one in that retailing business who was as frank as Alistair was in his about its prospects, and for this reason alone Marks and Spencer was to lose its way. I enjoyed going to its head office in Baker Street, however, and reminiscing with its managers and staff. It was a business with a tradition. It is important not to rely upon it. Alistair's hero was not a Marks, nor a Sieff, Israel or Marcus, but John Sainsbury, although, unlike John, he was falling back on no family experience or reputation. He was very first-generation, as Tom Spencer had been in the days when Marks and Spencer's shops were known as Penny Bazaars. It was Alistair, not John, however, who encouraged me to view retailing and retailers comparatively. Already before I met him I felt that I knew more about retailing than any other professional economic and social historian, but I learned from him far more subsequently than I thought possible. I was impressed by his many talents and by his immense charm, which impressed foreigners as much as his fellow countrymen.

He and Judy lived in what had been the great library wing at Tyninghame House, and, like me, he loved books. He had a wonderful collection of twentieth-century first editions, but he was as fond of Trollope as I was and welcomed more enthusiastically than I did the formation of a Trollope Society. I would have liked him to succeed me as President of the Brontë Society. His physical gifts were far greater than mine. He was a keen horseman and kept horses. In *Who's Who* he described his leisure interests as hunting, shooting, golf and gardening.

His business interests were not confined to Safeway. He was a non-executive director of Scottish & Newcastle from 1992 and its chairman from 1997 and at the same time a non-executive director of the Bank of Scotland from 1992. He was appointed Governor in the last year of his life. That would have taken him into new and different territory, but banking issues were very different in 2001 from what they are now. He had had no time to test the water when he died. I had no time, alas, to discuss with him my own plans for future writing. I was stricken with deep-vein thrombosis just before he died. Asked by Judy to speak at his memorial service in St Giles in Edinburgh I had the utmost difficulty in climbing the stairs up to the pulpit. I had never thought that I would ever do so, but as I looked down across the crowded pews of the great church I meditated on why I was alive and a friend far younger than me was dead.

Chapter 7

Writing and Reading

I have kept this chapter until quite late in my book, but it is obviously central. Apart from *Patterns of Peacemaking*, the book which I co-authored at Bletchley, I wrote only articles between 1945 and 1952. Volume II of the *History of Birmingham* appeared then. It too may have been thought of as co-authored, for Volume I, which was written by Conrad Gill, and my Volume II shared a common index. In fact the two volumes were written quite independently. I was fond of Gill and stayed with him on at least two occasions in his house off Morecambe Bay near Silverdale, but we did not spend much time talking about our individual responsibilities, let alone our judgements. I began my first chapter 'The Framework of a Community' not with what Gill had written but with the lament in 1781 of William Hutton, first historian of Birmingham, that Birmingham, 'one of the most singular places in the universe never manufactured an history of herself who manufactured almost everything else'.

I did not regard my *History of Birmingham* primarily as local history, although I was much concerned with the strictly local dimension of my book. I had read carefully, as had Gill, the two volumes of J. A. Langford's *Modern Birmingham and its Institutions*. Hutton was unduly cautious when, after noting that local history was 'much wanted', he observed that 'many an author by historically travelling all England might have made a tolerable figure had he staid at home'. He wrote this at a time when there were few, if any, professional historians but when the number of local histories was multiplying. I concluded in 1951 that 'the balance between detailed discussion of the local affairs of a city where I had not been born and important trends in national history was easier to strike in the case of Birmingham than in the case of many other cities'.

I did not add then that before deciding to write my *History* I had contemplated writing a biography of Joseph Chamberlain, following in the footsteps of the great journalist J. L. Garvin, but that I had not done so because the Conservative politician Julian Amery, with whom I always got on well, had already started doing so; the fourth volume of Chamberlain's *Life* that he wrote came out a year before my *History* with the sub-title *At the Height of His Power*. (Amery was MP for Brighton Pavilion in 1969 when I was Vice-Chancellor of Sussex and he completed the fifth and sixth volumes in that year.)

In retrospect, I am glad that in the late 1940s I was focusing not on a man but on a city. I was less interested in power than Amery was and more interested in what interested Charles Dickens – 'streets thronged with work people' where 'the hum of labour resounded from every house'. I drew more inspiration from America in writing of a great British city than from Britain, and while I was writing my history I became a friend of Bessie Pierce, who was writing about Chicago, which she knew intimately, and of Blake McKelvey, who was writing about the New York Rochester and who was to generalize about the making of American cities in his book *The Urbanisation of America*. By the end of the 1950s an international confraternity of city historians had come into existence. They looked to A. M. Schlesinger's *The City in American Civilization* (1949). I knew A. M. before I knew his more famous son, another A. M., who was to be a special assistant to President Kennedy and Lyndon Johnson.

To place myself in perspective I should emphasize that in these academic manoeuvres I entered the confraternity of English historians of all kinds without having taken a doctorate. That would become far rarer in the future. In 1944 I had been made a Fellow of a college in Oxford without a doctorate being a requirement. I could not, of course, have been in a position to write a doctoral thesis when I was in uniform at Bletchley. Still in uniform I was interviewed by C. M. Bowra, Oxford's wartime Vice-Chancellor and before and later one of its great characters. Worcester College was very much outside Bowra's circle, but the Fellows were circumspect enough to arrange for me to be seen by him. An interview over sherry took the place of a thesis. Bowra made me feel at ease at once and when I came to Oxford offered me ample hospitality. While I was settling in I wrote two important articles centring on Birmingham – one on Thomas Attwood, who became my substitute for Joseph Chamberlain, and one on the battle for parliamentary reform between 1830 and 1832 in Birmingham, Manchester and Leeds.

Both articles, I knew, broke new ground, but they were of a type that hitherto had not been approved of by J. R. M. Butler, author of *the* work on parliamentary reform, or, for that matter, by Richard Pares, then editor of the *English Historical Review*. As a result they appeared in the *Cambridge Historical Journal*, a periodical which did not care about reputations, and were greatly welcomed by highly reputable nineteenth-century historians. At once they brought me into touch with S. B. Checkland, who was studying what came to be called the Birmingham School of Economists. In 1941–2 he had been President of the National Union of Students, and in the 1950s he had as many contacts with American scholars as I did. What drew us together was an interest in nineteenth-century concern for currency politics. It inspired one of my rare *bon mots*: 'If Engels had lived in Birmingham rather than in Manchester,' I suggested, 'Marx would have become a currency reformer.' Another phrase of mine was to inspire international historical conferences, including one in São Paulo, Brazil. I called Manchester the 'shock city' of the early nineteenth century.

In writing my *History of Birmingham* I several times quoted the Australian Keith Hancock, born in 1898, who had been a professor in Birmingham from 1934 to 1944 before becoming for five years Chichele Professor of Economic History in Oxford. He was one of the first historians to lead me into drawing a contrast between Birmingham and Manchester. As I have explained, he was to invite me to Australia in 1959, a formative experience in my life. A few later historians thought (I believe wrongly) that I had exaggerated the significance of the contrast. For me it remained a key to much eighteenth- and nineteenth-century English history.

My work on Manchester and Birmingham stimulated my interest in sociology as well as renewed my interest in economics. A book I had greatly admired before I started writing my *History* was the American L. J. Marshall's *Development of Public Opinion in Manchester, 1780–1820*. The study of opinion seemed to me a major task both for the sociologist and the economist. Many later American students of cities greatly extended the scope of urban sociology, dealing with the images of cities as well as with their topography and their social structures: Kevin Lynch's *Image of the City* (1954) was a landmark work. Oscar Handlin, born in 1915, who from 1954 to 1965 was a professor at Harvard, gave his blessing to what became a 'movement', editing *The Historian and the City* in 1963. He invited me to lecture at a summer school in Harvard in 1956, where Peter Stansby was my 'assistant'. He was to have a distinguished career ahead of him, writing, among other books, important studies of William Morris. He did not, however, write about cities.

Geographers and demographers as well as historians did. An example of their contribution to urban studies was P. Hauser and J. N. Schnore's *Study of Urbanization* (1963). There were quite different complementary studies too. *The Urban Frontier* (1960) was written by Ralph Wade, Professor of History at Chicago, who was head of the History Department in the University of Chicago, where I was a visiting professor on several occasions, and two years later M. and L. White published their *The Intellectual Versus the City* (1962). Few of the intellectuals who disliked city ways and city values were born in cities themselves.

In Britain, a far older society and culture than the United States, as R. W. Emerson had stressed during the nineteenth century, there was some twentieth-century friction between 'antiquarians' on the defensive, and local and regional historians who pressed them hard to explore the recent past. I was firmly on the latter side and was a supporter too of Peter Laslett, Fellow of Trinity College, Cambridge, whom I had first known as a political scientist (and an authority on John Locke) and later as an indefatigable supporter of the BBC's Third Programme.

My long involvement in local and urban history turned me over the years into the total historian I wanted to be. I first used the term when I was writing about the history of Birmingham. I did not borrow it from *Annales*, the periodical founded in 1929 by Marc Bloch and Lucien Febvre which they called, in full, *Annales d'histoire sociale et économique*, using the order of the adjectives that Cole had insisted upon when he founded my readership. After it changed its name in 1946 to *Annales: economies, societiés, civilisations*. I was uneasy about the inclusion in the title of the word *civilisations*, drawn as I was already to G. M. Young's concept of culture. Meanwhile I cared nothing for what Febvre called 'the rules of the profession', refusing consistently to answer the questions 'what is your period?' or 'what kind of an historian are you?' I did not need the great Fernand Braudel to tell me that historians had to abandon the idea of unilinear time, or Emmanuel le Roy Ladurie, author of *Peasants of Languedoc* (English translation 1966), to suggest that quantitative history could be creative. I knew that long before.

The two books which I had published while I was Professor of Modern History at Leeds, in a very creative period of my life, established me – to use a dangerous word – as a professional historian. *The Age of Improvement, 1783–1867*, all my own work, and *Chartist Studies*, which I edited, both appeared in 1959, the centenary year of a Victorian *annus mirabilis* in publishing, the year of Charles Dickens's *Tale of Two Cities*, of George Eliot's *Adam Bede*, Edward Fitzgerald's *Rubaiyat of Omar Khayyam*, George Meredith's *The Ordeal of Richard Feverel* (which I only fully appreciated when I read all Meredith's novels in the early twenty-first century), Alfred Tennyson's *Idylls of the King*, John Stuart Mill's essay *On Liberty*, Karl Marx's *Critique of Political Economy*, Charles Darwin's *Origin of Species* and, what looks like, perhaps, the most relevant title for pulling together the material of this book, Victor Hugo's *La Legende des Siècles*.

The Age of Improvement was the ninth volume in a 'History of England' series consisting of ten volumes. All publishers like the idea of such a series, and W. N. Medlicott, who edited the Longman series, prefaced it with an introductory note emphasizing that while he had made no attempt to secure a general uniformity of style or treatment, the series had a unity of purpose: 'the authors have been asked, while avoiding excessive detail', to give:

> ... particular attention to the interaction of the various aspects of national life and achievement, so that each volume may present a convincing integration of those developments – political, constitutional, economic, social, religious, military, foreign or cultural which happen to be dominant in each period.

I (and G. M. Young!) would not have used the adjective 'cultural' in the way it is here, and I would not have put the whole proposition that way either, but I knew what Medlicott meant, respected him as an editor who never interfered with anything I said, and liked him as a man. I was proud to receive a Medlicott Medal at a meeting of the Historical Association fifty years later in 2009.

I was proud too that *The Age of Improvement* has withstood the test of time. When, after an exceptionally long interval, I produced a new edition of it in 2000 I did not change the chapter titles or sub-titles that were in the original edition. It was the footnotes that changed most. I added much new material and revised thoroughly what I had written about, for example, railways, in my view the weakest part of the first edition, or Victorianism about which I had written very little in 1959 except *Victorian People*.

I wrote what I regarded as an important article on the two editions in the *Times Higher Education Supplement*, the last periodical in which I regularly wrote reviews. I had come to the conclusion in the 1990s that I should cut drastically the amount of reviewing that I had done since the 1940s. Writing them was diverting me, I thought, from 'higher things'. At the beginning I had reviewed most frequently in the *Manchester Guardian*, *Yorkshire Post* and *New Statesman* when

Kingsley Martin was editor and Janet Adam Smith was literary editor. Kingsley I knew very well during the last years of his life. Janet, the daughter of a Principal of Aberdeen University, had been married first to Michael Roberts who died in 1948. I was deeply impressed by his attitudes both to poetry and to philosophy. He was an antidote to Oswald Spengler, whose *Decline of the West* was my favourite book when I joined the Army: I read it quietly on the evening before I joined up in 1942. Janet herself was an excellent writer whose *John Buchan, A Biography* (1965) was one of my favourite books at that time.

During the 1960s and 1970s I reviewed most in *The Economist, The Listener* and *New Society*. I also remained a regular reviewer in the *Guardian* until Bill Webb ceased to be in charge of its reviewing. I had had a special relationship with the *Manchester Guardian*'s great editor, M. P. Wadsworth. Whenever I was in Manchester I would visit his office where he always wanted to talk to me at length 'undisturbed'. The news of the day was not usually the main element in our conversations. The nineteenth century was.

I did not often visit Bill Oliver's office when he was dealing with books, but he became President of the Brotë Society before me and a personal friend. So, too, was Kenneth Young (and his wife, Phyllis) when he was editor of the *Yorkshire Post* from 1960 to 1964. He had had a varied career, starting in the European Service of the BBC in 1948 and moving on as a journalist to the *Daily Mirror* in 1949, the *Daily Mail* in 1950 and the *Daily Telegraph* from 1952 to 1960. In 1966 he wrote *Churchill and Beaverbrook, a Study in Friendship and Politics*. My favourite book of his was *Music's Great Days in the Spas and Watering Places* (1968).

To be an editor, the first job which I had thought of for myself when I was a boy, was almost as precarious as to be a regular reviewer. Some were deposed as were literary editors, and when they changed, reviewers usually changed with them. A change in the *Economist* books editor eliminated me from its pages. For a long period during the 1990s I was privileged to write reviews for the *Financial Times*; I regard them as some of my best. I was not unduly influenced, I believe, by the reviews that my own books received. Most of them were good, some surprisingly so. You almost always get one bad review, however: it is the price that you pay for being reviewed widely.

Some subjects seemed to persuade reviewers to write good reviews. Chartism was one, and the second book that I had published at Leeds, *Chartist Studies*, got exceptionally good reviews. It reflected my belief in local studies. Avoid generalizations until you were sure that you could make them. Stick to particularities. I was delighted to be able to persuade Ralph Pugh, general editor of the Victoria County History, always known as VCH, to write about Chartism in Wiltshire, my wife's county of birth. By 1959 I knew more about Trowbridge and Bradford-on-Avon than she did.

The volume as a whole changed the direction of Chartist studies, encouraging the study of particular Chartists as well as of particular places where Chartism was – or was not – strong. It marked an immense advance historiographically on Mark Hovell's *The Chartist Movement* (1925) and it led many of its readers back to the *Northern Star* and to a re-evaluation of Feargus O'Connor, 'the lion of the north'. It made J. L. and B. Hammond's *The Age of the Chartists* (1930) look anachronistic, although I continued to treat it as a classic. It compared the classical world with the world of industry.

For me the natural successor to *Chartist Studies* was *Victorian Cities* (1963). It was published by Odhams Press, which had earlier published *Victorian People*. I dedicated *Victorian Cities* to Rose and Bernard Gillinson, whom I missed very much when we left Leeds. I conceived of the new book as a companion volume to *Victorian People*. It would be the second volume in a trilogy that would culminate in *Victorian Things* (1987). As I said in my introduction, *Victorian Cities* was 'the product of many years of research'. I rightly described the existing literature of cities as prodigious both in its volume and its variety. I chose as my motto D. H. Lawrence's comment that 'the English are town birds through and through . . . Yet they don't know how to build a city, how to think of one, or how to live in one.'

I did not agree with Lawrence, but in my book I emphasized that I was just as interested in Victorian attitudes towards 'the city' as in the history of the six particular Victorian cities that I selected for the central chapters of my book. By the time that I wrote it I had become acquainted with the writing of Patrick Geddes, who seemed to me to be one of the first writers to understand that a great city could not be the product of one man, like Lutyens in India, or one category of men, like architects or engineers. I took as the six: Manchester, 'symbol of a new age'; Leeds, ' a study in civic pride'; and Birmingham, 'the making of a civic gospel'; but I moved into new territory in writing about Middlesbrough and the growth of a new community described by Gladstone as 'the youngest child of England's enterprise'; Melbourne, 'a Victorian community overseas'; and later Victorian London, what I called 'the World City'.

The two of my cities that I had not written about before, Middlesbrough and Melbourne, were particularly important to me. I worked on their history on the spot, making friends, not all of them historians, as well as poring over records. In both places I left behind me young historians whom I knew would continue my researches. My chapter on London suggested new ways of conceiving the changing relationship between metropolis and provinces. I would have liked to write about Glasgow too, but to have done so then would have required more time than I had at my disposal.

The Oxford historian A. L. Rowse shared my enthusiasm for encouraging young historians. Indeed, it was he who had first suggested that I should approach Odhams as publishers. One day in Broad Street, Oxford, he stopped his bicycle when he saw me and said with beaming face, 'Why don't you do for Queen Victoria what I have done for Queen Elizabeth? I know just the right publisher.' Lytton Strachey would have been amused. John Canning of Odhams proved to an agreeable and enterprising publisher and I liked to go to the rather old-fashioned Odhams office in Long Acre to talk to him. Curiously there was a link between John Reith and the Odhams family: his wife was an Odham. It was a link that neither of us ever mentioned. There was no shortage of personal links in 1963.

One American city, Chicago, featured in most of my publishing plans. There was much in its own short history that I would like to have compared with elements in British Victorian cities. Was Julian

Ralph, who described Birmingham as 'the best-governed city in the world', right to say of visitors to Chicago, 'those who go clear-minded expecting to see a great city will find one different from which any precedent then had led them to look for'? It seemed natural to me that historians in the University of Chicago took great interest in my work and invited me to spend terms there teaching, among others, students who had actually been born in Chicago. I was impressed, too, that the University of Chicago Press printed more editions of *Victorian Cities* than were produced in Britain.

The first person I worked with in Chicago, Alex Morin, whom I got to know as well as John Canning in Long Acre, had been born not in Chicago but in Russia and loved to take me round Russian markets in Chicago. He had never been to London. Later I got to know the chairman of the Press, Maurice Philippson. He wrote at least one novel as well as encouraging young English people to feel at home in Chicago. I did. I even had a few talks with Mayor Daley and then, fully at home, lectured on Victoriana in the magnificent Chicago Art Institute.

The third volume of my trilogy, *Victorian Things* (1988), was published by a very different publisher than Odhams or the Chicago University Press, Batsford, who had already published my *Friends of the People*. It was, I think, the most innovative of the three, although it was *Victorian Cities* that won almost universal praise. I particularly welcomed a review in the *Huddersfield Examiner*, an important provincial newspaper in a town which was not incorporated until 1868 and which I did not select for a whole chapter. '"We don't now live in the days of barons, thank God" exclaimed the ambitious Whig politician Henry Brougham, before Victoria came to the throne, "we live in the days of Leeds, of Bradford, of Halifax and of Huddersfield".' I am not sure whether he had even heard of Keighley, where one of the main roads leading out of the town was called Halifax Road.

I had an almost instinctive dislike of Whiggery as a young historian and did not need Herbert Butterfield to tell me about the Whig tradition in English history. In *Victorian Things* I had little to say of the places which I had described in *Victorian Cities*. In my chapter in it on the philosophy of the age I looked back to both Leeds and Keighley markets where people would go and try on spectacles without having their eyes 'tested'. I did not make that mistake, but the person who tested them was a German by origin, one of many who made their way to Bradford.

The chapters in *Victorian Things* which I myself now read most often are those on needles and stamps, the latter in perforated, gummed form a Victorian invention. My last chapter led me once more across the Atlantic, this time to Thomas Alva Edison's house and laboratory in New Jersey. Edison seemed to me to be the greatest inventor in the universe, and I much admired the scholars in Rutgers, the state university of New Jersey, and in other universities outside the state, who were publishing and carrying out research on his papers. I loved the library room in Edison's house, which he called his 'thought laboratory', and in which the objects he displayed included many that were testimony to the mysteries of electricity. They included a stuffed eagle from the 1889 Paris Exhibition, whose eyes shone from a miniature electric bulb in its head. Not surprisingly he was called a wizard and his house 'a House of Invention'. Besides making entirely new things, he tested natural products from all parts of the world as well as unleashing new natural forces. I dealt with one of these, steam, which had long been unleashed, in my *The Power of Steam*, published in 1982.

It is not difficult for me to move from *Victorian Things* or *The Power of Steam* to my book *A Social History of England* – I insisted on putting the *A* before *Social* in the title as I had done in all the volumes of my *History of Broadcasting*. While I write this page I have in front of me the Book Club Associates' edition of 1984. Stanley Remington, its chairman, liked it as much as my first commercial publishers Weidenfeld and Nicolson. In the lead-in to my own preface I quoted three passages from very different authors which brought out clearly my own view of English social history in what may have been my prime.

In the first passage Mandell Creighton, first editor of the *English Historical Review*, who went on to become Bishop of London, wrote in 1896, in my perspective an *annus mirabilis* in social history, that 'no nation has carried its whole past so completely into the present. With us historical associations are not matters of rhetorical reference on great occasions, but they surround the Englishman in everything that he does.'

In my second passage I quoted T. S. Eliot, American by birth, Englishman by adoption:

> A people without history
> Is not redeemed from time, for history is a pattern
> Of timeless moments. So, while the light falls
> On a winter's afternoon, in a secluded chapel
> History is now and England.

While I am writing, it is now a winter's afternoon, and Eliot's *Four Quartets*, which I read one by one when they first came out, are my favourite Eliot poems.

In my third passage I quoted a friend, the historian Henry Steele Commager, unmistakably American, whose *Britain Through American Eyes* appeared in 1948 when we were living in an unmistakeable age of austerity. 'The English Character is not only stable and uniform', Commager contended, 'but various and heterogeneous; it is at once obvious and elusive, and every generalization must be not so much qualified as confounded.'

All three quotations carry the same message. I feel that I need say little more of the contents of my book that followed. These would have been very different had I chosen as authors of two of my first three quotes to introduce it Karl Marx and Antonio Gramsci (so popular with intellectuals in the 1960s that he was treated as an intellectual genius). I do not know whom I would have chosen as my third author to go with them. It would have been difficult to avoid Friedrich Engels. J. B. S. Haldane would have been a totally inadequate substitute.

When in 1983 I travelled round the world to prepare my only television series, *Karl Marx and His Legacy*, to celebrate the centenary of Marx's death, Marxism still seemed to me to be very much alive. Yet while China and Cuba wanted us, the Soviet Union did not.

Some of the material in *A Social History of England* had been used in a completely different form in a series of twelve radio programmes on social history broadcast in 1980 on the World Service of the BBC, and before that I had been closely involved as a senior consultant on a pioneering series of programmes for home listeners, *The Long March of Everyman*, which combined original sources and commentary. I wrote two of the programmes myself, both of them focusing on recent history. One was called 'Semi-Detached', the other 'The People's War and Peace'. In the first I drew on my knowledge of towns, cities and the rise of 'suburbia'. In the second I drew on very diverse original sources. I picked out the famous line spoken by Mona Lott from Tommy Handley's *ITMA*, 'It's being so cheerful keeps me going' and ended with lines from T. S. Eliot's *The Waste Land*. My favourite 'quote' came from Beaverbrook's *Daily Express*, 4 September 1939: 'Pardon me but have I time to get to Victoria before the devastation starts? I have to get a train for Hayward's Heath.'

I recall a story of Harold Macmillan in the 1960s. Making his way slowly and with dignity to the Victoria platform where trains left for Hayward's Heath, the nearest station to his country home, he asked the ticket collector 'Is this the train for Hayward's Heath?' to which the ticket collector, who knew Macmillan, merely nodded. 'Wonderful train, wonderful service' Macmillan exclaimed.

The Long March of Everyman, 1750–1960 was edited by an economic historian, Professor Theo Barker, born in St Helens in the north of England. It was published in 1975 by André Deutsch, and a Penguin edition appeared three years later. Barker's books included two volumes of a revised edition of Christopher Savage's *Economic History of Transport*. That indeed was his way, as it was H. J. Dyer's way, into urban history. Barker's books also included *The Glass Makers: Pilkington, the Rise of an International Company, 1826–1976* (1977). Harry Pilkington was known in broadcasting circles for the report of the curiously selected Pilkington Committee which he chaired. He travelled to work on a bicycle.

Barker, secretary of the Economic History Society, was also the treasurer of the British National Committee of the International

Congress of Historical Sciences. Books for him were the basic source for his radio programmes. He did not acknowledge the pioneering contribution made to them by the BBC's Radiophonic Workshop, which could broadcast 'splendid sounds of tramping, note-counting, coin-dropping and hunting horns'. No fewer than 800 speakers' voices had also been recorded and 500 tapes used. The BBC producer, Michael Mason, the man behind the series whom I got to know exceptionally well as he pushed his researchers onward, thought of the programmes as symphonies. The audience listening to the programmes was as attentive, he claimed, as the readers of books.

I myself was anxious to understand the relationship between readers and writers, and, of course, I was a committed reader of books of all kinds. I built up an eclectic library not of first editions or of 'rare books' but of the works that mattered most to me as my life and thought evolved. Since I had begun writing the books I have mentioned I had drawn a distinction between books and articles that I read in order to write my own books, and books which had no such purpose and that I read by choice for pleasure. In practice the distinction between the two categories is not as clear as it first looks. Books in the second category have influenced my work as an historian as much as books in the first. I do not necessarily regard fiction as falling into the second category or, indeed, books about fiction. There is what Medlicott called interaction. If I had not read Trollope novels neglected by writers on Trollope, I could never have written my essay 'Trollope, Bagehot and the English constitution' in the *Cambridge Journal* in 1958 or my essay 'Trollope the Traveller' for *Trollope Centenary Essays* edited by John Halperin.

In examining the interaction broadcasts must be brought into the reckoning too. If I had not been the writer and presenter of the BBC television series celebrating the centenary of Marx's death I could not have written my little book *Marx in London*, published in two editions and translated into several languages, the first by the BBC the second by Laurence and Wishart. For the second I had a co-author, John Callow, with whom I got on perfectly. He was chief librarian of the Marx Memorial Library and he had written novels also.

In my reading I have never by choice read many historical novels, and I do not place John Fowles's wonderful novel *The French Lieutenant's Woman*, published in 1969, in that category. Nonetheless, I had a special relationship with Fowles, born five years after me. As a collector I liked the title of his first published book *The Collector* in 1963, and the content of his second book, *The Magus*, which appeared in 1968, held all my attention. It was to me entirely in character that he should bring out his *Poems* in 1977.

There were all kinds of 'coincidences' – or were they just that? – in my special relationship with Fowles. He was educated at Bedford School, which I knew well when I was living in Bedford and working in Bletchley. His agents, Anthony Shiel Associates, whom I introduced in Chapter 2 have the acronym ASA. The 'hero' of the last of his novels which I read, *Daniel Martin* (1977), bore the Christian name of my older son. Antony, the philosopher in the novel, turns out to have been teaching at Worcester College, Oxford. He and his wife Jane live in Beaumont Street just above the college. Not only does a cottage in Wytham Woods figure in the novel, but a flat in Notting Hill Gate in London where Susan and I had bought a small house. Dartington School seemed to Daniel Martin 'an enlightened place'. I knew its last headmaster, Richard Lambert, who was an alumnus of Sidney Sussex. An early pupil there was Michael Young, about whom I was to write my last big book. The German-born philosopher who meets Daniel and Jane filming in Egypt had been at a college where there was furniture – and a faculty – but no students. Reading about it reminded me of the United Nations University with which I was associated even before it officially opened. It was no wonder, therefore, that Fowles called my *Social History* excellent and that I praised what he had to say in a book about Stonehenge in which he drew on the first chapter of my *Social History*.

Fowles was in my judgement a great novelist, who could travel through time without having to divide it into different time frames. So, too, could Umberto Eco, the Italian novelist, essayist and semiotician, best known for one bestselling novel *The Name of the Rose*. Born in Piedmont in 1932, he was deeply interested in reader response criticism as I came to be. I never met him, but responded in depth to all that he wrote, particularly about 'intertextuality', the interconnectedness of all literary works. He rejected single meanings. The rose, for example, was a ubiquitous symbol which you should not try to particularize: 'A rose is a rose is a rose'. He liked lists, and he kept his huge personal library in two places (I keep mine in three). He started with the Middle Ages, as I did, but he went on through broadcasting (with RAI, Radiotelevisione Italiana) to open up the field of semiotics. I have read him equally intently for what he has had to say about communications and about 'things'.

I read Isaac Asimov and Kurt Vonnegut while I was reading Fowles and Eco, but I confess that I have never read *How to Enjoy Writing: A Book of Aid and Comfort* (1987) by Asimov and his wife Janet. One year older than me, Asimov had a crater on the planet Mars named after him in 2004. He was the writer of science fiction whom I read most regularly. That, however, was not all that he wrote. Some of his writing was about Shakespeare, some about the Bible. Much of his writing was about history; I found much of this pertinent to me, but I was just as interested in his approach to the future as to the past. He was one of the authors who influenced me in joining the board of advisers of the periodical *Futures*. One of Asimov's projects was called Project Gutenberg: it linked the study of time with the study of communications. So did his widely discussed investigations of robotics, a word that he may have invented.

At the beginning of his novel *Nemesis*, published in 1980, Asimov insisted that from the start that the 'cardinal rule' in all his writing had been the need to be 'clear', and he kept to this rule assiduously even to the point where he virtually eliminated local colour and, indeed, description of any kind from his novels. He chose deliberately to write 'practically, not symbolically or experimentally'. This, he claimed, helped him to win many awards for his writing. Over the years he also established a warm relationship with readers like myself who have never set out to write science fiction. His short story 'Nightfall' was voted the best short science fiction story of all time by the Science Fiction Writers of America.

It was Asimov who first made me ponder on the implications of the term 'psychohistory', which he may also have invented. Paul Krugman, a Nobel laureate in economics, claimed that it was Asimov's psychohistory that made him an economist. There is one penetrating study of Asimov, published in 2002, by a professor of English, Donaki Palumbo, *Chaos Theory, Asimov's Foundations and Robots*. Two years earlier, Asimov himself had published *The Science of Science-fiction Writing*, and he wrote two autobiographies – *In Memory Yet Green* (1979) and *Asimov, a Memoir* (1994) which appeared two years after his death. He left behind many friends, including Gene Roddenberry, creator of *Star Trek*. Indeed, he earned a screen credit on *Star Trek: The Motion Picture* for advice he gave during production, confirming to Paramount Pictures that Roddenberry's science-fiction extrapolation made sense. Asimov suffered from ill health in his later life after having triple bypass surgery in 1983 and had contracted HIV from a blood transfusion given him during the operation. From 1985 to 1993 he was President of the American Humanist Association, an honorary title, and on his death was succeeded by his friend Kurt Vonnegut, who is the second of the writers of science fiction whom I read avidly.

Born in Indianapolis the year after me, Vonnegut blended science fiction with satire, irony and black humour. It is not easy to take all his work seriously, but he was old enough to serve in the war in its last phases, crossing the frontier identified by Fowles, and partly for this reason catching the mood of the 1960s and 1970s. As a US Army infantry private he became a prisoner of war in the Battle of the Bulge in December 1944, which I have described in *Secret Days*. He was imprisoned in Dresden, a city which he has placed on the world map far more than Indianapolis. I have spent time in both cities largely because of him, not as a pilgrim but as an explorer. He was repatriated by Red Army troops at the border between Saxony and Czechoslovakia, one of Europe's frontiers which I know best.

The Vonnegut novel which I have read and re-read most is not his semi-autobiographical *Slaughterhouse Five* (1969) which deals with 'carnage rampant' in Dresden and afterwards, but his *Cat's Cradle*

(1971) which the University of Chicago wisely accepted in lieu of a thesis when Vonnegut secured an MA degree there in 1971. It took note of its anthropological content, present also in Asimov and in a quite different way in Eco. Nevertheless, to me its political content seems more significant, an adjective he would have questioned. To me *Cat's Cradle* is most interesting, not because it begins neutrally with a would-be historian's attempt to find out in retrospect just what happened in the mindless mind of the man who made possible the dropping of the atomic bomb on Hiroshima on 6 August 1945 or his later invention of K-9, the ultimate weapon that would destroy the whole world, but because it furnishes me with a concept, that of the *karass*, that has influenced me profoundly in the way that I think of myself and my relationships outside as well as inside this book. I shall return to it at the end of the book.

Chapter 8

Travelling and Lecturing

Since my name first appeared in *Who's Who* in 1956 I have always described travel or travelling as my one recreation; and my delight in travel has been singled out many times, then and since, often mischievously, by fellow historians and commentators. Hugh Trevor-Roper, Lord Dacre, is said to have remarked of me 'Lord Briggs can't see a Concorde in the sky without thinking he ought to be on it.' My travels by plane preceded and outlived Concorde, but in recent years after deep-vein thrombosis and a slight stroke in 2001, what was memorably called a 'double event', I have travelled more by sea, my favourite form of travel, than by air. With strictly limited mobility I am now safer at sea than on dry land.

It was not until 2005, however, that Susan and I celebrated our golden wedding by fulfilling an old ambition of mine and travelling via Brazil, Uruguay and Argentina around Cape Horn, to visit Chile and Peru before for the first time traversing the Panama Canal eastward, admiring the great lake in the middle of it, a surprise to us. Three years later we fulfilled a great ambition we shared, that of travelling round the world, crossing the Atlantic, going through the Panama Canal from the east, crossing the Pacific, reaching Australia and later South Africa, rounding the Cape of Good Hope and reaching home via Namibia, Ghana, Portugal and the Bay of Biscay, as calm as a mill pond. I had been to many of these places before, often more than once, but I had not assembled them together in my mind.

I did not give any lectures on these great ocean voyages, although years previously I had lectured to British sixth-formers and French *lycéens*, male and female, on old liners carrying them through the Mediterranean or the Baltic. I met one of them, now a Member of Parliament, in February 2012. Cities were one of my favourite themes. I have never forgotten how, on one trip to Leningrad as it was then called – and as I thought that it would be called for the rest of my life – the Soviet post office by the quayside ran out of stamps, almost provoking a riot. I remember too that on the same occasion just before our ship moved off a girl 'in my charge', who was asked only at the last moment to make a speech thanking our Russian hosts, picked up a megaphone and addressed them in excellent Russian. I felt very proud of her.

On commercial cruises I have I listened to many other people lecturing, some excellent, some poor. Some of them have become friends. I have always refused to lecture on ships dedicated to learning with erudite lecturers from British universities, some of them friends of mine already, choosing to visit places that they already know well and sometimes have already written about. Not being a good listener to lectures, I have felt only a limited interest in listening to what they had to say at sea. I prefer talking to them after they return home and reading their books at my leisure.

I like travel books as a category; they were already treated as one in Victorian England, sometimes in series described as 'home and colonial'. I treasure a privately printed offprint going back to an earlier period, made by my friend L. H. Stickland, whom I always called Andrew, at his Triton Press, of a letter written by Sir Isaac Newton in 1669 offering advice to a young gentleman about to travel. The main advice was ' to let your discourse be more in queries and doubtings than peremptory assertions or disputings'. More purposeful advice was to collect information whether the Dutch have 'any tricks to keep their ships from being all worm-eaten in their voyages to the Indies' and whether 'pendulum clocks do any service in finding out the longitude &c'.

Andrew's wife Irina enjoyed helping me look up sources for books or articles that I was writing, among them a foreword to a Sotheby's loan exhibition of 1986 on *Sussex and the Grand Tour*. She helped me with preparing a sequel, which we never completed, to *How They Lived: An Anthology of Original Documents written between 1700 and 1815* which appeared in 1969. I myself enjoyed preparing that book, working on my own, in 1969. I had written earlier *They Saw It Happen* (1960). It was published by Blackwell and I dedicated it to Susan. The genre appealed to me and I wrote a preface to the *Observer of the 19th Century*, a book of extracts from the Sunday newspaper selected by Marion Miliband, the mother of two socialist politicians, whom I have never met, one the present Leader of the Opposition.

In general, I prefer books to lectures and, recognizing that most ships' libraries are not very well stocked even with relevant travel books or necessary works of reference, when I travel by sea I have had to carry far too many books of my own with me. I have done much of my writing 'confined' in a ship's cabin, and when I go on deck I have a book with me. I love watching night skies, the moon and stars. Yet, in 2010, on the only trip that I had then made by sea to Hong Kong, I never saw a single star. I was writing then not on recent history nor, indeed, on global history, but on the text of this book, and I plan before my last chapter is complete to travel there again by sea. The University of Hong Kong is celebrating its centenary in 2012.

Hong Kong is a very special place for me and my personal relationships there are equally special. Sadly many of my closest friends there are no longer alive. One who is very much alive and whom I always greatly look forward to seeing, T. L. Yang, is a previous Chief Justice, from 1988 to 1996, and was a candidate in the elections for the Chief Executive of Hong Kong when it was handed back to China. A bond between us – and there are several – is that he writes knowledgeably about longevity, one of the subjects which began to interest me long before I became old. I now move on dry land with the help of a powerful walking stick which he gave to me. Before I needed a stick at all the only stick that I possessed was an elegant rather than a sturdy one; it had been given me by J. C. Masterman.

In retrospect I find it remarkable how much lecturing and travelling I did in the ten years between 1945 and 1955, making up for my

Bletchley Park years when I could not travel abroad at all. Many of my contemporaries had been in physical combat then in foreign lands. I admired their courage, the quality in people that I have always respected the most, and I wept when from time to time news came through of deaths, several of my friends among them. I sometimes knew more about what they had been doing from the vantage point of Hut Six in Bletchley Park than they themselves did.

After the war I travelled both on business, as I regarded lecturing to the troops or to university students, and for pleasure. I liked when possible to mingle the two. I have kept two old passports, crowded with visas and immigration stamps. They record my post-war travel movements, along with details of foreign exchange transactions for travelling expenses, which are meticulously listed in the last two pages of each of them. Each page is firmly headed 'No entries to be made on this page except by a Bank or Travel Agency in the United Kingdom'. I drew only slight consolation from the fact that on the travelling expenses page of my passport for 1949 the Barclays Bank stamp read North Street, Keighley.

On the cover of my first post-war passport are printed the resounding words 'We Ernest Bevin, Member of His Britannic Majesty's Most Honourable Privy Council, a Member of Parliament, etc., etc., His Majesty's Principal Secretary of State for Foreign Affairs, requests and requires' that the holder of the passport be allowed 'to pass freely without let or hindrance'. By the time I acquired my second passport there was no Foreign Secretary's name on it, but the request and the requirement were the same. In both of them I was promised 'such assistance and protection as may be necessary'.

Fortunately it was very seldom that I needed it. Once when I had my passport stolen in East Berlin, a frightening experience, I was given a precious slip of paper to help me get past the Wall to the airport in West Berlin, but the immigration officer did not even bother to look at it when I returned to Heathrow. This was because he had been preoccupied and ruffled during his interrogation of a young, not very attractive, foreign woman just in front of me, who doubtless could not understand, let alone answer, the questions he put to her. After passing her over to a superior 'Oh, go through' was all he said to me without looking at my piece of paper or at me. A few years later, travelling from Aix-en-Provence to Bordeaux with a high-ranking British diplomat and his wife, our car was broken into while we were trying to look at a monastery and our passports were stolen. We noted after the theft that we were not the first to undergo this ordeal. There was broken glass everywhere. We did not even see the monastery. It was locked. We got temporary travel papers in Bordeaux.

Bevin, who died in 1951, would have liked travellers to be able to cross frontiers without passports, but it would have needed an ideal world very different from the post-1945 world for that to have happened. I never read anything that he said or wrote about visas. Some of the pages of the passport which was issued to me in his name are covered with transcriptions of multilingual visas, some of them in unreadable languages. Some of them bear rows of specially printed fiscal stamps of the country which I wanted to enter, sometimes only in transit. On the third page of my 1945 passport where, had I then been married, the photograph of my wife would have appeared, Syria (or was it Lebanon?) filled up the space with a stamped transit pass, bearing mysterious messages in Arabic. The Lebanese/Syrian frontier was about as difficult to cross then as now.

On the foreign exchange page Barclays Bank noted that my basic allowance for the year 1946/7 was £40 and that £5 had been refunded to me. Although many of my travels were on official business, I could not escape the vicissitudes of exchange rates. I was angry when, in 1947, the use abroad of any money of my own was banned, but I suffered silently at the time of the convertibility crisis (conversion of dollars to pounds) of that year when I was stranded without any foreign exchange in Belgium by the devaluation of the pound from $4.03 to $2.80. Teaching economics in Oxford at the time I knew, of course, 'all about the dollar crisis': Tommy Balogh at Balliol talked about it unceasingly.

I was trying to get to Maastricht of all places with a British friend, Donald Murray, wounded during the war, who subsequently became a British diplomat, serving for a time as Ambassador to Libya (though he never met Gadaffi). I wish that I had gone out to see him there: he told me that it was a favourite occupation to dig up ancient Roman coins from the sandy shore. In 1947 we were trying to meet an American friend from Oxford in Maastricht who was going to lend us money, and in order to get there we had to play bridge for money and win. We did.

Some of my post-war travel did not involve using my own strictly limited pounds. It was organized for me by the Army Education Corps, whose London office in Kingsway I got to know at first hand, visiting it many times. This followed naturally from the work that I had done at the Formation College in 1945, which I described briefly in *Secret Days*. I was never a member of the Army Education Corps, but it was under its auspices that on my first visit abroad after the war, in 1946, I flew from Northolt Airport (there was then no Heathrow) to Gibraltar where I lectured to British troops on the topics that we had devised in Bedford. It was fascinating to discover in the officers' mess in Gibraltar that there were officers there who were engaged in trying to calculate the weight of the great Rock. Could it withstand an atomic bomb?

I was to visit Gibraltar several times between 1946 and the 1990s, sometimes to lecture there not to servicemen but to its citizens, and it was in the 1990s that I was to explore the Rock's fascinating interior corridors, not revealed to me in 1946, and to learn about its eighteenth-century as well as its Second World War history. Never again, however, did I hear anyone discussing the weight of the Rock. On two occasions I stayed with the Governor, Richard Luce, in his venerable house, once a convent, where the roof had been neglected for so long that buckets had to be kept in some of the corridors to catch water pouring in from above.

Richard was the first civilian Governor and Commander-in-Chief of Gibraltar. I had first met him when he was Member of Parliament for Arundel in 1970 when I was Vice-Chancellor of Sussex University, and in 2000, soon after leaving Gibraltar, he was to become Lord Chamberlain of the Queen's Household. It was with him in Gibraltar that I visited the great mosque that had recently been built to look out, it seemed to me portentously, over the whole Mediterranean. I enjoyed visiting the Gibraltar Museum and Art Gallery where I learned as much about Iberian birds as about Iberian people.

As I write this chapter, I am reading the first article in *Seven*, the *Sunday Telegraph* magazine, written by Alex Hannaford, which paints a picture of a very different rock from the Rock of Gibraltar and points to a quite different danger from that contemplated by the defence forces in Gibraltar in 1946. Hannaford's article is called 'Collision Course' and is sub-titled 'The Space Rocks that Threaten our Lives'. Among these is 'the rock falling from the skies that could take us back to the Stone Age'. In the twenty-first century there is less talk of a 'Space Age' than there was during the 1970s and 1980s, and I myself have never been to Cape Canaveral, let alone travelled in space, but having read volumes of science fiction I am not reassured to be told by Hannaford that NASA (one of the most common post-war acronyms) has twenty-five years to destroy a 20-million-ton asteroid now hurtling through space.

Hannaford himself is not reassured by the comment of a NASA research scientist that we must keep the risks in context with others like climate change and natural disaster which are 'close and present dangers'. As I revise these pages for my publisher NASA itself seems to be changing the perspectives. It is planning with the help of rockets to probe the surface of Mars, the planet which has most thrilled or chilled science fiction writers. The literature of Mars may prove to be more exhilarating than the planet itself. What happens when we confront illusion and reality?

I felt that I was free of all illusions when, after Gibraltar, I visited post-war Germany. In my old passport there are two permits allowing me to enter the British Zone in Germany in 1947, one of them very carelessly giving my name as Assa Briggs. The name Oberhausen, central point of the British zone of occupation, meant more to me then than Aachen, the capital of Charlemagne's empire. The most illuminating of my visits to occupied Germany was not by grace of Britain's Control Commission but entirely on my own initiative. Along with a well-known journalist, William Clark, I lectured at the

University of Münster in 1948, approaching my lecture room only with difficulty across the remains of a ruined city. The university dated back to 1773. Clark, who had pursued an interesting career before I met him, had been a lecturer in humanities in the University of Chicago from 1938 to 1940, and he and I were the first British lecturers to address German students since 1939. Herbert Butterfield, I believe, had been the last person to lecture to them before the war.

I gave some of the same lectures in Münster in 1948 that I was then giving in Oxford. They were up-to-date and dealt not with the war or with security after the war but with the problems of and opportunities of a 'welfare state'. It was a term that was to pass into history, although it was not liked by Beveridge, who continues in the twenty-first century to be associated with its inception. It was not much liked in Konrad Adenauer's Germany either, but with Cole's blessing I was committed to taking the implications of the adjective 'recent' seriously in the title of my Oxford readership. In any case I preferred it to the adjective 'contemporary'. The terms of my readership required me to lecture not to read, but I read all that I could lay my hands on which dealt with citizenship and welfare. Oxford undergraduates appreciated that there was one person at least at that traditional university who was doing so. My early morning lectures in Worcester College were overcrowded, and I could not help pausing in my delivery when I saw late-comers sitting on the hot plate from which breakfast had just been served.

In 1948 my profession was described simply in my passport as University Tutor and Lecturer. I recall one of my more distinguished Oxford colleagues, the historian E. L. Woodward, telling me what difficulties he had confronted in explaining to immigration officials what the word Bursar in his passport meant. No one in Oxford could have been in any doubt. There were bursars everywhere, labelled 'domestic' or, more grandly, 'estates'.

The name Oxford mattered more to Münster professors then than any description I might have chosen to put in my passport, more too than the topics I was lecturing about. How did Clark's passport describe his occupation? In 1955/6 he was to become Public Relations Adviser to the Prime Minister, Anthony Eden, a task that he did not relish, and in 1974 he was to become Vice-President for External Relations at the International Bank for Reconstruction and Development. In *Who's Who* he gave 'travel' as one of his three recreations; it came after writing and talking. More to the point in the context of this book, in 1968 he published a novel called *Special Relationships*. I have never been able to find it.

There was a moral dimension to my own thinking and even more to my feeling in 1948. While at Münster I was determined to take no advantage from the fact that I had travelled there with military permits. I quite deliberately ate the same rations as my German colleagues, mainly potatoes. Only once, when some of them took me out into the countryside, did I eat a little home-produced meat. When I returned from Münster to England via Belgium I found that I became ill after eating rich Belgian restaurant food in Bruges and had to return to England earlier than I had planned. I was greatly impressed – and moved – by the presence in Münster of a group of Dutch students, victims of tough German repression during the war years, who were now clearing rubble in the streets around the university.

I later visited other ruined German cities before the German 'economic miracle', including, notably, Cologne, where the cathedral had been saved, it seemed miraculously. There I met a German student, Ferdinand Esser, who, like me, was interested in film (and comic strips). I found him agreeable company, unspoilt by the war in which towards the end he had been forced to serve. I gave him funds to visit Oxford and sent testimonials on his behalf to an American Catholic university, Latrobe. He subsequently settled successfully as a businessman in the United States. I often stayed at his large but cold house in the woods of Ridgefield, Connecticut, where he and his Boston-born wife, Betty, and large family, were excellent hosts. They were interested too in my own children. They even said that they would bequeath a section of woodland to my younger son, Matthew.

One of the most vivid of my memories of Münster is of getting to know a young British woman who had been married to a German who was later killed on the Eastern Front. She had lived in Berlin and other German cities throughout the war and she moved around warily after the war ended. She liked confiding in me. Far more trivially I remember a German professor of English there who loved P. G. Wodehouse and could quote him at length. I also remember going to a small academic party given by him and other colleagues where we were offered mysterious drinks, which I was told later were based largely on hospital alcohol. I never went to another party in the city!

French wines, offered me in Belgium, where they were abundantly available, damaged me in 1948 as much as Belgian food. I had appreciated them as a schoolboy. Later I was to write of them as an historian during the 1950s. Before that I was to dine in excellent Belgian restaurants with Raymond Georis, who with great skill directed the European Cultural Foundation. I came to love Bruges, one of my favourite cities in the world, where good Belgian friends of mine, the Van der Elsts, François and Danielle, who also owned a charming home in the country, lived in a wonderful medieval house beside one of the city's canals. I liked Brussels, too, before it began to be ruined by over-large and uncharacteristic European Commission buildings. Many of my British friends worked in them. Meanwhile, Peter Carrington, living in a beautiful part of the city, introduced me to NATO, of which he was Secretary-General between 1984 and 1989, and a colleague in Worcester College travelled with me to Waterloo.

Münster in 1948 had been a journey on my own initiative. So, too, were highly mind-changing journeys in the early 1950s to the United States, to West Africa and to the Middle East. These were followed by an Army lecturing tour to Malaya, then in a 'state of emergency', and, as a kind of reward, my first visit to Hong Kong, then largely a naval base, where I stayed in a long since abandoned Gloucester Hotel. Through these journeys the world was opening up to me, but Europe still mattered most. Italy beckoned. France unfolded. My most special experience was in 1948 when I was offered a bursary, along with young historians from other European countries, to study the revolutions that had swept across Europe a century before. Thereafter Paris became more of an international reference point for me than London, which I got to know better than I had done during the war but still not well.

My Paris was essentially the Paris of the left bank, at first the area round St Germain des Prés, later in streets beyond the Champs de Mars with the Eiffel Tower in full view. I liked going up in it and I liked travelling on the Metro, appreciating the often historic names of the stations and sometimes getting out to see what kind of territory surrounded them. When I crossed the Seine I got to know the Louvre far better at first than the Place de la Concorde, the Champs Elysées and the Place d'Étoile, but the last of these thrilled me when my colleague Ladya Carych, director of the European Institute of Education in Paris, a body which I chaired, drove me round it as fast as he could. Raymond Georis was often a fellow passenger. We created a ritual.

I was surprised by what happened to me in Paris in 1948. Having crossed the Channel by rail and ferry and travelled from Calais by rail to the Gare du Nord, I ensconced myself on the left bank in a hotel room in the Rue de l'Université. From there I reported to the *comité d'acceuil* in the Boulevard Raspail and asked their representative where my fellow historians were living and where and when we would meet to discuss our academic plans. There was no immediate response. Nor was there any response later. Not pressing too hard, I picked up a cheque and never heard from the *comité* again. Virtuously, however, I made my way to the Bibliothèque Nationale, where, as I have noted, my unusual name secured me careful attention, and started looking for links between the French revolutionaries of 1848 and the British Chartists who marched from Kennington Common.

I soon concluded that it would have been more relevant to my research to have gone to Brussels instead of Paris, following in the footsteps of Karl Marx, whose early writings I read attentively for the first time in my life during this period. I found out more about revolution by exploring bookstalls along the Seine than sitting in the library. I came to know which books different booksellers specialized in, and, fortuitously, I met there several of the fellow researchers that the *comité* had summoned to Paris but had not told me about. They included the one I got to know best, Kevin Nowland, from Dublin, another favourite city of mine. It was in the Paris of 1948 that I also read James Joyce for the first time.

I very soon decided that it was better to enjoy the Paris of 1948 than to return to the Paris of Lamartine and Louis Blanc, and I had a wonderful time making the most of the city until my funds ran out. On one memorable occasion a colleague from Worcester College, the French tutor Richard Sayce, who was already a friend, recommended that we have dinner at a famous Paris restaurant by the river, La Pérouse, and it lived up to our highest expectations. I drank my first Pernod there before dinner; it and the dinner swallowed up a sizeable proportion of my total academic stipend. Much of the rest of it went on buying old books and pamphlets, not all of them by the river – there was then one particularly good shop in the Rue Jacob – and newer books about occupied France during the war.

I was often by myself and happy to be so, often eating alone, simple but agreeable meals in small restaurants, like Le Dragon, which I revisited many times, chatting to their *patrons*. I chose many dishes which I had first eaten with the Cordonniers before the war. I also had two or three meals in Richard's lodgings where his far from young landlady provided rooms full of greedy cats for a few academic guests. She found me a better listener than Richard, boasting proudly about her intimate knowledge of Paris – '*Je suis Parisienne de sept générations.*' She did not know that Richard had already informed me correctly that she had come to Paris from Alsace only just before the Second World War.

That war was already receding into history by 1948, but, as Isaac Newton had advised travellers in the seventeenth century, it seemed sensible not to talk too much about it to French strangers, male or female, including the young as well as the old. You were not sure which ones among them had favoured Vichy and which ones had taken part in 'the resistance struggle', themselves a very mixed collection. Some talked a lot, but the former were usually silent or at best reticent if pressed to recall it. I had a few academic friends in the Sorbonne, but found it easier to talk to a young Frenchman of my own age who pointed out to me in a small restaurant Henri de

Montherlant, a Left Bank character of dubious politics. A little beyond the Rue de l'Université I liked sitting at a table in the Deux Magots or the Flore, although nobody pointed out to me there Jean-Paul Sartre or Simone de Beauvoir.

I was not well-informed at the time about existentialism, but I knew the Boulevard St Germain better than the Boulevard Raspail, and I liked strolling in the Jardins du Luxembourg. I also went occasionally to cafés in the Boulevard St Michel, then far less expensive than they were to become in the twenty-first century. One of my favourite places was a small cinema in the Rue de Bac. It was a cinema which I was to revisit time and time again. At later points in my life I watched Woody Allen films there. He seemed to belong there as much as to Manhattan.

As a post-war traveller I never felt that I completely belonged to Venice as naturally as I belonged to Paris. Yet Venice is a city which I adore. I visited it for the first time in 1950, spending almost a whole long vacation there with two pupils of mine in Worcester College, who through the vagaries of war were only slightly younger than myself, in a villa, the Palazzo Bonlini, in San Trovaso. It belonged to the Somers-Cox family, and we leased it thanks to Simon Townley who was writing in Oxford about the origins of Italian opera. We had a Romanian maid who used to go to the nearest market to buy food that she would cook for us. Free as we were from chores, we were able to live a beautifully balanced life in Venice following our own timetables – working in the morning at our books; swimming in the afternoon or exploring churches and museums; and going out in the evening to opera or to concerts. It was mainly Ruskin whom I read. Very much a non-tourist, as he had been, I was determined to understand Venice. Yet I never restricted my reading to Ruskin. I found a perfect book-binder who bound for me many of the paperbound books I had bought in Paris. I added Italian books to them, including Vico and Vilfredo Pareto.

Venice had been at the centre of its own world, which stretched far beyond Europe, and before 1954 my travels had already taken me far beyond Europe also. The first stage in what would now be called my globalization was a journey by air to West Africa. That was then the

geographical name given to a huge area covering separately admin-
istered territories still governed, with the exception of Liberia, from
Europe. I arrived in Accra, in what was then called the Gold Coast, in
December 1951 on the initiative of Thomas Hodgkin, Director of the
Delegacy of Extramural Studies in Oxford. A periodical called *West
Africa*, edited by David Williams, with whom Hodgkin was in close
touch, paid my travel expenses there in return for my writing six
articles on the current political situation in what was soon to become
Ghana, an old African name for a different part of West Africa.

The building where the central administration was organized was
Danish. It was not only the Portuguese, the Spaniards, the French, the
British and last of all the Germans who came to Africa in the years of
the slave trade. Relics of the trade are everywhere so that I was able to
talk easily at once to Eric Williams, author of *Capitalism and Slavery*,
whose work had largely been ignored by British historians, when I met
him years later in 1974. We were both on the Governing Body of the
United Nations University. He had then become Prime Minister of
Trinidad.

The timing of my visit to Accra in 1951 was just right, for a charis-
matic young leader, Kwame Nkrumah, who had founded a new-style
popular political party, the Convention People's Party (CPP), in 1949,
had been released from gaol by the Governor of the Gold Coast, Sir
Arden Clark. In 1951, after winning a general election, the country's
first, and forming a government, Nkrumah had been called Leader of
the Government. Later he too became Prime Minister. I found the
situation exciting, an adjective I had rarely used before.

Nonetheless, I did not find it exciting immediately on my arrival
in Accra, after what in an odd page or two of a rare diary I called a
'rapid journey', that I found no one to greet me at the airport and was
irritated by what I described as 'a rather fusty and self-conscious
bureaucracy'. Eventually two representatives of the People's Education
Association (PEA), a body bearing an unmistakable Hodgkin imprint,
who claimed that they had been there all the time, discovered me in a
quiet corner reading a detective story. They drove me through the
jumbled streets of Accra, which did not impress me either, to the home

of David Kimble, founder of the PEA, and his wife, who was a Cambridge graduate.

A cobbler's son from East Sussex and a graduate not of Oxford but of Reading, Kimble was almost as remarkable a man to meet as Nkrumah himself. He had first arrived in Accra in 1948, sent there, like me, by Hodgkin, and in an incredibly short space of time he had built up a remarkable team to develop the PEA. He was so successful that he went on to become the first Director of the Institute of Adult Education in a new University College of Ghana. Hodgkin was not alone in paying tribute to his 'remarkable energy, resourcefulness, freshness of mind, tremendous capacity for work and devotion to the objectives for which he was working'. He was a researcher and writer too. In 1948 he wrote a Penguin book, *The Machinery of Self-Government*, and in 1960 he was awarded a doctorate by London University for a thesis which two years later was published as *The Political History of Ghana*, Vol. I, *1850–1928*. He and his first wife Helen, who had four daughters while he was working in West Africa, were also to edit an accessibly cheap West African Affairs series for the Bureau of Current Affairs in London.

At my own meeting with Kimble, about whom I then knew nothing, he gave me a rapid and vivid introduction to Gold Coast life, which he knew intimately, and thereafter I was 'plunged' at once into a round of activities, which by the time I went to bed made me feel that I had been in the Gold Coast for several years. The next day, 'damp and hot', I saw a new building called the Community Centre, which had been designed by the architect Maxwell Fry, architect along with Jane Drew of many Gold Coast buildings, particularly schools. The Community Centre was sponsored by the United Africa Company, which played a big part in the then relatively rich Gold Coast economy. I also went to look at Achimoto College, which under a 'benevolent Methodist headmaster' had 'moulded its pupils in as efficient a way as any public school'.

In the evening I went to a dance given by old Achimoteans, 'a very grand occasion' with more than a 'suggestion of lunacy'. 'The dance dresses were superb: the men's dinner jackets were of various cuts, but none of them would have disgraced a London nightclub.' I liked dancing, then the passion of Oxford, and quickly responded to the rhythms of 'high life', but by the end of the evening I had decided, prematurely it proved, that I did not like old Achimoteans at all, prematurely because I found out later that there were old Achimoteans inside both the PEA and Nkrumah's CPP. I could not have foreseen then that within a few years Nkrumah himself would be photographed dancing with Queen Elizabeth.

Meeting Nkrumah face-to-face for the first time was an extraordinary experience. I went to see him in his modest house at six o'clock in the morning, the earliest time of the day that I have ever had an interview with anyone, and at once I fell for his charm and for his intelligence. He communicated to me immediately his commitment not only to creating an independent Ghana but to pan-Africanism, a term neither of us employed. Kimble had first met him 'hiding under a bed'. Nothing seemed to me to be hidden from me when I first met him, and while I was in the Gold Coast it was with his active help that I got to know the whole of his entourage and travelled with some of his closest friends along the long coast belt that linked Accra and Sekondi-Takoradi.

They were happy to talk to me, and I was placed on the platform just behind them when they addressed political meetings. Perhaps because of that I decided that I must travel by myself through other parts of the Gold Coast. I went alone, therefore, to Kumasi to meet the Asantehene, tribal chief of the Ashanti, who received me in full tribal dress and presented me a roll of locally produced Kente cloth. By occupation he was a railwayman. I also had an all too brief trip to the larger Muslim north where the writ of Nkrumah did not then run. The visit out of Accra that I most enjoyed was to Togoland with one of the two full-time extramural tutors, Lalage Bown. (The other was Dennis Austin.) Before 1914 Togoland had been a German protectorate, and between the wars had been administered as a League of Nations mandate by France. In 1951 we needed visas to go there. Togo resisted determined attempts by Nkrumah to merge it with Ghana. My memories of my visit to Togoland in 1951 – with an excellent

A busy Workers' Educational Association office. Here as President I am dictating letters. On my far right is Elizabeth Monkhouse, who supported my predecessor as President of the Social History Society, H. L. Beales, in his old age.

Distance education. Having been involved in establishing the Open University in 1968/9, I became the main planner (with 'Sonny' Ramphal of the Commonwealth), when the Commonwealth of Learning was created. I became its President. On this visit in 1989 with my Chief Executive James Maraj (*on my right*), I met Rajiv Gandhi who warmly welcomed me to India.

I lectured in India in 1960 where I met for the first time Lionel Knights (*far left*) and David Daiches (*right*). It was on this lecture tour that I decided, on his suggestion, that David, then at Cambridge, should join me as a founding father of Sussex University.

Crossing frontiers (*above and right*). I have loved crossing frontiers as I have travelled widely. I have also loved crossing disciplinary frontiers in my work as an historian.

I got to know China before the events in Tiananmen Square in 1989 virtually ended the life of the Society for Anglo-Chinese Understanding. I later became involved with the University of South East Asia and addressed a meeting in the Great Hall of the People's Palace in the Square.

Seeing China for myself.

Harold Macmillan, whom I knew in Sussex, visited Worcester College, as Chancellor of Oxford University, for its seventh centenary celebrations in 1983. We are seen here emerging from the College Chapel, which has a magnificent William Burges interior. The Fellows wore surplices when they attended Chapel services.

The Victorian Society brought John Betjeman and me together. Here we are shown presenting prizes for the best parish church guide.

26 VESTA DRIVE, TORONTO

Carson and Anne Kilpatrick
    Are beautiful children to me.
Carson is strong and his hair is long
    And his eyes are blue as the sea.

Anne has a peach complexion
    And elegant curves and hips
When she looks in her brother's direction
    There's a secret smile on her lips.

For they help at their parents' parties
    Where the men have a healthy tan
The eye runs off where the heart is
    To fall at the feet of Anne.

I look through a leaded window
    Over the neat, mown grass
As a small wind moves in the maples
    And the stately Cadillacs pass.

Oh rye-on-the-rocks forever!
    And I'm glad that I'm still alive
While Carson and Anne Kilpatrick
    Are living in Vesta Drive.

On a great trip with John Julius Norwich and Hugh and Reta Casson, John and I explored Victorian Canada. In Toronto we admired its great banks and visited interesting houses. In one of them, John copied out this poem 'for Asa and Susan'.

A poster that I kept for all to see in my office when I was Vice-Chancellor of Sussex.

> MAY THE
> People awake to the
> Recognition of their Rights;
> HAVE THE
> Fortitude to demand them;
> The Fortune to obtain them,
> AND HENCEFORTH
> Sufficient Wisdom and Vigour to
> DEFEND THEM;

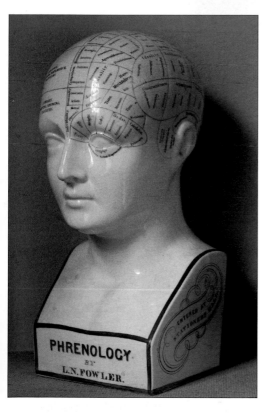

I bought this phrenological head in York. Phrenology was a serious subject in the mid-Victorian era.

This late silhouette was a ninetieth birthday present to me from my friend Mary Teakle.

The handsome head of a wise friend. Alistair Grant, my neighbour in Tyninghame, with whom I discussed, among other subjects, both literature and retailing.
(Photograph by Jane Bown, for The Observer*)*

African chauffeur and guide – are as much of nature as of politics. We saw a wonderful waterfall and more small blue butterflies surrounding it than I have seen in the rest of my life.

I was to see nature transformed on a second visit to Ghana, as it had then become, in 1965 when I was a guest of the new University of Kumasi at an international symposium discussing the resettlement problems created by the building of the huge new Akosombo dam, completed that year. It created one of the world's largest man-made lakes, covering over 3,000 square miles. As early as 1954 Nkrumah had formulated in public the idea, not his own, of a Volta River project. He had seen it through as President of the new Republic of Ghana from 1960 and in retrospect, as at the time, it was regarded as his supreme achievement. Yet it did not save him from being ousted from power in 1966, the year after my visit.

When I started that visit I had a long argument about Nkrumah with Conor Cruise O'Brien, a well-connected Irish politician, who had been appointed Vice-Chancellor of the University of Ghana in 1962. The quarrel between them seemed to me to have something in common with that of Henry II and Thomas à Becket in the Middle Ages. Before I left Accra for the symposium O'Brien asked me on which plane I would be leaving Accra when the celebrations had ended, telling me that he might well be on the same one: he expected Nkrumah would soon dismiss him from his vice-chancellorship.

O'Brien indeed got out of Ghana in 1965 and moved across the Atlantic to become Albert Schweitzer Professor of the Humanities in New York University. There were multiple African resonances in that title. Schweitzer established his reputation in Africa, and O'Brien had already been concerned with Africa before he moved to Accra, having been employed in Katanga, a contentious province of the former Belgian Congo, working with the Secretary General of the United Nations, Dag Hammarskjöld. In 1962 O'Brien had described his experience in *To Katanga and Back: A UN Case History*. Like me, he described his recreation in *Who's Who* as travelling.

By 1965 'the African awakening' already had its historiography as well as its history, and long before that it had begun to interest me.

Indeed, as early as 1951, the year of my first visit to the Gold Coast, four writers, two of whom figured prominently in my own life, published a Penguin Special, *Attitudes to Africa*, which I took with me in my baggage. The two were W. Arthur Lewis and Martin Wight.

Lewis was born in the West Indies in 1915 and in 1948 had been appointed Professor of Political Economy at the University of Manchester, where I got to know and like him, and to discuss with him his views on economic development. When he was sent out to the Gold Coast he disagreed sharply with Nkrumah on what would later be called the strategy of development. Lewis prescribed the expansion and modernization of agriculture: Nkrumah demanded rapid industrialization.

The other co-writer, Martin Wight, was interested not in economics but in politics. In 1951 I knew him less well than I knew Lewis, but I was to get to know him far better than Lewis ten years later when he joined me as one of the founding deans of the new University of Sussex. In 1951 he was Reader in International Relations in the University of London, having served in Chatham House with Arnold Toynbee, whose multi-volume study of history, hailed by a few as a masterpiece, never greatly appealed to me. In 1947 Wight wrote *The Gold Coast Legislative Council* and four years later a more general book, *British Colonial Constitutions*.

I do not think that he ever met Nkrumah, but he knew J. B. Danquah, who having entered politics as a young man, had invited Nkrumah back to the Gold Coast to be General Secretary of his political party, the United Gold Coast Convention. This was to be a party appealing to an elite: Nkrumah was to demand instead a 'mass party' under new leaders. The two chose different slogans too. Danquah's slogan was 'Self-government in the shortest possible time', Nkrumah's was 'Self-government now'.

In June 1949 Nkrumah created the new mass party, the People's Convention Party, which went on to acquire power after the first Gold Coast elections. On the same day as he launched his party he also launched a newspaper, the *Accra Evening Post*. 'As long as we remain under an imperialist government', it told its readers, 'we shall continue to be poor, unemployed, ill-used and continually oppressed, enslaved and exploited [a word that was highly charged, and rightly so, in the Gold Coast]. To ameliorate our condition we can do nothing but ask for self-government.'

In achieving his mission Nkrumah was helped by two lieutenants in particular, who were themselves to become rivals, Kofo Botsio, who in 1951 accompanied Nkrumah to his old American university, Lincoln, located in Oxford, Pennsylvania, where he received an honorary degree, and Komla Gbedemah, an impressive platform politician who acted as my chief guide after I had seen Nkrumah. After he became President Nkrumah was in a position to rule his country as he wished. I did not myself suspect his motives in 1951. He seemed to me both practical and curious to find out what was going on in Britain, where the Labour Party was in trouble and where he knew he would have to work with Conservatives. He seemed to hold nothing back from me, providing me with more material than I had space to write about even in six articles. Indeed I wrote several more for the *Fortnightly*, a review which had been founded by Anthony Trollope in 1865. In the number in which my own article 'Nationalism in the Gold Coast' appeared, there was an adjacent article by 'A Correspondent' entitled 'Syria is not a Democracy'.

Syria was a country which fascinated Hodgkin before the Gold Coast, as it fascinated my young Cambridge supervisor Otto Smail, and as it fascinates (and horrifies me) in 2012. In 1951 I nevertheless focused most of my interest in foreign politics on Africa, as Hodgkin did. In the epilogue to his *Nationalism in Colonial Africa*, published in 1957, he concluded that, as it was clear that 'the period of European ascendancy in Africa' was drawing to an end, everyone should try to ensure that its end 'does not inflict avoidable suffering upon Africans, Asians or, indeed, Europeans themselves'. He had much to say in his survey about the Sudan, a country which I was to visit, not under his auspices. Hodgkin gave me a copy of his book inscribed in his neat handwriting 'with gratitude'. Like Nkrumah he was a Pan-African, but he was a Pan-Arab too. He never ignored East Africa, and his book included five references to Jomo Kenyatta and two to Mau Mau.

I had never been to Kenya – and subsequently never have been – but in a rare letter to the press I warned against making too much of Mau Mau adherents swearing oaths. I pointed to nineteenth-century English parallels and drew on the work of Manchester anthropologists. The next book on Africa that I read was Andrew Cohen's *British Policy in a Changing Africa* (1959), not knowing then that it would be with his assistance and blessing that in 1964 a new Institute of Development Studies would be set up in Sussex, directed by a friend of mine from Oxford, Dudley Sears, who was as remarkable a figure on the international scene as Cohen himself.

I enjoyed being chairman of the board of the Institute, never an entirely easy task, given its very diverse membership. I felt that its being located on the Sussex campus was a natural outcome of our being the first university in Britain, old or new, to link together African and Asian studies. I was encouraged by the fact that one of the first nine academics at Sussex in 1961, Michael Lipton, recently and rightly honoured, joined the Institute and made a major contribution to its development.

In that year Roland Robinson and John Gallagher's much publicized *Africa and the Victorians* appeared with the sub-title *The Official Mind of Imperialism*. They did not compare that 'official mind' with pre- or post-Victorian minds. On my bookshelf I place their book between Vincent Belepatu Thompson's *Africa and Unity: The Evolution of Pan-Africanism* (1969) and Philip D. Curtin's *The Image of Africa*, sub-titled *British Ideas and Action, 1780–1850* (1964), a brilliant study which is basic to any historiographical analysis. During the 1960s the number of books on Africa was increasing significantly, but outside Sussex University there was little attempt in Britain to compare 'the Dark Continent' with other continents or one kind of imperialism with another.

The year after I went to West Africa I made my first encounter with an old continent, Asia, which I began to compare with Africa and, indeed, with America, north and above all, south. This time I was again under military auspices: I was invited by the Army Education Corps to travel to Malaya, since 1948 in a state of emergency, where I was sent to the heart of the jungle and attached mainly to the Royal West Kent Regiment. I felt that I was back in the Army again, this time at last in conditions of combat. I went out with them heavily camouflaged on night patrols. Along with the 1st Battalion of the Suffolk Regiment they were on very active duty, but they seemed interested in my lectures about life in Britain. I gathered lots of information from them on life in Malaya. When I arrived in September 1952 I learned from them of the killing in July of Liew Kon Kim, the 'Bearded Terror of Kajang'.

There was no Kimble to give me a complete picture on my arrival, but within hours I was well briefed about my namesake Lieutenant-General Sir Harold Briggs (no relative), who had produced a co-ordinated civil and military plan, to be known to soldiers, politicians and historians as the Briggs Plan. It remained the basis of British strategy until the end of the Emergency, although Briggs himself, on grounds of ill health, had to resign his post of Director of Operations in November 1951 and died in October 1952. Under the plan, Chinese squatters and others who were considered to be in danger from the Communist rebels were moved to 'new villages' protected by barbed wire and by Malay Police and a Chinese Home Guard.

The settlement process had something in common with the settlement process in Ghana when the Volta Dam was built, but the motivation was different. I heard very little in Ghana about communists: in Malaya I was told about little else. Nevertheless, being an historian, I tried to find out about Malay and Chinese political alignments and arranged to get an interview with Tunku Abdul Rahman, the leader of the United Malay Nationalist Organization (UMNO), who in 1955 was to form a government known as the Triple Alliance, a coalition of UMNO, the Malayan Chinese Association (MCA) – I had met one of its representatives in 1952 – and the Malayan Indian Congress. In August 1957 Malaya gained complete independence, but it was not until 1960 that the 'Emergency', as it was called, was formally declared to be over.

When I finished my brief Malayan tour in 1952 I was rewarded by a short visit to Singapore and to Hong Kong. Singapore was to follow its own pattern of development. So, too, was Hong Kong. When I first visited it there was little sign that it was about to be anything more than a naval headquarters. I bought Ming plates there, however, and spent a day in Macao, for which I required a visa. It was still Portuguese.

There had been big changes in international political alignments before Rahman came into power and the process went on afterwards. Asia and Africa were drawn closer together at a conference in Bandung, Indonesia, in 1955 which was attended by representatives of the Gold Coast, soon to be Ghana, Liberia, Libya, Sudan, Ethiopia and Egypt. I kept in touch with what was going on as much as any private individual could do, using to the full the resources of the Royal Institute of International Affairs at Chatham House.

I also believed in learning through travel. Egypt figured in the third of my world travels, Egypt before Suez. In article 1 of a draft constitution of 1952 it was stated quite simply that 'Egypt is an Arab state'. In fact, President Nasser, who came into power with Neguib in 1952, and succeeded him in 1954, was deeply involved in African politics, proclaiming, for example, 'the unity of the Nile Valley'. The journey that I made in 1952 to the 'Middle East' with Rupert Murdoch, then a pupil of mine at Worcester College, Harry Pitt, a Fellow of the College, and George Masterman, another Australian undergraduate, ended in Egypt. It still stands out in my mind, not least because, like most of my early travels, it was a journey without any formal academic commitments.

It had started for Harry and me in Athens, my first visit there, where we saw the Acropolis, like Ephesus at that time only very incompletely restored. We met there a Labour MP from Lancashire, also called Harry, Harry Hind, who was interested to learn that we were on our way to Turkey and appreciated that in doing so we would follow some of the journeys of St Paul. The comment he made still rings in my mind too – 'I didn't know that St Paul was a Turk.'

We met Rupert Murdoch and George Masterman, no relative of the Provost of Worcester, in Turkey, in what had been Constantinople and was now Istanbul. Rupert had travelled there with his father in a brand new Ford Zephyr, which he had promised his father that he would send back to Australia by sea from Port Said. They had had trouble, as I would not have had, in crossing Yugoslavia: I would have been welcomed in Belgrade. Curiously Rupert was to have trouble too in Jordan. King Abdullah had recently been assassinated, upsetting the whole balance of power in the Arab world, and there were many signs of tension in all the places on our journey beyond Turkey through Syria, Lebanon and Jordan. There were Arabs who thought that the name Murdoch was associated with the Jewish name Mordecai. Coincidentally the biggest greengrocer in Keighley was called Mordecai Barker; he was no more of a Jew than I was. No one seemed suspicious of me even though my name might seem Jewish.

There was more rumour and suspicion in the Middle East of 1952 than I had ever encountered in my life and sometimes I felt that we were being unduly caught up in it. We certainly would have been had the Arabs had any intimation of the Rupert Murdoch-to-be. Turkey seemed more stable than any other country through which we travelled, and in Istanbul we were warmly welcomed when we appeared, somewhat dishevelled, at a formal party in the garden of the British Consulate. The city appealed to me more than Athens. I was thrilled by the sight of St Sophia, once cathedral, later mosque, but I loved even more the blue mosque at Bursa. I also went to Scutari by myself in search of Florence Nightingale. None of my companions wanted to accompany me.

The long journey beyond Istanbul through Turkey and into Syria was not easy, not because of political tensions but because there were few really modern roads. Nevertheless, we made our way uneventfully to Ankara and visited the restaurant where the wartime German Ambassador, Franz von Papen, was said to have gazed across the room and caught the eyes of the British Ambassador. Both knew everything that there was to know about spies. While we were in Ankara it was inhibiting not to be able to talk of wartime Bletchley to my companions. For most of our long journey through Turkey, however, we talked freely to each other but not to the Turks about the fate of the Ottoman Empire and the rise to power of Atatürk, one of my schoolboy heroes whom I dragged into sixth-form essays when there was no need to do so. His presence in the Turkey of 1952 was ubiquitous; he seemed still to be alive despite his death in 1938.

Whenever we stopped for a meal on our journey across Turkey we would be approached by Turkish teachers of English, who wanted first to discover what we felt about Shakespeare but who quickly switched their question to what we thought about Atatürk. Turks then knew more German than English, and since I was the only one of the four of us who understood any German my own halting conversational German often had to be brought into play. It would have been easier for me had we been engaged in a conversation about Panzer Korps and the Luftwaffe.

Meanwhile, we had to order Turkish food in the kitchens of tiny eating houses by pointing at dishes that appealed to us. Though I had been brought up in a greengrocer's shop, it was my first encounter with aubergines: they could be delicious. We did not always know what we were eating. The only Turkish word I learnt was that for bread. Ordinary Turks, who spoke no English or German, were extraordinarily kind to us, and when we were camping they even gave us food of their own, usually roasted corn, to share with them. The women would sit apart from us, almost hidden from view. Atatürk would not have liked that. He taught his fellow citizens ballroom dancing.

The roads played havoc with the Ford Zephyr, and I was amazed by the skill of Turkish mechanics in coping with the havoc. In Aydin we had to have major repairs done, and we felt that, even if we did not have to spend the night in gaol because of Rupert's mischievousness in tossing out of the window a small piece of local handicraft which he was taking back as a gift, we might at least have the car confiscated. I recalled all this on a visit with my wife to Ephesus early in 2011 when I saw signposts pointing to Aydin. In 1952 we had seen what little there was of ruined Ephesus, but archaeological work there had barely started. There and elsewhere we often had to sleep in the open air; we had taken sleeping bags with us. The Turkish police were very suspicious about our doing this, particularly it seemed to me outside

Nicea, which I alone among our band of companions was determined to see. I felt that I should recite the Nicene Creed in the place where it was formulated. I did so, but in the night we were abruptly awakened by the police. I felt then that we were living in a very different past: we had no news of what was happening that day in the world outside.

Eventually we crossed the frontier with Syria – no talk then of Baathist politics there or in Iraq – and spent the night in relative comfort in a hotel in Aleppo. I had contacts there, and we spent another night with English friends living in that great city. We went on to Palmyra, Resafa and the great Crusader castle of Crac des Chevaliers, which Otto Smail had told me about before he himself went to war. Norman-looking children were playing outside it. On to Damascus, one of my favourite cities in the Arab world, and across via Baalbek – no talk then of Hezbollah – to Arab Jerusalem. We were not allowed to cross into the Jewish sector of the divided city which I was to visit many, many times later. Just how the city was divided I never then found out, but I collected a phial of water from the River Jordan, which we used a few years later at the christening of my older son, Daniel, by the Bishop of Ripon, a good friend who had never used it at any christening before. Anthony Sampson, his godfather, had never met a bishop before.

On setting out on this great trip I had promised the Oxford theologian Canon Lightfoot of Christ Church to try to get to Petra at all costs, but we never managed that. 'For God's sake, go to Petra', he had called out up my staircase in Worcester College just before we started our trip. The best I could do – with some trepidation – was to let him read a diary I had kept. It was not a great piece of literature, but it was the first long diary that I had kept since Kirkcudbright, and it was far more revealing. I wanted to get into it everything that mattered – landscape, memorials, customs, politics.

The next part of our journey took us into Lebanon, where again we slept in the open, sleeping more comfortably and less disturbed in banana groves. The atmosphere at the border itself was unpleasant. The Lebanese did not like the Syrians any more than the Syrians liked the Israelis. I discovered at once, however, what a great city Beirut is.

We saw it at a time when there was no thought of civil war. Money changers dominated the centre of the city, and I was delighted to exchange there a large Italian note which I thought I would never be able to get rid of. At this stage of our journey we were all short of money, even Rupert, and we made contact with the father of an Oxford postgraduate student known to Harry who generously offered to lend us what we needed. We arranged to meet him in the market the following morning and have coffee with him. What followed was one of the strangest stories of my life. Our benefactor did not turn up. He had died during the night. He had arranged for us to have the money, however, and all that we could leave behind by way of heartfelt thanks were our blessings.

We crossed over the Mediterranean to Port Said from which we had ocean tickets back to Southampton on a ship which had started in Australia. Once there – and it was then a filthy place, specializing in all varieties of filth – we decided to go by train to Cairo, where I sold for cash on the train a pair of light trousers that I had bought, or rather had foisted on me, in the Damascus *suk*. Cairo, as always, is a city of secrets and again I regretted that I could not talk to my fellow travellers about what I had known about it while at Bletchley. We visited Shepheard's Hotel, however, and went on a camel ride at the pyramids. Keeping all my wartime secrets to myself, I felt almost as sphinx-like as the sphinx. Back in Port Said we found that the ship was full of dissatisfied British emigrants returning from Australia who had taken advantage of cheap tickets to go out and settle there. It had not worked out for them.

It is not difficult more than fifty years later to conjure up Rupert's language about these 'pommies', stronger than he ever used about the Egyptians. He was at his most Aussie then. Throughout most of our trip I had learnt from him for the first time in my life just how strong spoken language can be. Since he left Oxford I have kept in touch with him only irregularly and I was glad to receive a handwritten letter from him on my ninetieth birthday; he had appeared in person by surprise at my seventieth in Oxford. I have chosen never to write about him or his remarkable career but to have left him out of the strange context which I have been describing in this chapter would have been absurd. In 1952 he used his own Aussie influence to get a far better cabin than I did and got off the ship at Marseilles, our next port of call, and travelled back to London by train. Harry, who was to criticize Rupert passionately later, went with him, so that I and the fourth member of our party were left to make our own way back to England.

Not long afterwards I was to have the incredibly difficult task of telling Rupert of the death of his father. His mother, Elisabeth, a great woman who has done an immense amount for Australia and for Australian art, rang me and asked me to tell him. He was deeply shocked and returned to Melbourne at once. Thereafter there was a great silent bond between his mother and me. I saw her last in her house outside Melbourne just after her hundredth birthday.

I went to Australia several times between 1952 and 1999 and got to know and like the Capons in Sydney. Edward Capon was Director of the New South Wales Art Gallery and I last saw him in 2008 when Susan and I went on our world cruise. He was immensely helpful and allowed me to tarry in the room housing the Gallery's English pictures, very Victorian. I loved some of the twentieth-century Australian paintings, particularly the Drysdales and the Nolans. I got to know well the largely self-taught Sidney Nolan, four years older than me, and our conversations about Ned Kelly and Australian history linger in my mind. Oddly most of them took place in England rather than in Australia. The first of them was in Aldeburgh and a later one was in Covent Garden. Painting and music met.

I had no other Australian friend with whom I could talk about music, but whenever I was in Sydney I went to the architecturally exciting Opera House, opened in 1973. Susan enjoys opera as much as I do.

Listening to music is usually followed for me by meditation, and my meditations usually take me back to all the countries where I have travelled and through all the centuries when music was played. They take me back too to all the writers who had something to say about it, musicians and non-musicians alike. I was interested, for example, to hear the comments of the humanist Kurt Vonnegut in a DVD of 2002:

'Music is to me proof of the existence of God. It is so extraordinarily full of magic, and in tough times of my life I can listen to music and it makes such a difference.' I share the thought. I still meditate on it when times for me are tough.

Chapter 9

Words and Music

This chapter, which I began to write on an unseasonably cold and grey day during the Edinburgh Festival of August 2010, might have been placed after any of the earlier chapters in this book. Throughout my adult life words have been linked with music, although I have written far more about words than about music. Nevertheless, I have assembled a good library of books about music and about music festivals in particular, starting with the first Birmingham Festival for 'the benefit of the General Hospital' in 1768. I gave the Hesse Lecture on the history of festivals in Jubilee Hall in Aldeburgh in 1992.

I first went to the Edinburgh International Festival in 1972 when Jack Kane was Lord Provost and Peter Diamond was Director in succession to Rudolf Bing, Ian Hunter, Robert Ponsonby and Lord Harewood. I never knew Bing, a refugee from Hitler, who was general manager of Glyndebourne Opera when he was appointed Festival Director, but I knew Ian Hunter well, largely through the Brighton Festival, Robert Ponsonby through the BBC and the Proms, and Lord Harewood, who directed the Festival from 1961 to 1965, through the city of Leeds, where I first met him, and through the Institute of Recorded Sound, where I was a member of the committee which he chaired.

Bing had talked to Audrey Mildmay, wife of John Christie, founder of Glyndebourne Opera, about Edinburgh as a possible venue for a festival on a visit to the city in 1939, after Glyndebourne had staged a performance of *The Beggar's Opera* there, but after the war the national economic, social and cultural context of music, like every-thing else, had completely changed. The first Edinburgh Festival of 1947, a festival of hope, a great artistic success, was not national but deliberately international in character. Bruno Walter, reunited with the Vienna Philharmonic Orchestra, proclaimed that the war was at last over, while the *Manchester Guardian* observed that, 'The Vienna Philharmonic' stood for nothing less than 'the unconquerable spirit of European civilization'. It noted at the end of a historic leader that Bing himself had become a naturalized British subject only in 1946.

The idea of a very different kind of Edinburgh Festival had been proposed in 1815, at the end of a much earlier and even more protracted war, by Henry Cockburn. It was a festival that 'sprang more from charity than from love of harmony', but the music, Cockburn had been told, 'was good' and the 'Outer House', Parliament House, where it was performed, was 'not ill calculated to give it effect'. There were to be no more nineteenth-century Edinburgh festivals, but there was no shortage of music in Edinburgh. On one occasion Chopin played his own compositions in the Hopetoun Rooms, and on many occasions songs and later quartets were staged in St Cecilia's Hall.

It was more than a gesture, therefore, when at the tenth anniversary of the twentieth-century International Festival the composer Arthur Bliss travelled north to conduct a new overture 'Edinburgh' as a tribute to the city which had supported it. Bliss was careful nonetheless to pay an indirect tribute to Glasgow and to Scotland as a whole. In his overture he quoted the old tune of the 124th Psalm which the Glasgow Orpheus Choir under its conductor Hugh Roberton had performed many times, and he ended his overture with his own interpretation of Scottish reels. He even danced a few steps himself on the rostrum.

When I first went to the International Festival it was twenty-five years old, and in his foreword to the souvenir programme Lord Provost Kane, whom I had come to know through the WEA, wrote generally of the problems that festivals, like individuals, faced with advancing age. One of them was 'the tendency to become institutionalised and to rely more heavily on tradition'. Looking back in the light of my experiences as described in previous chapters, I regard twenty-five years as a very young institutional age; and the twenty-five years after Kane wrote of the Festival's jubilee, which saw a huge growth in the Festival's 'fringe', seem more exciting than the first twenty-five.

After Diamond two successive directors left their mark – John Drummond, who while in the BBC was, like Ponsonby before him, to take charge of the BBC Proms, and Brian McMaster, who in 1991 moved from Welsh Opera, which he had directed for fifteen years, to Scotland. Both of them became my friends in their pre-Edinburgh days. While I was writing my history of broadcasting for a time I had an upper room near to Drummond's inside the then Langham building of the BBC opposite Broadcasting House, and in breaks from our work we used to talk and drink there together, discussing both music in general and BBC music in particular. My connection with Welsh Opera had nothing to do with the BBC. I had friends in Cardiff who kept me well informed about the Welsh Opera, which I came to love and whose board I was invited to join. I got to know its lively conductor, Richard Armstrong, who was himself to move to Scotland to Scottish Opera. He was a brilliant musician. Barbara Stewart and Ian Douglas were the friendliest of administrators

McMaster's successor as Edinburgh Festival Director, Jonathan Mills, a vigorous young Australian, whom I took to at once, used the verb 'converge', which inspires the title of the last chapter of this book, in his 'Welcome to Festival 2010'. The items in his festival programme for that year were based, he wrote, on 'the expansive imaginative territory between places [countries and continents] of extraordinary cultural diversity'. 'Diverse cultures, separated by vast oceans, converge on Edinburgh.' This has been a theme close to my heart as I have been writing my book.

I begin my narrative in this chapter not with my old age, or indeed with my middle ages, but with the life of a child brought up very differently from myself but who certainly belongs to my *karass*, Denis Forman, four years older than I am and a friend over many years, who loves the Edinburgh Festival. His brilliant autobiography covering his childhood, *Son of Adam* (1990), I have just been re-reading. It stops short at his arrival in Loretto School, when he already knew far more about music than I did when I went to Bletchley Park years later. I first met Denis just after the war when he was Chief Production Officer of Films with the Central Office of Information. I was chairman then of a small, largely expert, committee which chose non-commercial British films for international film festivals. In that capacity I remember attending memorable film festivals at Cork in Ireland, where I met Jack Lynch with whom I could talk about Irish politics and drink the best Irish whiskeys, and at Cracow in Poland, where I drank superb home-made vodka with the then father-in-law of Norman Davies, an historian friend, who brought European history, west and east, to life. I also talked over academic – and Marxist – politics with the Rector of the University. He told me that he was delighted that the University was to appoint a Pole as Professor of Russian for the first time since 1945.

I got to know Forman best during 1971 and 1972 when he was Chairman of the Board of Governors of the British Film Institute, on which I served as a governor from 1970 to 1979. I saw much of him too from 1974 to 1987 when he was a wonderful Chairman of Granada Television which he had first joined in 1955 as a production executive. Denis proved himself then and later to be a more cogent and persuasive spokesman for public service broadcasting than anyone working in Broadcasting House or in Television Centre. Perhaps Denis's greatest quality was that he was quite incapable of talking or writing jargon. It was the content of what he had to say or write, however, which mattered most to me.

I was drawn to Granada around the time that Denis began his own Granada career. The company, based in Manchester and chaired by Sidney Bernstein, was the first television company to stimulate television studies in universities, and in setting up a University Fellowship not in Lancashire but in Leeds, while I was Professor of Modern History there, it drew Leeds into pioneering studies of the language of television scripts. Joseph Trenaman, in charge of the studies, showed through detailed scholarly research that many viewers did not understand many of the words that were being used in television programmes. Through the sponsorship of this research Granada not only introduced me to Trenaman and to Bernstein but reintroduced me to Gerald Barry, who took me into his confidence concerning his experiences as Director of the Festival of Britain in 1951.

In Denis's *Son of Adam* he describes the 'Big House' in south-west Scotland, Craigielands, where he spent his early childhood. Laid out on a Palladian model, it was the home of a privileged household with eight women servants, and in the adjacent farm there were below a headman, two housekeepers, five agricultural workers and a boy, sometimes two. Flora, the widow of the businessman who bought Craigielands, James Smith, kept everyone in place during Denis's childhood, members of the Forman family, including Denis, as well as servants. Flora composed music as well as sang it, playing it on a soft-toned upright piano in the snuggery next to her bedroom. In the hall there was a Steinway grand piano, imported from New York, in the drawing room a Broadwood grand and in the billiard room two seven-foot grands.

The musical regime of Craigielands mattered more to Denis's parents themselves than the pianos, for in music as in everything else at Craigielands adults believed that there was a right and a wrong. Beethoven was right. So was Brahms. Chopin was wrong. So was Liszt. Mozart was a dilettante who wrote pretty-pretty tunes. Denis's mother and father were Wagnerites. Most modern music was dismissed as rubbish, except that of Delius and Elgar.

On the Forman side of the family there was a tradition dating back to the early eighteenth century that each first-born son was called Adam, and Denis's father Adam followed the pattern, which incorporated both Craigielands and Loretto, to which Denis was sent off to school. The pattern was broken when Denis came back to south-west Scotland after his first term there: Craigielands, which probably belonged to Flora, had been sold. For Denis a whole era had now come to an end.

Denis had already learnt before he left home that there was more to music than just listening to it, or worse judging it within a regime, yet it needed Loretto for him to be able to take 'a great leap forward' and in his words 'grasp the true shape and meaning of the main classical forms'. Denis's *Mozart Piano Concertos* (1971) was the first of his books that I read, and I have it in front of me now as I write. There is nothing pretty-pretty within it.

The first book of Denis's which I should have read was his auto-biography, which he published when he was Deputy Chairman of the Royal Opera House, Covent Garden. In 1992 he gave a copy to my wife, who knew and knows more about music than I do, and who had earlier arranged with little outside help a series of concerts in Sussex University's then somewhat disturbed Arts Centre, which had been opened in 1969. She bypassed internal quarrelling by entertaining performers and composers in beautiful Ashcombe House where we lived on the edge of the Downs. Our copy of Denis's *Son of Adam* was inscribed for the two of us 'with love', and for both of us it has become a much-loved book. It stands in my bookshelves side by side with Alec Hyatt King's *Mozart Chamber Music: A BBC Music Guide*, first published in 1968. Alec, a Deputy Keeper of Printed Books and Super-intendent of the Music Room in the British Museum, had been a fellow member of a course in cryptography in Bedford in 1943. I have described the experience in *Secret Days*. In one month in Bedford with him I listened to more Mozart than I had listened to in the whole of my previous life.

As far as music was concerned, and indeed all that surrounded it, my own childhood had contrasted completely with that of Denis. I was brought up in a small house in a long street. Nevertheless, our household was not completely unmusical. We had one solid upright piano which my father played enthusiastically and quite well, revelling in noisy Victorian set pieces, and my mother, who played the piano far less well, sometimes gave soprano solos in her Chapel choir. Neither my sister nor I were taught to play the piano, although I strummed on our piano contentedly, playing tunes, mainly hymn tunes, entirely by ear. My sister and I were taught very little music at school. The limitations of our own homes were taken as much for granted as the comforts of Craigielands. Yet one boy in my class at Keighley Grammar School, Hubert Cowgill, whose mother doted on him, played the piano brilliantly. He wore spectacles that were even thicker than mine, and I considered him a genius. I found it strange that my school paid little attention to him. The so-called music room in the basement of the old Mechanics' Institute was used more for debates than for recitals, and in old age it is the debates, not the recitals, that I remember most clearly.

It was while working in wartime Bletchley Park that for the first time my musical horizons widened significantly. The BBC Symphony Orchestra had been evacuated to Bedford and I used to listen to it regularly. I came to admire Sir Adrian Boult as a conductor long before I started to write the history of broadcasting in 1957. Boult had been made Permanent Conductor and Director of Music of the BBC as long ago as December 1929, two years after the BBC had 'taken up' the Proms, founded by Henry Wood in the Queen's Hall in 1895. For a few years when I was writing my history of broadcasting my BBC office was in Henry Wood House, on the site of the Hall.

Before Reith enthusiastically welcomed the Proms, Boult's BBC predecessor, Percy Pitt, had inaugurated the daily *Foundations of Music* series, which was to have what the men who got rid of it in 1936 called 'a long innings' before it was dropped. I cannot remember listening to even one *Foundations of Music* programme, but inside Bletchley Park I got to know well one of the members of the BBC's Music Department, later to become its head, Herbert Murrill. I was deeply impressed that he had completed a string quartet in the year war broke out. A sergeant, Murrill took to uniform even less happily than Alec King did to cryptography.

On a related cryptography course at Bedford I had met the future Minister of Education and Vice-Chancellor of Leeds University, Edward Boyle, a devoted admirer of Saint-Saëns, whose music, to use the language of the future, was his 'private passion'. *Private Passions* was the title of the composer and critic Michael Berkeley's still-running post-war radio programme. It was a coincidence that it was

Edward who introduced me to Michael's father, the composer Lennox Berkeley, whom I got to like. I first met Michael years later at a party given by Jeremy Thorpe and his wife Marion, a wonderful person, always deeply involved in music, who had earlier been married to Lord Harewood.

In my personal perspectives Marion, trained as a pianist, linked London, Leeds and, above all, Aldeburgh. In Leeds she had been co-founder of the Leeds International Piano Competition with Fanny Waterman whom I got to know and admire. In Aldeburgh she was a trustee of the Britten–Pears Foundation and lived for part of the year in the Red House which Britten and Pears had shared. The person at the London party who introduced me to Michael Berkeley was the musicologist Donald Mitchell, four years younger than myself, who devoted much of his abundant energy to the life, letters and music of Benjamin Britten, and was executor of his estate in 1976. From 1986 to 2000 he was Chairman of the Britten Estate Company. The two volumes of Britten's selected diaries and letters, which Donald edited and published in 1991 and 2004, are indispensable to musicians and historians.

It was an older book of Donald's, however, *The Language of Modern Music*, published in 1963, that changed the whole of my attitude to contemporary music. Again there had been a coincidence in our initial meeting. His wife, Kathleen, Headmistress of Pimlico School, whom he married in 1956, was a valued colleague of mine on the Heritage Education Group. Another of his books which I have in front of me as I write this chapter is *The Mozart Companion* (1969), which he co-edited, a book which very quickly made me realize that there is no single approach to the work of a musician, least of all to Mozart. By then I had also read much musical biography and criticism, some of the criticism being more egotistical than stimulating. I like to make my own judgements on musical performance (as I do on pictures).

At the same time as I read *The Language of Modern Music* I was being influenced by changes in the BBC's whole approach to music. It was being transformed (controversially) after William Glock,

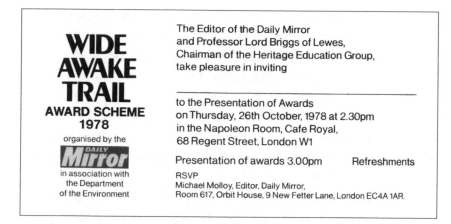

WIDE AWAKE TRAIL
AWARD SCHEME
1978
organised by the
Daily Mirror
in association with
the Department
of the Environment

The Editor of the Daily Mirror
and Professor Lord Briggs of Lewes,
Chairman of the Heritage Education Group,
take pleasure in inviting

to the Presentation of Awards
on Thursday, 26th October, 1978 at 2.30pm
in the Napoleon Room, Cafe Royal,
68 Regent Street, London W1

Presentation of awards 3.00pm   Refreshments

RSVP
Michael Molloy, Editor, Daily Mirror,
Room 617, Orbit House, 9 New Fetter Lane, London EC4A 1AR.

Part of the Heritage Education Group's activities.

chairman of the music committee of the International Society for Contemporary Arts, was appointed Controller of Music in 1959. This was an appointment that surprised his own personal friends as well as his future colleagues in Broadcasting House. One of them told him he felt as though he was 'a citizen of Wittenburg [*sic*] in 1556 and had received the news that Luther had been elected Pope'.

Glock stayed in post until 1971, and I not only got to know him well but also some of the bright young men he brought into the BBC. The brightest of them all, I felt, was the composer Alexander (Sandy) Goehr, born in 1932, who worked with him from 1960 to 1967 before later becoming West Riding Professor of Music at Leeds University – I loved this geographical designation – and Professor of Music at Cambridge University in 1976, the year when I moved from Sussex to Oxford. I have never seen enough of him.

When academics were talking about introducing music at Sussex I frequently drew on Sandy's advice, as I did on Glock's. It was always stimulating to argue with Sandy; the Music Faculty in Cambridge did not always think so. Sandy's advice also sometimes clashed with that of Donald Mitchell, who became first Professor of Music at the university. Sandy's book *Notes in Advance: An Autobiography in Music* (1990) is about as different from Denis Forman's childhood autobiography as any two autobiographies could be.

Three other people figured in the Sussex story. The first was László Heltay, a political refugee from Hungary after the ideologically as well as politically important Hungarian revolution of 1956, which was brutally put down by Russian tanks. I had been in charge when at Leeds of a welcoming team helping to settle refugees in Britain. A pupil of the composer Zoltán Kodály, about whom he loved to tell extraordinary stories, he developed an orchestra and a choir at Sussex University and extended his activities to Brighton, conducting with aplomb the Brighton Festival Choir.

The second person who figures, Robert Mayer, far older, had also been an immigrant, in his case from Germany. He was a very special person, born in Mannheim in 1879. As a boy aged eleven he had met Brahms, in the 1890s a very special qualification. Brahms was still staple fare in the 1960s and 1970s at the Sunday afternoon concerts in the Brighton Dome. In 1890 Mayer was a young musical performer, who at the age of eight had played Beethoven's Sonata No.5 for Violin and Piano – in his own words, he won 'considerable applause partly for my playing and partly for the fact that I was too small for my feet to reach the pedals'. Three years later Mayer's teacher invited him, in the year he met Brahms, to a performance of Wagner's *Meistersinger*. In old age well-known on both sides of the Atlantic, Mayer delivered an informal address in 1971 at the British Institute of Recorded Sound, which I heard, that he called 'My First Hundred Years'. He had not quite reached that landmark in 1971, but he went on to celebrate his centenary, then a remarkable event in itself.

I much admired Mayer's imaginative efforts to promote concerts for children and later teenagers. Before the sixties began he had started a series of youth concerts in 1956 at the Festival Hall; Norman del Mar conducted them. In 1959 they switched to Sadler's Wells Opera. All the season tickets for four concerts were quickly sold out, and on the first night the enthusiasm was overwhelming: 97 per cent of the audience had never seen or even heard an opera before. Mayer then created student youth orchestras, and in 1959 a National Youth Orchestra gave three concerts in Vienna. A year later three British orchestras gave concerts in Bayreuth.

A third person deserves a paragraph to herself for her distinctive contribution to Sussex music. My wife, Susan, was drawn into what were then the somewhat troubled affairs of the Gardner Centre, the university's performing arts centre, which had been initially endowed by Lyddon Gardner, a perfume manufacturer and benefactor in many ways of the University. I placed great trust in him, and his untimely death was a great blow to me as Vice-Chancellor. The Centre was more devoted to the theatre than to music (and the visual arts) and it was troubled not only for financial but for management reasons. Susan entirely by herself brought distinguished musicians to the university who gave their services free. She provided publicity. She herself used to go down to the centre to check that the posters were in place. She loved to entertain the performers in our beautiful house, Ashcombe, as I did. Among them were Gerald Moore, the great accompanist, Clifford Curzon, a close friend, and Charles Rosen. On one occasion Susan persuaded John Pritchard, whom we both knew well, and the whole Glyndebourne cast of *Così fan tutte* to come to the Centre.

The Allegri Quartet, artists in residence, led by Hugh Maguire, were always welcome guests who felt at home with us at Ashcombe. There were all kinds of interactions in this. The then wife of the cellist Bruno Schockler had been born in Keighley, not very far away from me. Patrick Ireland was an alumnus of Worcester College. Just before we left the University Susan was given a special concert in the midst of a great heatwave by the Academy of St Martin-in-the-Fields. I was deeply moved.

One of the most famous visitors to Sussex – and to Ashcombe – playing unaccompanied Bach privately for us in a nearby barn – was Mstislav Rostropovich (Slava), to whom we gave a Sussex honorary degree, the first such that he received in England. He was then in trouble in the Soviet Union, where his gramophone records were no longer on regular sale, and he was deeply concerned about his future. On his journey back from Brighton to Heathrow he asked the University driver, Mr Osbourne, the name of the place they were passing through and when he was told Redhill he replied 'Redhell, that's where I am going back to.' Nevertheless, despite his fears, he never lost his reputation in Russia, and when he was ill in hospital at the age of eighty in 2007 Vladimir Putin visited his bedside.

Rostropovich, like the Russian composer Shostakovich, who dedicated his cello concerto to him in 1960 (it was played at the Edinburgh Festival), became closely associated with Benjamin Britten and even acquired a house in Aldeburgh. I was thrilled when Britten, the first composer whom I got to know really well, entered my life; he was influenced more by Tchaikovsky than by any other Russian composer. I never talked to him either about Tchaikovsky or Shostakovich. In the music I like most I would place *Eugene Onegin* among my six or seven favourite operas and at least two Shostakovich symphonies and much of his chamber music.

Of course, there would be a lot of Britten in my selection, and I felt it to be a very special coincidence when he became a peer in the same very short honours list of 1976 as I did. He was the first person to telephone me after our names were announced. 'I have a question I must put to you, Asa', he began. It surprised me. 'Shall I call myself Lord Britten or Lord Benjamin Britten?' I replied that the latter would be better for him, but that (with Lord George Brown in mind) I had no intention of calling myself Lord Asa Briggs. Sadly he died without ever being able even to go to the House of Lords.

I knew Ben, as I called him, as a composer before he became a friend. I had been one of the privileged audience who heard the first Sadler's Wells performance of his *Peter Grimes* in 1945. I took to the opera at once, but I did not get to know him well for another fifteen years when I was writing the second volume of my *History of Broadcasting*. By then I had heard much of his music in many places. By then too I had got to know Peter Pears, and since Ben had received honours everywhere and Pears only praise, I persuaded Sussex University to give him an honorary degree in 1971. In what was then an unusual element in the ceremonies Peter sang and Ben played the piano. Peter loved travel as much as I did and, unlike me, kept diaries. The first dates back to 1934, a year before his friendship with Ben began. A far later diary records a journey he made with Ben to the Far East and describes their encounters with Balinese gamelan music and Japanese Noh theatre.

Whatever honours Sussex conferred on Peter and Ben, I felt that I had been offered a great honour myself when I was invited to open a new Britten–Pears Library in Aldeburgh, directed by Paul Banks. I have been there many times since and on more than one occasion have even worked in it. One of its first publications was a full-size facsimile of Britten's composition draft of *Peter Grimes*, which reflects the composer wrestling with text and music. The Library has not neglected visual arts and has staged a number of exhibitions, including one in 2007 on Peter before he met Ben, with good photographs and paintings as well as old programmes, of which I have a collection myself.

On my own visits to Aldeburgh I usually used to stay with Gilly Cave, who became a close friend. She was a great supporter of the Festival, and kept me fully informed about musical activities in the town. Her house looked out across a beautiful garden to the reedy Suffolk marshes. Her hospitality was legendary and she was a knowledgeable and dedicated gardener.

I had – and have – other music-loving friends in Aldeburgh, among them Humphrey Burton, who has a long and interesting experience of musical broadcasting, Hugo Herbert Jones, an alumnus of Worcester College and one-time mayor of Aldeburgh, who lives in a wonderful house that reminds me of a ship, and Paul Zisman, a more recent alumnus of Worcester and one time captain of the Boat Club, and his wife Sybella. Paul pays eloquent tribute to the power of Aldeburgh and the area around it to attract highly sophisticated (and intelligent) people to live there. Years ago I used to meet there Princess Margaret of Hesse, who endowed the Hesse Lectures, and Peter du Sautoy, when he was chairman of Faber and Faber, publisher of Britten. It was he who invited Donald Mitchell to join his board, on which T. S. Eliot also sat.

I have bought many books, pictures and artefacts in the town of Aldeburgh, and watched many interesting films in the local cinema, including the world premiere of *Carrington*, about the woman who had been at the heart of the Bloomsbury set. Not far away in the town, near to the stony beach, is the Wentworth Hotel, which figures in my own life among a number of diverse Wentworths – Wentworth Woodhouse, the great house where the depot of the Intelligence Corps was lodged in the stables, and Wentworth Street in east London which I knew in a quite different period of my life. Other Suffolk places have figured too apart from Aldeburgh – Thorpeness to which I used to walk; Blythburgh, where festival concerts continue to be held in its beautiful church; I explored Suffolk churches, where Festival concerts were presented; Orford at the mouth of the River Alde beyond which you cannot go; and villages across the cornfields far from the sea, like Framlingham.

Whenever I went to Aldeburgh I saw as much as I could of Hugh Maguire, who had been leader of the BBC Symphony Orchestra and of the Allegri Quartet, often in residence at Sussex, who taught in the Britten–Pears School at the Maltings, where a perambulation of the marshes is a necessary journey in the intervals between parts of a festival concert. For many years Hugh lived in a cottage on the Verney estate in Buckinghamshire. I had a special relationship with Ralph Verney, who had a fascinating historical pedigree, including Florence Nightingale connections, and his wonderful wife Mary. They were not directly concerned with Aldeburgh, but they used to put on concerts themselves at Claydon, their historic house, in which musical performers of world reputation took part. Both the Verneys loved music and Mary herself was a regular performer. It was at a Verney concert that I heard one of the last recitals given by Clifford Curzon. It was deeply moving, ethereal indeed. Curzon seemed at times to be on the point of ceasing to play.

In a tribute to Britten on his fiftieth birthday Curzon had recalled a wartime visit of Ben and Peter to his cottage in Cumbria. They arrived on the night train from London and took the bus to the last stop before Clifford's cottage, and then, against a background of howling wind and pelting rain, Ben and Peter played *Peter Grimes* on an old upright piano.

Cumbria was not quite as distant from London as Wexford in the Irish Republic, where my own musical education was further extended. Hearing of the humble beginnings of the Aldeburgh Festival and knowing the delights of Glyndebourne, with which I will conclude this chapter, T. J. Walsh, a local doctor, born in 1911, with a great love of music and opera in particular, wrote to Compton Mackenzie, editor of *The Gramophone*, in 1950, inviting him to visit Wexford to give the inaugural lecture to a Circle which Walsh had founded. Mackenzie, born in 1883, said yes, but enquired of Walsh why Wexford, a town where he felt thoroughly at home, should be content with studying operatic records. Why did not Wexford produce an opera for itself? It soon did. In 1951, the year of the Festival of Britain (a coincidence), Michael Balfe's opera *The Rose of Castille* was performed in Wexford with professional singers in the leading parts and a chorus consisting of singers from the neighbourhood.

What happened thereafter seems in retrospect logical. The first step was Mackenzie becoming the first President of the Wexford Festival for Music and the Arts, which always won the approval of the powers that be in Dublin. Erskine Childers, latest member of a family that fascinated me, Minister for Posts and Telegraphs and later to become President of Ireland, gave a speech in the theatre. His father had written *Riddle of the Sands*, a spy story which belongs unmistakably to the pre-1914 world, the world into which Mackenzie was born. At the end of the 2001 festival the President of Ireland, Mary McAleese, unveiled amid cheers a plaque commemorating Tom Walsh.

Records are almost as important as festivals to me in my musical life not only because I listen more and more to them the older I get, but because they have brought into my life, though not directly, Compton Mackenzie. Mackenzie belongs to my *karass*. Two years after I was born he started his magazine *The Gramophone*, and he calls his autobiography, published in 1955, *My Record of Music*. It was a long record, and it was through Mackenzie that records figured prominently in the early history of the BBC. Mackenzie describes unforgettably an interview with John Reith before the BBC was converted from a company to an institution. He describes Reith as the most startling man he had ever met, a prophetic figure who saw clearly long before recording of whole programmes became technically feasible how the presentation of individual records could figure in day-to-day broadcasting. Mackenzie's brother-in-law and business partner, Christopher Stone, who presented record programmes, became one of the best-known broadcasters in the country. I knew his name as well as I knew the name of the Boat Race commentator John Snagge.

Selection of records and skill in presenting them became an art in itself on both sides of the Atlantic. 'Favourites' were identified long before *Family Favourites* established itself as a record-breaking popular programme. As early as 1927 a symposium on the gramophone brought together thirty-four well-known men and women, including Max Beerbohm, Noël Coward, Ivor Novello, Hilaire Belloc and D. H. Lawrence, who were asked questions about their favourite composers. Lawrence selected Mozart. So did Belloc. Coward chose Gershwin, Novello Wagner. Asked what were their favourite arias (and singers) Beerbohm chose 'Voi Che Sapete' as his. Only George Bernard Shaw refused to answer any questions. He regarded the whole exercise as a 'monstrous insult', adding that 'only people in a deplorable elementary stage of musical culture have favourite tunes'.

Susan and I have collected records and have often been given them by composers and performers. We treasure them; among the most delightful were those given us by the accompanist Gerald Moore, whom we welcomed to our house in Sussex. It was extremely moving to be given later in our lives a set of classical 78s by Leonard Woolf; he and Virginia had listened to them together. He told me how reluctant they had been to dispose of their favourite possessions. In the attic at Rodmell they kept all their old newspapers.

When Mackenzie died in 1972 he was succeeded as President of the Wexford Festival by a very different man, Alfred Beit, a rich former Conservative MP at Westminster. His family's fortune had been made before 1914. He had first attended a Wexford opera in 1952, the year he moved to Ireland. This was the second opera to be performed in Wexford, Donizetti's *L'Elisir d'Amore*. Beit was to remain President until 1992. I never knew him well, but he and his wife once visited us in Worcester College, and I can remember him sitting at our piano and enthusiastically playing and singing Irish songs.

My own first connections with Wexford had been through Worcester College, not when I was Provost but as a young Fellow. The College had a strong musical strand in its history going back to Henry Hadow, who would have been chosen as Provost in 1917 had he not moved to Sheffield as Vice-Chancellor, where he became best known for his contribution to education rather than to music. I treasure, therefore, a copy of his *Studies in Music* (1893) which was dedicated to Charles Hubert Parry, who became Professor of Music in Oxford in 1900.

When I was installed as a Fellow of Worcester in 1945 the History Fellow of the College, who had drawn me there, Henry Vere Fitzroy Somerset, was as devoted to music – and to musical composition – as any fellow of any college could ever be, and he loved to play extracts of his Mozartian opera, *The Imbroglio*, on the piano in his study, to his pupils and to colleagues outside and inside the college. In 1953, one year after Beit's first visit, he invited me to go with him to the third Wexford Festival, my first visit to Ireland, a country which I came to love. We saw Donizetti's *Don Pasquale*. One of our surprise delights had nothing to do with Donizetti, however. We found two adjacent Wexford shops called Somerset and Briggs. On all my subsequent visits to Wexford – and there were many – I never met a Somerset or a Briggs, but I did find a tailor, Corcoran's Menswear, in Wexford's Bull Ring – so different from Birmingham's – from whom I bought my first Donegal tweed suit.

After I left Worcester College in 1955, the year of my marriage, my links with Wexford multiplied. Our first visits there were with Bryan Moyne, who lived with his large family at Knocmaroon in Dublin. It was he who introduced me to Phoenix Park, to the city, to de Valera and, not least, to the Guinness works, where the staff canteen provided meals of a quality which I had never encountered in any factory. They were accompanied by piped Guinness of a type that I immediately liked. Guinness backed the Wexford Festival, ensuring that in a year of crisis for the company, when because of a dispute there was very little Guinness in Dublin, there was never any shortage of it in Wexford.

On one trip south with Bryan we combined bird watching in the marshes near the town, a pursuit that delighted him, and listening to opera – *Don Pasquale* again in 1962 and Mozart's *La Clemenza di Tito* in 1968. The Festival was now winning world attention for the willingness of its artistic directors to put on operas, sometimes by well-known composers, which had seldom been widely staged after they were first performed, and sometimes by little-known composers. In 1962 Amilcare Ponchiolli fell into the latter category. Who had heard of him? There was more Balfe, however, in the next year and more Donizetti in 1964.

The theatre had been closed in 1960 after being extended and greatly improved, and after a break of my own, when I became Vice-Chancellor of Sussex, Susan and I most enjoyed going to Wexford with the painter Derek Hill, who became a good friend and who did portraits of us both for our home (with lots of drawings) and a large portrait which hangs in Hall in Worcester College. As he painted Derek wore what looked like a butcher's smock, but he was very much a talking butcher. There was never any lack of conversation. Each year he used to give a party in London at which he showed very early Hollywood films. Buster Keaton, not Chaplin, was his favourite. Back across the Irish Sea, he was a great benefactor to the Republic. The pictures of his which I like best are those of the Atlantic coast. Sadly I do not have one.

Wexford, like Aldeburgh, became a regular part of my annual calendar, and I wrote a piece for Karina Daly's book *Tom Walsh's Opera* (2005) called 'The Wexford Experience' in which I stated that from the start I had been drawn into the local community as well as into the Festival. I have a copy of it in front of me, lent me by Tom Walsh's daughter, Victoria, who is a friend and neighbour of ours in Sussex. She spent several years working in Glyndebourne. I place the two festivals as musts in my diary if I can possibly get to them, as I do Promenade Concerts where I am sometimes a guest of the BBC. On the invitation of Nicholas Kenyon, then head of Radio 3, I took part in the planning of a symposium in 2007 on the jubilee of the BBC taking over the Proms in 1927. I also gave a lecture at the symposium, which was based entirely on original sources, on the beginnings of the BBC regime.

Kenyon's room, where the planning committee met, was in Henry Wood House on the site of the old Queen's Hall destroyed by German bombs during the Second World War. I had a room there myself when I was writing my BBC history, which was decorated in very different and less adventurous style from Kenyon's, which was full of colour. I do not know which one would have been approved of by Wood, whose statue is prominent in the Albert Hall to which the Proms moved in 1941. In my own home I have kept a collection of Prom programmes. That for 1976, when Robert Ponsonby was the BBC's Controller of Music, began with an American musician's comment in the 1920s that 'even a casual attendance at the Proms is provocative of thought . . . The listeners at the Proms in their alertness remind an American of the stadium rather than of the Carnegie Hall public [in New York] with its fads, its snobberies and its boredoms.'

I went to many concerts at Carnegie Hall and got to know it well in a very different phase of its history. With or without fads, snobberies and boredoms, its atmosphere remained very different, however, from that in the Albert Hall, where the organizers of the Proms set out each year to balance what is acknowledged to be 'great music' with the best of what is unfamiliar, ending with a 'Last Night of the Proms' which now incorporates broadcasts from provincial cities as well as the metropolis. During the last ten years technology has greatly influenced the pattern of public musical entertainment just as in the nineteenth century it influenced the making of musical instruments.

Roger Wright, Controller of Radio 3, who took over the management of the Proms in 2010 in the year of the 150th anniversary of Gustav Mahler's birth, introduced a Henry Wood Day on Sunday 5 September, 're-creating' the programme that Wood had conducted at the last night of the Proms in 1910 with the addition of what Wood called a 'novelty'. Most of the items were short, many were excerpts. The first item was the overture to Wagner's *The Flying Dutchman*, the last the waltz and polonaise from Tchaikovsky's *Eugene Onegin*. The 'novelty' was a 'dark pastoral' composed by David Matthews from the surviving movement of Vaughan Williams's Cello Concerto (1942). On the last night, 11 September, the soprano was Dame Kiri Te Kanawa, born in a distant continent. In the previous year the Welsh singer Bryn Terfel had performed.

Earlier programmes in 2010 had featured 'varieties' as well as novelties. The great Russian conductor Valery Gergiev is a favourite of mine. I heard him in my ninetieth birthday year conducting in Edinburgh what to me is one of the most absorbing and extraordinary of operas, Richard Strauss's *Frau ohne Schatten*. Reading some music critics' accounts both of the opera and its production I stand firmly behind my own judgement, not theirs. Shadows have a long history in myth, literature and art.

I have left almost to the last in this chapter my love of opera and of Glyndebourne. I served there as a trustee for longer, I think, than any other trustee has done, from 1966 to 1991. I was first invited, I believe, through my role at the University of Sussex, but while I treasured – and treasure – the connection between Sussex University and Glyndebourne, it was not that connection which has given me the greatest pleasure. I derived that from being drawn into an intimate world of family life and of fascinating musical relationships. George and Mary Christie became close friends, as did a series of 'administrators' beginning with Moran Caplat, a very capable but friendly colleague. From the start I appreciated that these were very special relationships. It was part of my general education to serve under the chairmanship of Gerald Coke, who was Chairman of Rio Tinto, a huge international business concern, the history of which has been full of twists and turns, and Tony Lloyd, whose father was my main link with Lewis's when I was writing my study of that remarkable retail business, *Friends of the People*. I also knew and liked – through Sussex local politics – the father of Tony's wife, Jane, Corny (Cornelius) Shelford. How he got his first name I do not know.

My main contribution to Glyndebourne was a double one. First I gave my wholehearted support to Glyndebourne Touring Opera when it was most needed. It was the only Glyndebourne operation which received any public funding, what Glyndebourne's founder John Christie himself called 'State jellyfish', a curious description, and not every trustee was in favour of accepting it. In 1951, a year which I have picked out for special attention , there had been a once and for all state guarantee of £25,000 against loss when an all-Mozart Glyndebourne Festival was featured as part of the Festival of Britain celebrations. Finance thereby became available that virtually doubled the seating capacity of the old theatre to 592. In 1968 the Touring Company made a pioneering publicly supported provincial tour to Liverpool, Manchester, Sheffield and Oxford, which I strongly backed. Then and later it gave new opportunities to under-studies and attracted an extended and often musically and socially different audience from that in Glyndebourne itself.

So in a different way did television, first BBC television and then in my time Southern Television, of which I was a director. So too were George Christie himself and Lady Rupert Neville, friend of us both. I felt in 1966 that through my own knowledge of television and people directly involved in television, the first of them Humphrey Burton, I could double my individual contribution to Glyndebourne history. In the process of doing that I became a surprising 'authority' on broadcast opera inside and outside Britain.

Glyndebourne did far more for me in return than I gave to it. It introduced me to music I might never have heard – Monteverdi, 'rediscovered' in Germany by Sandy Goehr's father; the widest possible range of Handel, Haydn and Richard Strauss operas; wonderful performances, sometimes the best, of operas that I had often seen. In the process I got to know some of the conductors well, among them Raymond Leppard and John Pritchard. I talked often to directors, particularly John Cox, whose productions I greatly admired. I met singers whom I would never have otherwise have met, among them Elizabeth Södeströhm, Janet Baker, Thomas Allen and Geraint Evans. From close at hand in board meetings I admired the financial genius of Sir Alex Alexander, and later shared the enthusiasms of Emmanuel Kaye. All these people were far more than names. Nor were our relationships centred entirely on Glyndebourne.

With Geraint we went to an Eisteddfod, where in a BBC tent gin was disguised at water. It was the only place on the premises where it was obtainable.With Emmanuel, through his unparalleled generosity, we twice went to the Salzburg Festival, outstanding among all festivals. Because we were on the Glyndebourne board we could get tickets for Bayreuth, and we went there with Tony and Jane Lloyd to watch the performances of Wagner's *Ring* conducted by George Solti, whom I knew and admired independently of the Lloyds through Leeds and Chicago, where I listened to lots of music whenever I went to teach at the university. I made friends there with the great oboist Bayard Still. Even before I married Susan I made my way through icy and intensely cold Chicago to Chicago Symphony Orchestra concerts.

Seeing and hearing *The Ring* at Bayreuth with the Lloyds was an unforgettable experience even in a hot and crowded theatre. Between operas we would take a picnic (Glyndebourne style) to quiet places in the beautiful Bavarian countryside where we would look at the score of the next opera that we would see. Curiously Wagner had been performed before Mozart at Glyndebourne. In June 1928 Act III of *Die Meistersinger* was performed (complete with printed programme) in the organ room in the house in which late in my life I would watch on a screen performances in the new theatre.

In 1928 there was no old theatre and John Christie had not yet married Audrey Mildmay; the Festival itself did not begin until 1934. John had been to a Bayreuth Festival, however, taken there by the Precentor of Eton, by a coincidence also called Lloyd, no relative of Tony, who was himself a prominent figure at Eton. Charles Hanford Lloyd, forty years older than John, had launched the Oxford Musical Club as an undergraduate in 1872 and had been Eton's Precentor since 1892. John's visit to Bayreuth with him accounts for the preponderance of half-morocco folio editions of Wagner's full scores in the Glyndebourne music library.

There was no Wagner at the Glyndebourne Festival until the year when I am writing, 2011, when I saw *Die Meistersinger* in the impressive new theatre. The theatre that John Christie created for Audrey Mildmay he conceived of essentially as an addition to the house where he lived, although it was to be extended during the post-war years. When I became a trustee it had 768 seats with a box at the back which was placed at the disposal of each trustee once a year and to which the trustee could invite guests. Trustees also sat in it *en bloc* once a year after an annual meeting and during the long Glyndebourne interval dined in the house.

John Christie died three years before I became a trustee, but a few days before his death I had gone to an unforgettable performance at Glyndebourne of Monteverdi's *L'Incoronazione di Poppea*, conducted by Raymond Leppard, which John would have loved to have seen. I was in the theatre but not in the box. Richard Lewis was Nero and Magda László Poppea. I was in the theatre for the last night before the old opera house closed. The night's performance of *The Queen of Spades* focussed more on death than renewal.

The highlight of my Glyndebourne experience was participating in the fascinating but not always easy discussions about a new Glynde-bourne opera building, sometimes with the architect present. I admired George Christie's determination to get it built, a deter-mination which at times involved an element of daring. His success was as exciting as the 'curtain up' of old Glyndebourne in 1934.

I was also to be involved indirectly in the making of a new Covent Garden Opera House, having known the old Covent Garden well when Garrett Drogheda was Chairman of the Board and later Claus Moser and John Sainsbury. I first met Claus just after the end of the war when he was a young lecturer in statistics at the LSE, and I welcomed him to Oxford when I was Provost of Worcester and he became Warden of Wadham. We worked together closely on 'Music in Oxford', which offered regular concerts in the Sheldonian building and in the Town Hall.

I end this chapter, which could have been much longer, not in Covent Garden, Oxford, Glyndebourne or Bayreuth, but where I began it – in Birmingham. I started the chapter with festival pro-grammes and mentioned the first Birmingham Festival of 1768. As an historian I am more interested in the works that were performed during nineteenth-century festivals than in the performers, and for this reason alone I find my programmes highly informative.

One of them dates back to the last years of Queen Victoria's reign. It refers to a composer very different from Wagner, Felix Mendelssohn, whose oratorio *Elijah* was performed in the sixteenth concert of the Hallé Orchestra in its forty-first season in Manchester, 1895. The oratorio had been first performed in Birmingham, conducted by the composer himself in 1846, the year of the repeal of the Corn Laws. Fittingly the first Manchester performance was in the Free Trade Hall. The oratorio was an immediate success in both cities in 1846. In Birmingham no fewer than eight items of the oratorio were encored, among them 'If with all your hearts', 'O rest in the Lord' and 'Come everyone that thirsteth'. A special train from Euston had conveyed soloists, orchestra (described as 'band') *and* composer to Birmingham in 1846. In the following year a revised version of *Elijah* was to be presented to the metropolitan public in Exeter Hall, home of Evangelicalism and one of my favourite Victorian locations, quintessentially Victorian.

Books have not figured primarily in this penultimate chapter. Yet in the period covered in it I co-authored one book on the Victorian era which was not published, *Music in the Queen's Reign*. My Lewes co-author, Janet Lovegrove, had read music at Cambridge and knew well a host of Cambridge musicians, many of whom had made their mark. We worked out a perfect division of labour which (almost) involved breaking one of my rules. I never think of history in terms of decades, yet to have divided the Queen's reign into three, as was my wont, could not work in writing of Victorian music. We settled, therefore, for double decades, 1837, 1857, 1877, 1897, ending as seemed appropriate at her Diamond Jubilee. There was nothing conventional about that. Choosing two decades was like choosing a bicentennial. I am sad for Janet's sake as much as my own that all our researches came to nothing. No one may ever know how we judged the Queen or her contemporaries.

Chapter 10

Connections and Convergences

When I was finishing off the first version of this book in August 2011, with summer rain pelting down, I awoke from a vivid dream in which I was reading a surprising review of a book of mine that had been published just fifty years before. This was my first volume on the history of broadcasting in the United Kingdom which, while not intended primarily to serve that purpose, over the years had come to be treated as an essential work of reference. After covering in a careful and probing manner the way in which I had handled the main themes, the reviewer confessed that what he liked best in the book was neither my narrative nor my analysis but my presentation of the judgements that some of the leading characters in the book themselves made about their own contemporaries and 'their own times'. He picked out the comments of John Reith, curiously ending his review with President Sarkozy whom he claimed greatly admired Reith.

Has the French President even heard of Reith? I asked myself still in my dream. They shared neither the same times nor the same place in space. Nevertheless, when I awoke I decided that in my final version of this last chapter I should make an attempt not only to explore the connections and convergences of my birthday year but to reflect with the help of quotes on the judgements that the leading characters that I have introduced into this book have made about past, present and future. How far back in time has their sense of time taken them? Did that part of the recent past which they actually remembered influence their attitudes towards the present and the future more than older perceptions of a distant past that was beyond their memory? How far ahead did their future reach? Was it longer than the duration of one Parliament? One of the most depressing features in the background (for once I will use this word) of my birthday year has been the fact that none of our three major politicians – David Cameron, Nick Clegg or Ed Miliband – has much knowledge of, or interest in, Britain's own history. I have found nothing that any of them have said or written about the past of the slightest interest.

When I woke up from my dream I asked what I regard as leading questions because I recognized quickly that I myself was the reviewer who featured in it. I knew even in my dream that for me past, present and future constitute a continuum. Not everyone does. I was less concerned with my birthday, which was an unrepeatable event, than with the duration of a life far longer than I expected, covering a 'present age' which has seen immense change. I recall the words of the French historian Fernand Braudel, himself preoccupied with time. although I did not remember them in my dream:

> Let us agree on what we mean by the expression, 'the present age'. Let us not judge this present on the scale of our own individual lives, in the daily slices, thin, insignificant and translucent [I would not have chosen those adjectives] represented by our own personal existence.

Most people do.

From the moment that I had first contemplated writing this book in 2008 I had never doubted that I should conclude it with what I knew would be 'a year of connections and convergences' in my own life which had more than private significance. I knew, in particular, that my birthday year would mark the fiftieth anniversary of the arrival of the first students to join the new University of Sussex and the fortieth anniversary of the entry of the first students at the new Open University in 1971. These were crucial dates for me, each worthy of celebration as well as commemoration, the kind of combination that

I associated in my boyhood with chapel anniversary services in the northern villages and towns where I grew up. On those occasions an outside preacher would endeavour to cast a spell over his congregation, reminding them equally of the past and the future. He would combine sometimes personal and public themes with a biblical text sometimes treated as timeless.

Sussex and the Open University were not the only two universities in my life which would be looking back to their beginnings. Another university that I knew well through different phases of its history since the 1950s, the University of Hong Kong, would be celebrating its centenary, and I was determined to try to travel out there again by sea and take what would probably be my last look at Hong Kong. I had first visited it in 1952 before it became a city of skyscrapers, a completely new kind of city. I had known personally all of its post-war Vice-Chancellors, except the first one and the present one. In 1975 I had joined the Hong Kong University (and later Polytechnics) Grants Committee, which in the twenty-first century is still operating in a similar fashion to the British UCG when I was a member of that body.

Thanks to the History Department in the University of Hong Kong, with which I have maintained academic connections through the years, and the indefatigable efforts of Professor Priscilla Roberts, I was able to achieve my ambition. I owe an immense debt to her. She was imaginative as well as indefatigable. My lectures were described as contributions to Pharos II. The name sounded Egyptian. Pharos, however, was an acronym for 'Postgraduate History Archival Research'.

I have already described in this book a last and very different centenary in 2011 that I had been fully prepared for before the year began, that of the Confraternitas Historica in my old Cambridge College. It is, I believe, the oldest institution of its kind in the country, founded not by dons but by undergraduates. The centenary already stands out in my mind as one of the landmark events of 2011. Less of an event, but more widespread in its implications and its ramifications, would, I knew, be the sixtieth anniversary of the founding of *History Today* in 1951, which was itself, as I have suggested, a year of institutional conjunctions. *History Today* is a periodical to which I have devoted much of my time and interest. I cannot do without it for, like me, it is concerned with all kinds of history, with all historical periods and with all parts of the world. Its very existence forces me to confront the notion of 'the past' with the challenges of writing critical history

There was to be one item in my own personal conjunctions of 2011 which I was not prepared for before the year began, another ninetieth birthday, that of the Institute of Historical Research in London. Because of the very particular conjunction in its life and mine, which its Director, Miles Taylor, foresaw, it organised a symposium on various aspects of my work as an historian and how they were related to each other. Ninety years do not carry with them the aura of a century, but the occasion of a joint birthday stimulated a very lively event which, like this book, concerned places as well as people. It had its own aura. Two historians I had never met dealt, for example, with my professorial years in Leeds and in Canberra. They used original sources that I have never seen, and I learned much about myself that I did not know before. I hope that a book will result out of this double birthday event.

The occasion had something in common with an Oxford 'collection' during which tutors report orally on work done by under-graduates under their care during the previous term, choosing whether to be frank or 'diplomatic'. The head of the college sits in the chair and listens attentively to what both the undergraduates and their tutors say. As Provost of Worcester I was responsible for moving collections from the Senior Common Room to the Provost's Lodgings. When I was a young Fellow they had taken place in silence in the College Hall. When I returned to the College in 1976 they were held noisily in an upper common room: the undergraduates queued to be seen and high spirits made the event jocular rather than dignified, or indeed useful. With the move to the Lodgings behaviour was better. When the Cambridge historian Norman Stone, who had been appointed a University Professor in Oxford to succeed Richard Cobb, burst into the Lodgings during a collection not knowing what was going on, and I slipped away from the ceremony briefly to welcome him, he told me that what he had looked at resembled the Spanish Inquisition.

The event at the Institute of Historical Research, which had been moved from the Institute to a different room in the Senate House building of London University, could never have been thought of in that way. It started with an introduction by David Cannadine, a former Director, whom I had known well for many years, in which he ranged briefly over the whole of my work. This was followed by the presentation of a paper by one of my most intellectually able former research students, now a professor, Martin Hewitt, who noted correctly – and very much to the point – that in his own field I myself had been more interested in the Victorians than in Victorian studies. This made me sit up.

I have never been a great lover of seminars, and Victorian studies, pursued as diligently in Bloomington, Indiana, as in Leeds, are not the only field where I deliberately limited my attendance at scholarly meetings that were designed to promote specialized fields of knowledge. For example, as urban studies developed I was more anxious to write about cities than to be involved in committees seeking to organize a new field. I was glad that, starting with a simple typed newssheet, a sizeable organization run by Jim Dyos took over their direction. Likewise, I preferred to write about topics in labour (and business) history which I had selected for myself rather than to watch over the affairs of the Labour History Society, of which I had been a founder, or of business history societies, of which there was more than one.

Listening in the Institute of Historical Research symposium to papers covering aspects of history, but by no means all of them, to which I had made a personal contribution, I became for that day at least a subject of historical research rather than an historical researcher. It was by no means like a collection, but the writers of the best of the papers delivered that day assessed my work rather than described it, drawing on primary sources. I was particularly glad that my successor as historian of the BBC, Jean Seaton, gave a paper on my work on the history of broadcasting. I had always found it impossible to separate off that element in my work from my work on the history of books and of other media. As BBC historian, she has to work in conditions very different from those I worked in and I hope that I have been helpful when I have discussed her work with her. I had urged the BBC in vain to immediately appoint someone to succeed me. The last BBC Director-General whom I dealt with, John Birt, still thought of the post as that of official historian. The special relationship that was as crucial to her success as to mine was full support from the BBC Archives, archives that had to be sorted out and catalogued before she could begin to write.

Several aspects of my historical writings which were not named in the printed agenda of the Institute symposium were raised in a swift-moving discussion in which I fully participated. Two have meant a lot to me. The first was the history of wine, the second the history of sport. Both of them I have referred to in other parts of this book. They fit in. I was drawn into both kinds of largely undeveloped history through personal relationships. Eric Colwell, who participated in a course which I ran, bringing in both civil servants and businessmen, drew me into the first. In 1971 he took over the management of the Victoria Wine Company, the oldest 'wine chain' in the country, founded in the City of London in 1865 by an enterprising wine store keeper, William Winch Hughes.

Hughes's idea was simple – to sell wine for cash in shops to customers who would never be visited by a specialized wine merchant. In doing so he opened up new horizons. 'From the earliest ages of mankind wine has been drunk', a knowledgeable contemporary of Hughes wrote in that year, 'and it is only reasonable to suppose that everything is known respecting it.' 'Reasonable' it may have seemed. Untrue it was. I enjoyed telling the story of wine within the context of a new approach to wine and spirit retailing, which was to go through new phases after my book on Victoria Wine appeared in 1985. Super-markets led to the abandonment not only of local high street shops but also the demise of chain stores.

When Hughes died in 1886 he owned ninety-eight shops in towns and cities from Norwich to Bristol and from Birmingham to Brighton. To assess his achievement, I went back to local history again, exploring with the enthusiastic help of Susan Hard scattered newspaper items and obscure collections of local records. My work, which incorporated a study of advertising, followed naturally from my earlier work on other branches of retailing. I also studied in detail temperance records of a different kind – jugs and plates and printed ephemera. Inevitably my researches involved politics as well as economics. As in so many of the contexts that concerned me William Gladstone played a major part: he lowered duties on French wine in 1860.

I found myself covering, but in a quite different way, ground covered by my Oxford friend Brian Harrison, who was as interested in temperance as he was in drinking habits. My book, with a foreword by John Arlott, a real celebrity, whom I got to know well while writing it, included pictures of the interiors of wine shops, wine lists and national statistics of wine (and beer) consumption. Arlott himself collected mainly topographical books and had a great collection. He moved from Hampshire to the Channel Islands in the later years of his life.

A second book on wine that I published in 1994 could not have been more different from my first. In *Haut-Brion: An Illustrious Lineage* I crossed the seas to Bordeaux, and took up a very different story, fortified by a letter I had read from the first American owner of the great vineyard, Clarence Dillon, who had acquired it in 1935. He wanted a history of Haut-Brion to be written, he had told his nephew, that would be of interest to anyone 'whether he was particularly concerned with wine or not'. 'My only thought', he wrote, 'is that you should consider someone other than a wine enthusiast for preparing this volume.'

I had loved French wines since I went to stay with the Cordonniers in my teens, but having written about claret I have become as uneasy as Dillon was about the use of the term 'wine enthusiast'. I have always been sceptical about 'experts'. Some writers on wine are superficial in their thinking and otiose in their language. I have learnt an immense amount about claret not from wine writers but from wine producers other than the Dillons, especially Antony Barton, and about the importance to vineyards of *regisseurs*, a term quite inadequately translated into English as 'vineyard managers'. Jean-Bernard Delmas at Haut-Brion, who was my guide through vineyards and cellars, was one of the greatest of them. In writing my book I also learned much both about the great city of Bordeaux and its institutions and about family politics. Philippe, duc de Mouchy, who married Joan Dillon in 1978, was a direct descendant of a great eighteenth-century *intendant* of Bordeaux, chief administrator and royal representative. Philippe, educated at Eton, was the only man in my life who criticised my English – I used too many pluperfects, he said. Fortunately we both loved oysters. We used to buy them in a Bordeaux fish market. I happily ate more oysters with Philippe than any other person in my life.

Joan Dillon had previously been married to Charles, Duke of Luxembourg, by whom she had two children, one of whom, Charlotte, became an undergraduate at Worcester. I had long talks both with her and with her brother, Robert. Joan restored the glories of the château of Haut-Brion, entirely redecorating and refurbishing it, making it a far more beautiful place than it had ever been. I did much of my work not there but in La Mission Haut-Brion, a *grand cru* property on the other side of the main road leading into Bordeaux. I found out as much as I could about its religious associations. Its economics appealed to me too. I could just afford to buy and drink La Mission.

As I wrote my book I found the story of Haut-Brion full of surprises. My first surprise, which surprised many of my readers far more even than me, was that Château Haut-Brion had no Irish O'Brian in its long history. Its first owner, Jean de Pontac, born in 1488, lived to be 101 and had fifteen children. 'When we have such genuine romance', I wrote in my first chapter, 'we do not need legend. What true story of a vineyard could start as dramatically as that of Haut-Brion?' I noted that Clarence Dillon, who died in 1978 at the age of ninety-six, last visited Haut-Brion in 1967. 'I will not come back' were his last words to Joan. There were fascinating connections for me to follow in the vineyards that I loved to wander through – connections with Pepys, with Locke, with Jefferson, with Talleyrand and with Kennedy. I set out to follow all of them, choosing words to introduce them from the historian Lucien Febvre, 'The historian is not the man who knows, but the man who seeks to find out.'

I would not have chosen this motto for any of the works or articles that I have written almost in parallel on the history of sport, which seldom disentangles news, gossip, legend and scandal. Sport has changed more in my lifetime than I would ever have thought possible when I was a boy, largely but not entirely due to the influence of the media. This is not the book in which I have space to identify or assess the changes, but I would like to do so in a different book that would show how and why historians have come to specialize in the history of sport, bringing in parallels with the history of religion, and with the history of the sciences. Sport has been significant in my life for other reasons. I have treasured a long relationship with Roger Bannister before and after he became Master of Pembroke College, Oxford, and his wife, Moyra, a talented artist. Through him, in my mind I have linked the history of sport with the history of medicine, another aspect of history that I have no time to investigate in this book, but which retrospectively I consider to be one of the main strands, if not the main strand, in my historical writing. I was not tempted, however, to accept an invitation to join the Sports Council or to write articles on sport of the kind that I wrote about the history of wine in *Field* magazine. Sport links the academic and the non-academic in a way that is, I believe, distinctive in this country and in its former 'dominions', but it has not shaped all my special relationships in 2011.

On the actual day of my ninetieth birthday I talked on the telephone to a former neighbour in Keighley with whom for years I had lost touch, Jack Taylor, who was born very near to me in Keighley on the very same day. I was told about this conjunction by his grandson; and preceding, as it did, a party for me given by my son, it made my day. I have talked several times since by telephone to Jack. He remembers some details of my early life, of my family and of the town far better than I do. So did my sister Emmie, who was a pupil at Keighley Girls' Grammar School. She died, alas, when this book was already in the press. I would love her to have read it.

On her first day at school Emmie was placed in the form taught by the future Edna Healey, then Miss Edmonds. Edna remembered my sister. I often examined that strange conjunction with them both. Over the years I got to know Edna Healey well as a friend, a Sussex neighbour and a versatile author. We talked at length about each of her books as she was writing it, in the same way as I had talked earlier with Elizabeth Longford.

Two boys whom I had known well at Keighley Boys' Grammar School have figured in my ninetieth year, Howard Stowell, who has written memorably about his days in Keighley immediately after leaving school, and Brian Baldwin, now living in Australia, whom I taught at the school in my brief but enlightening period as a teacher between taking my degree and putting on uniform. Both lived, as did Leo White, in the Highfield district of Keighley, very different from my Lawkholme. After leaving school Howard was employed in the office of a large textile mill in Keighley, Cloughs, which at the peak of its prosperity attracted enough foreign trade to need a foreign correspondent at its mill headquarters. Brian won an Exhibition to Peterhouse, Cambridge, and subsequently joined the British Council. I went to see him in Coimbra in Portugal when Salazar was still in power. Over the years I have had many continuing connections with Portugal long after Salazar. Indeed, I have a special relationship with the country, still regionalized but not as Spain is. Portugal, I had been taught at elementary school, was 'our oldest ally'.

It may be of interest to any reader of this book who is concerned with vocabularies – and my Spanish vocabulary is almost as good as my Portuguese – that the words in the title of this last chapter 'connections' and 'convergences' are only two of the many words beginning with 'c' that I might have brought into it. I hesitated before leaving 'coincidences' out of the title, having already decided to omit 'conjectures', 'circumstances' and 'commemorations'. All these 'c' words are presumably of Roman origin, many with French echoes. Century, centenary, centenarian and centennial are others. One of my favourite ones is *consuetudines*, a word used in the oath that I had to take as Provost of Worcester College. It too translates, with different connotations, into a modern English word, beginning with 'c' – customs.

The most general of all the 'c' words is, of course, communications, since the 1950s one of my major preoccupations as an historian. The title of the *Festschrift* – it was not so described – that was edited by Derek Fraser, a research student of mine at Leeds, and subsequently Vice-Chancellor of the new Teesside University, was *Cities, Class and Communications*. It appeared in 1990 on the eve of my seventieth birthday. I deliberately and explicitly preferred the plural in the title. Why did British Telecom choose to call its public affairs quarterly *Communication* in the singular?

The word connections is the title of two news bulletins, of two completely different bodies, which I regularly read, the Commonwealth of Learning, which has its headquarters in Vancouver, and the local staff newspaper of East Lothian National Health Services, which I read whenever I go to my doctor's surgery there. Associated with the word is the aphorism 'All Things Connect': this inspires the title of the bulletin of One World Media: 'Connected'. Every chapter of this present book is connected for me.

Words and how we use them, as I have insisted throughout all my scholarly work, provide insight into thought, emotion and social relationships. Not all of my own words have entered Raymond Williams's invaluable book *Keywords*. Like him, I enjoy differences in connotation, another c-word. I like to put side by side, for example, two uses of the word foolish: 'Dear Lord and Father of Mankind, forgive our foolish ways', and Eric Maschwitz's 'These foolish things remind me of you'.

Moving in this last chapter from words to the events that I have already mentioned, the entry of the first students to Sussex University and the Open University were landmarks that stand out fifty and forty years later respectively. The UGC had not expected Sussex students to enter the University so soon. Its 'administrators', appointed before its professors and lecturers, had necessarily been required to select, the first students. I have in my own archive a historically interesting letter, headed 'The University College of Sussex' and dated 9 June

1961, from Geoffrey Lockwood, 'Administrative Assistant', to a would-be undergraduate who wished to study geography:

> The position with regard to admission in October of this year is that the last date for applications was January 21st, that all of the fifty places available have already been filled on either a definite or a provisional basis, and that there is a long waiting list for any vacancies which might arise through withdrawals. Thus any further applications have only a very limited chance of success, but the University is willing to consider such applications and I am enclosing the necessary application forms.

Lockwood, a future Registrar of the University after the first Registrar, R. C. Shields, who shared a birthday with me, had moved from Brighton to be Registrar of the University of Adelaide, also enclosed a prospectus. In it he pointed out that there would be no geography department at Sussex but that the subject would eventually form a 'specialism' in several of the schools.

He knew already that the first nine academics, who had had nothing to do with the choice of this initial group of students, would agree on this objective at least. The word 'department' did not figure, therefore, in the Royal Charter of the University promulgated on 16 August 1961. Despite its absence, the Charter seemed to me, as a member of the University Grants Committee, to be an almost purely derivative document that ignored all the discussions that were taking place in the new universities sub-committee of the UGC, of which I was a member. Consequentially, I looked very carefully at the language employed by the Privy Council in founding each subsequent new university.

The first nine academics at Sussex did not take up residence until September 1961 – and we were still being paid by the universities which had been employing us. Nevertheless, we had had a few meetings in the huge house in Grand Avenue, Hove, complete with an impressive billiards room, where John Fulton, the first Vice-Chancellor, had been installed. To begin with he was called Principal as he had been in Swansea University College from which he came. I was determined that we should abandon any memories of a university college as quickly as possible.

The great house was subsequently pulled down and replaced by a huge block of flats. So too were the two partially converted Victorian houses in Preston Road, Brighton, where we, 'the faculty', were to teach the first students. I did not know on what terms these properties were acquired. In retrospect, however, it seems as if someone had issued an order stating that all traces of our occupation of them were to be obliterated as quickly as possible.

We held our first faculty meetings in a famous Brighton inn, the Old Ship, a place near the seafront that was renowned for its age and its history. One fact in its history that particularly appealed to me was that the virtuoso violinist – and composer – Paganini had played there. Yet, soon after we arrived in Brighton, our meetings were moved to another old and handsome Palladian building, Stanmer House, built by the Pelham family of Lewes, who had acquired the property, which included a deserted medieval village, in 1712–13. Thomas Pelham became first Earl of Chichester in 1801.

In the twentieth century the finances of the old and established Pelham family were to be undermined by a rapid sequence of calamities entailing the payment of huge death duties, and in 1947 the property was acquired by Brighton Council. Yet it was not the Council but the University that paid for its interior restoration. This was to be lost money, for although the University leased Stanmer House after its move in 1962 to the Falmer campus, using the house for a variety of purposes, it surrendered its lease in 1980. Ironically the last time I went to Stanmer House was on the occasion of the seventy-fifth birthday of the first Press Officer of the University, Fred Newman, who did not take up his post until some time after the University was established. Very few visitors to Stanmer House knew or know of its origins. Very few knew of the period when Robert Rhodes James and Mary Kaldor were University of Sussex faculty working there.

I myself did not first arrive in Sussex (ahead of my own family) until the eve of our first working term. I travelled down to Lewes, in a car driven by a colleague and friend in Leeds University whom I have already mentioned several times in this book, the sociologist Brian Wilson. I was to draw him into the affairs of another new university which years later I helped to create miles away from Leeds or Sussex in an old Portuguese colony, Macao.

Another colleague of mine – and family friend – in Leeds, the historian Maurice Hutt, arrived around the same time to live in Brighton. He had asked me to be one of his referees when it was announced in the press in 1959 that there was to be a university in Brighton. I never thought then that I would be joining the university myself. Once it was announced that I would be going to the new university I was the recipient of scores of letters from academics in other universities asking me if I could find a job for them too.

Maurice wrote an extremely thoughtful chapter on undergraduates and their problems in *The Idea of a New University*, which made an extremely important point not about students but about faculty,

> A new university cannot just 'happen'. It has to be made and adapted. Unlike Bagehot's bureaucrats, the faculty must not conceive 'the elaborate machinery of which they form a part . . . to be a grand and achieved result', but instead 'a working and changeable instrument'.

I compared this comment with one made by C. W. Elliott, President of Harvard, in the *Atlantic Monthly* in 1869:

> A university, in any worthy sense of the term, must grow from seed . . . It cannot be run up, like a cotton mill, in six months to meet a quick demand.

Perspectives change. In 1961 no one thought of comparing running up Sussex with running a cotton mill.

Our first year as professors and lecturers at the University of Sussex in its Preston Road premises was a unique experience. The word 'experiment' was frequently used to describe it. Women students were in the great majority, thirty-seven of them out of fifty-one. I said at the time that the atmosphere reminded me of a kibbutz. Some students (and faculty) found it claustrophobic. Granville Hawkins, who recalls the visit of a BBC film unit to Preston Road, described the move to Falmer in 1962 as 'quite traumatic'. 'We felt suddenly that we were dispensable units in a large impersonal plan.' The Common Room in Preston Road was a crowded place where a number of students talked relentlessly deep into the night. Sadly the first bursarial staff of the University did not contribute much to our mutual welfare. There was a shortage of bookcases in Preston Road, and I was dissatisfied in particular with the number of bookcases provided for me. I also did not have enough files. Before arriving in Brighton – and having not been entirely happy with my own experiences with bursarial staff at Leeds – I had specified the exact quantities that I required. This was a poor start. Fortunately there were later bursars who did an excellent job for the University as it grew. Forgetting my complaints, in our first year I enjoyed meeting and talking to our first students when we gathered in Preston Manor, an impressive house owned by Brighton Corporation. There were fresh flowers on the platform.

In our first term there were splendid occasions to follow. All the students and all the faculty were invited along with the Council of the University to a lavish dinner in the Royal Pavilion. I was more impressed by this event than the students were, for I knew that it was unique. I kept my menu; few of the students did. The main speaker was David Eccles, Secretary of State for Education. I did not quite realise then how much his very presence irritated the civil servants working in the offices of the University Grants Committee on which I was serving. The Secretary of State was not constitutionally responsible for universities. The UGC reported to the Privy Council not to him. Eccles, ambitious and proud, who over the years became a personal confidant and friend, had no intimations that the supreme authority over him, the Prime Minister, Harold Macmillan, would soon relieve him of his post – along with a number of other senior ministers – in a great political purge. He was replaced by Edward Boyle, whom I had got to know first not in Sussex, which he knew well, but in Bletchley. Neither of us had the slightest intimation that he would end up as Vice-Chancellor of Leeds

No two of the early years of the new University of Sussex were the same. There were no scientists among the first nine academics, and it was not until October 1962 that the first science professor arrived. I had signed up the theoretical physicist Roger Blin-Stoyle on Oxford Station. John Maynard Smith, a brilliant scientist, became the founding father of a new School of Biological Sciences in 1965. In the same year John Clifford West, one of several future Vice-Chancellors of other universities, became first Dean of a new School of Applied Sciences. Martin Black joined the school as a biomedical engineer a year later. We were in a vanguard.

In 1962 there were 400 students. According to Fulton a 'cracking pace' was being set. He expected there soon to be 1,800 students and by 1972 3,000, his optimal size. He had left Sussex by then, the campus having changed as much as the faculty. In the words of Sybil Oldfield, who worked at the University from 1962 to 1995, we got used to the presence on the site of 'men in hard hats', bulldozers, the churning up of mud and planks across it. 'That's how it had to be.' All of the country's seven new universities, whatever the differences between them, shared this experience.

The first students graduated in Falmer House in June 1964, and they continued to graduate on the campus until we had to move to the Dome in Brighton ten years later. By then, much was happening in the University that had not been planned, particularly in the development at Sussex of 'cognitive studies', a term not in general use in 1961. What were described as 'brain sciences' were being directly related to 'artificial intelligence' projects and a new map of learning was being drawn. With my interest in Asimov I was thrilled when robotics took its place on it.

I do not think that the UGC understood what was happening. I draw more than a chronological distinction, therefore, between the arrival of the first students at Sussex in 1961 and the entry of the first students to the Open University ten years later. By then the UGC had as its Chairman John Wolfenden, whom I had known when he was Principal of Reading, and under whose chairmanship I served for a time before I became Vice-Chancellor. I was happy neither about his grasp of university politics nor his style in chairing meetings. 'Subject committees' were appointed to deal with curriculum questions. The peer group recovered power. Innovation was discouraged. Universities seemed to me to be losing their autonomy step by step. Wolfenden moved to the British Museum before his 'reforms' had been tested.

I was happy that the Open University deliberately had no connections at all with the UGC. It was financed directly by the Department of Education and Science, though its initial financing had not been straightened out when the first OU students, around 20,000 of them, were admitted in 1971. Much has been written about their reception. No first-year students have ever been subject to such scrutiny. In 1974 Jeremy Tunstall published a book called *The Open University Opens* and the journalist Brian MacArthur, whom I had known as a student when I was at Leeds, wrote an interim history of the University. In Paris the European Institute of Education and Social Policy, of which I was Chairman from 1975 to 1990, published a study of the University by Alan Woodley in 1981.

The first Vice-Chancellor, appointed as early as he possibly could have been, in June 1968, Walter Perry, previously Vice-Principal of Edinburgh University, took over his new post in January 1969 as did the Secretary of the University, Anastasius Christodoulou. Together the two men, along with only four members of staff, handled organizational and curricular issues which had quite deliberately been left over for them by the OU's Planning Committee. It had been a privilege for me, I felt, to be a member of that body, which had been appointed in 1968 and was very effectively chaired by Peter Venables. My colleagues on the committee included Sir William Alexander, General Secretary of the Association of Education Committees, Eric Briault, Deputy Education Officer of the Inner London Education Authority, and Arnold Goodman, Chairman of the Arts Council, all very powerful figures in the management of education. There were also five Vice-Chancellors on the Committee, among them Sir Eric Ashby, then Vice-Chancellor of the University of Cambridge. This strategic Planning Committee had been appointed by Jennie Lee following the publication of the White Paper of February 1966.

She was the real heroine of the story, resolute, determined and able to confront Labour Party leaders who were not committed as she was to creating a real university of quality. Some were actually opposed to it. I choose the designation heroine deliberately. In retrospect I feel that no one but Jennie, backed by Goodman – and, just behind the scenes, by Harold Wilson – could have done it. Economic circumstances were working against it. In effect, Jennie de-politicised planning procedures. No social targets were set. The University, she insisted, was not a working-class university, nor was it a university college, it was an open university. The first Chancellor, Geoffrey Crowther, defined what 'open-ness' meant. The University was open to all students with or without qualifications for entry; open to different modes of learning; open to ideas.

In writing my own account of the founding of the Open University, which received its Royal Charter on 30 May 1969, I have fallen back on primary sources as well as my own still active memories. I wanted to be fully involved in the process until the point where the first Vice-Chancellor was appointed, and I could get back to my own university. From the start I knew that Perry would require support from other universities and that some of them were very unwilling to offer it. I start my account therefore with Perry's first report which deals with the period from January 1969 to December 1970. It is what can rightly be described as an historic document.

'The period under review is the gestation period of a wholly new kind of institution,' Perry began. 'In consequence what I have tried to write is a chapter of history rather than a formal recitation of the facts. As this story unfolds the mistakes will be as obvious as the successes, and it is only over time that a pattern, largely unforeseen at the outset, will gradually emerge.' In 1977 Perry was to publish a substantial book, *The Open University*, which is less concerned with 'atmosphere' than with achievement. For the former I still turn to John Ferguson's *The Open University from Within* (1975).

In those first days I was almost alone among the few members of the Open University Planning Committee openly to take part in OU television programmes from Alexandra Palace, a great Victorian building on the outskirts of London with a great Victorian organ. I was very familiar with broadcasting and knew well the BBC producers who worked with me. I also knew the BBC administrators who worked closely with Perry, notably Richmond Postgate, the Controller of Educational Broadcasting, and Donald Grattan, who had made his mark in schools broadcasting. I tried as far as I possibly could to avoid being drawn into discussions on administration and policy, preferring to work at the grass roots with 'course teams' planning special courses than to make high policy. Yet I was more than relieved when, after the Conservative victory in the election of 1970, Margaret Thatcher, in charge of education, made it possible for the OU to go ahead. I had no thought then of becoming the University's Chancellor, which happened in 1979. It was a very different university from what it had been in 1971.

I spent most of my fifteen years as Chancellor looking to the future more than to the past and so I do in 2012, when I write about both the fortieth anniversary of the entry of the Open University's first students and of the fiftieth anniversary of the entry of the first students to Sussex. A history of Sussex edited by Fred Gray in 2011 was called *Making the Future*. Gray was drawing on a quotation from John Fulton who called education 'making the future' and the book ends with an afterword, 'Navigating the Future' by Michael Farthing, the present Vice-Chancellor. Farthing rightly stresses the importance of links with other universities, including common programmes and projects, adding, as I do, that 'the future cannot be trusted just to happen. It needs to be planned for. It needs to be invented.'

The Open University employs similar language. It is now the largest academic institution in the United Kingdom in terms of student members, and since it was founded it has enrolled more than 1.6 million students. It has thirteen national and regional centres and 350 study centres across the UK. It is involved also in fifteen partnerships, established in twenty-five countries. Its own partnership with the BBC is strongly based and stretches far into the future. It adapts to new technology, however, and is a university of which Jennie Lee would be proud.

*

I end this book not with pasts, presents and futures or with people and places and institutions, but first with other books and then with trees. Before I travelled to Hong Kong by sea I read two new novels by two very different authors, Julian Barnes and Penelope Lively, which I believed would be of special interest to me in writing *Special Relationships*. I would have read Julian Barnes's *The Sense of an Ending*, which won the 2011 Booker Prize, if only for its title. As it was, Barnes approached time in the same broad way as this book was already doing. On its first page we are offered a general comment by the main character, Tony Webster:

> We live in time – it holds up and moulds us – but I've never felt I understood it very well. And I'm not referring to theories about how it bends and doubles back, or may exist elsewhere in parallel versions. No, I mean ordinary, everyday time, which clocks and watches assure us passes regularly: tick-tock, click clock.

I knew at once that this was a novel for me and that I wanted to read on.

Tony Webster proves no hero – and no authority – but his reflections are always pertinent. On page two he talks of 'memories which time has deformed into certainty', and in looking back on his schooldays he recalls a definition of history made by a more clever sixth-former than he was, Marian Fish, that 'history is that certainty produced at the point where the imperfections of memory meet the inadequacies of documentation'. At the end of the novel, which is about life and death not books, we are left with a sense of 'great unrest'.

I read *How It All Began* by Penelope Lively, a previous Booker Prize winner (in 1987), whose novels I have read since she began writing them. It is a novel which contemplates not unrest but chance and promises a 'long unknowable future'. I do not know Julian Barnes, although I have read many of his novels. Penelope is a friend, and it was in her Oxford flat that Susan and I decided to get married way back in 1955. *How It All Began* was an even more inviting subject for me in 2011 than *The Sense of an Ending*.

In her first chapter Penelope introduces an aged professor of history, who represents the 'last gasp' of the Namier school of history, the insistence that events are governed entirely by politics and persons, and takes him to Manchester, Namier's old university, where for the first time in his life the professor is humiliated in public as he forgets obvious names and incidents in the eighteenth century and gets everything muddled and 'unstuck'. 'The age in which he has moved with absolute confidence became uncertain, betraying.' *Anno domini*. As he recovers from Manchester, however, he now confronts delusion, and in seeking to by-pass it he never comes to understand how the vanguard past is related to the future.

The two novels made me think and feel, and I did not particularly want to read anything else on my way to Hong Kong to give two lectures. I am on my way there now in the Year of the Dragon, and contemplating dragons is more tempting than preparing lectures. Nevertheless, in an ill-stocked ship's library (not one guide to China) I found one book I had not read before, which influenced my thinking and feeling about the final version of this book, Stephen Fry's *The Fry Chronicles* (2010).

Fry's book, the second of two volumes of autobiography, followed his first oddly-titled *Moab is My Washpot*, published in 1998, which I had read and which gave an account of his childhood, very different in all respects from my own. Moab too was an even less familiar name than Asa. This time he turned to what both of us would call our 'formative years'. Imagine my surprise when I discovered that, bolder than I am, he started each of his fifty-four chapters with a title beginning with the letter 'c', among them Cambridge, Caledonia and Chichester, Class, Committees and Computers and 'conspicuous consumption'. So far so good, but I never expected Côte Basque or, without a 'c', places like 'a shabby set of rooms in London that belong to Granada Television' and two places that have featured in my life, Draycott Place and a flat in Pembridge Place.

I am glad that Fry also included in his book Kennedy's *Latin Primer*, which I dealt with in my history of the House of Longman; 'the marvellous Bamber Gascoigne', the first man to chair *University*

Challenge, which has twice been won by the University of Sussex; Russell Twisk, editor of *The Listener*, who in his judgement had a surname of 'unsurpassing beauty'; Ned Sherrin, who bequeathed (for how long?) the word 'Sherrinry' to the English language; and for good measure Leslie Evershed-Martin, who pioneered contact lenses and the Chichester Festival and introduced me to my first Livery Company, the Spectacle Makers. All these men were friends of mine, not just members of my *karass*, but they belonged to that too.

I end this book with trees. I am writing it in a raging gale which is destroying trees across the country. It is as wild as the gale that destroyed beautiful trees in the middle of Brighton in 1987. A dead tree figures towards the end of Penelope Lively's novel *How It All Began*: it lies on its side on Hampstead Heath and children have been scrambling on it for a generation. 'I think a dead tree does not go away', an attractive character in the novel remarks, 'unless someone takes it to burn it.' The same character, Anton, we are told on the penultimate page, carries a little acorn in the pocket of his black leather jacket. 'His fingers reach for it daily. It will be there for a long time to come', but it will never grow into a mighty oak

A great cedar tree at Tyninghame, the oldest tree in an estate renowned for its trees, fell, not in a gale, in 2007 two minutes before Susan and I were leaving the house in a car driven by our nearest neighbour, a true friend, Daphne Merrells. Had Susan been quicker in getting to the car we would all have been killed. This book was not then in mind. I have long associated cedars of Lebanon with the Bible, however, and mulberry trees with silk as well as with fruit. There had been an old mulberry tree in Worcester College garden in the land beyond the lake, and when I was Provost from 1976 to 1991 Susan claimed that the Provost had the privilege of eating the fruit that it produced. There was a mulberry tree too in the University of Sussex, a young tree planted by John Fulton, which over the years has grown, and in the Grange Garden opposite our house in Lewes there is a very old mulberry tree which now needs to be fenced in. The house in the Grange Garden was built from the ruins of the pre-Reformation priory and was once lived in by John Evelyn.

Allegorical or metaphorical trees were in my mind long before I started this book – prints of trees of life, of which I keep several specimens on the stairs at Tyninghame, all of them bearing moral messages, and trees of knowledge, explaining how one subject is connected to another. That was my preoccupation in my fifteen years in Sussex when I knew that the University was an acorn that would grow. And so it has.

'Finis'.
Sketch by Susan Briggs, c. 1965.

Index of Names